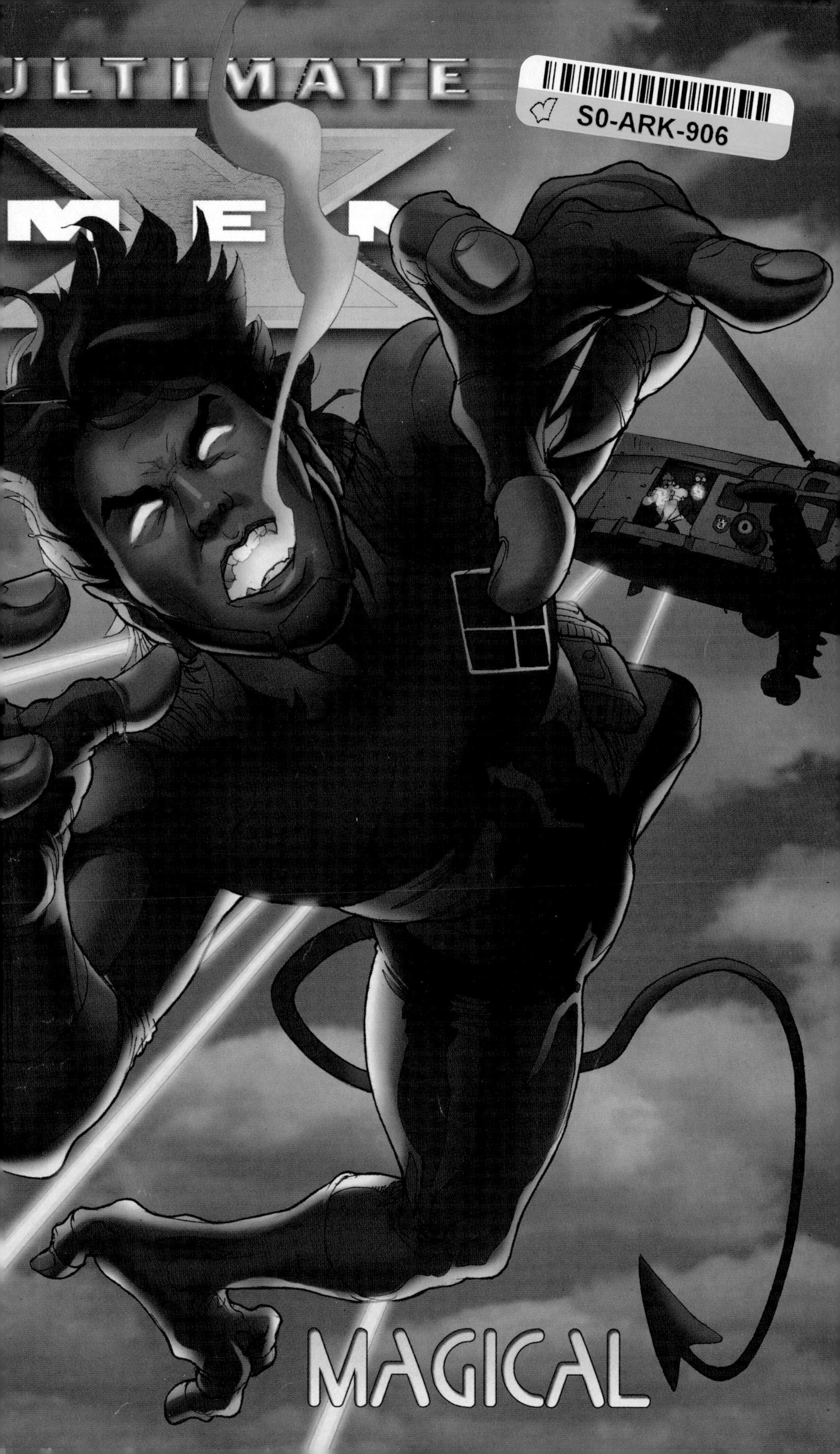
ULTIMATE
X-MEN
MAGICAL

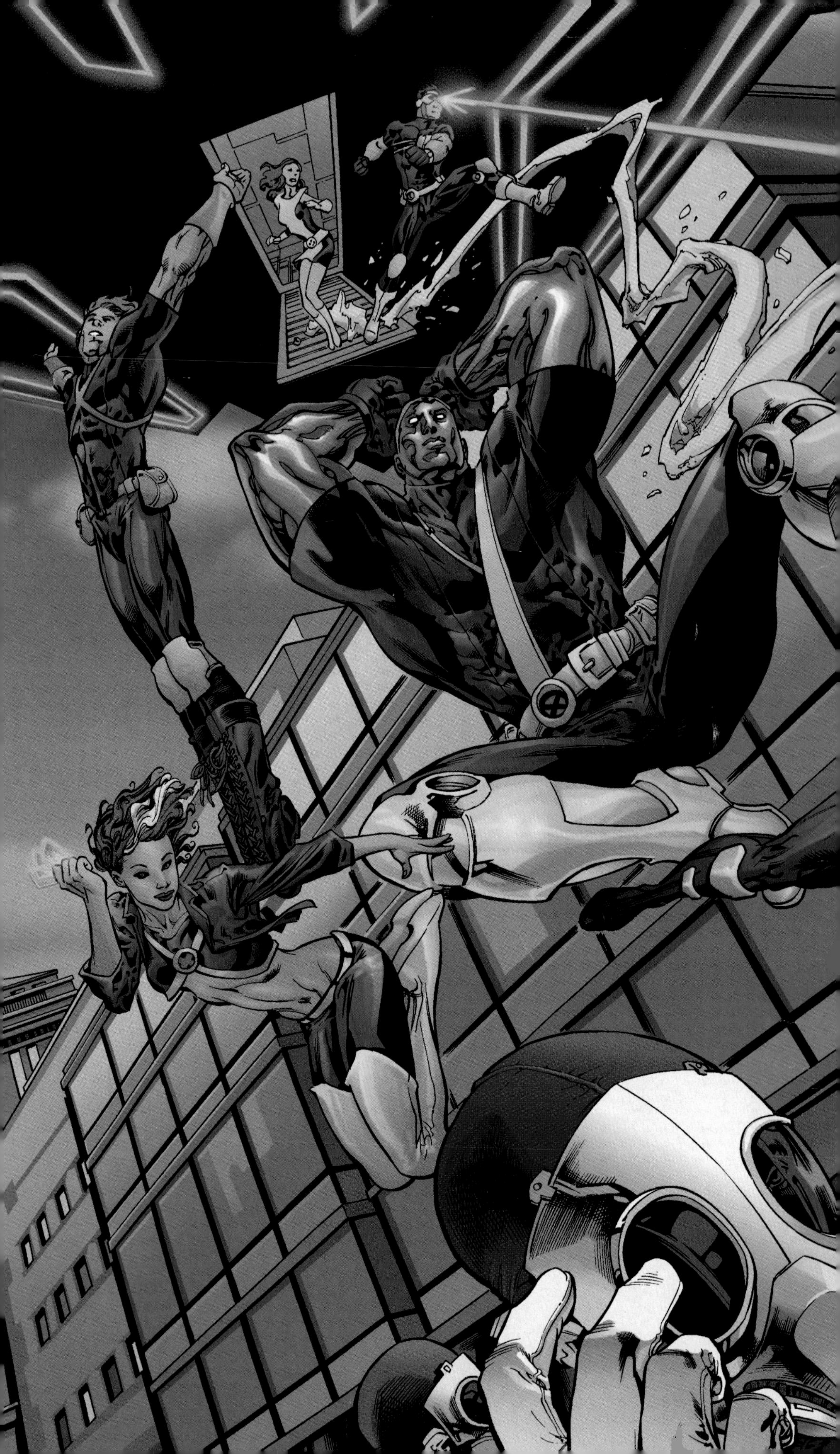

MAGICAL

Writer
Robert Kirkman
Issues #72-74
Penciler (breakdowns on #73-74):
Tom Raney
Inker (finishes on #73-74):
Scott Hanna
Colors:
Gina Going-Raney with June Chung
Letters:
Virtual Calligraphy's Joe Caramagna
Covers:
Tom Raney & Richard Isanove

Annual #2 Art:
Salvador Larroca
Art, Bonus Feature:
Leinil Francis Yu
Colors:
Jason Keith
Colors, Bonus Feature:
Dean White
Cover:
Salvador Larroca & Richard Isanove

Associate Editor:
John Barber
Editor:
Ralph Macchio

Collection Editor:
Jennifer Grünwald
Assistant Editor:
Michael Short
Associate Editor:
Mark D. Beazley
Senior Editor, Special Projects:
Jeff Youngquist
Vice President of Sales:
David Gabriel
Production:
Jerron Quality Color
Vice President of Creative:
Tom Marvelli

Editor in Chief:
Joe Quesada
Publisher:
Dan Buckley

Margaret E. Heggan Free Public Library
208 East Holly Avenue
Hurffville, New Jersey 08080

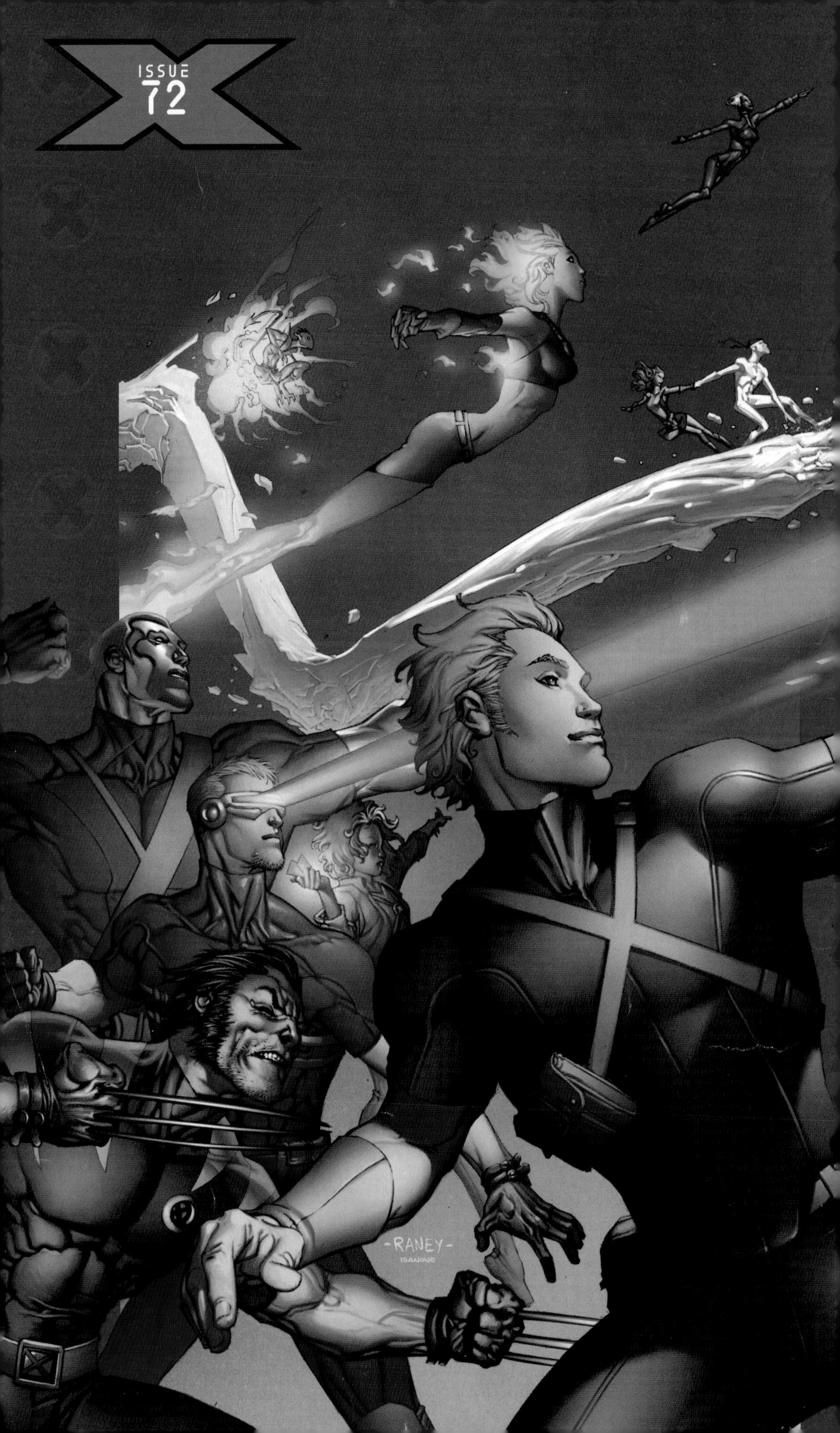
ISSUE
72
-RANEY-
ISANOVE

REVIOUSLY IN ULTIMATE X-MEN:

orn with strange and amazing abilities, the X-Men are young mutant heroes, sworn to protect a world that fears and hates them.

on being tested by the Church of Shi'ar Enlightenment, Jean Grey has learned that she is mentally unbalanced--not the ensely powerful entity known as the Phoenix, which the Shi'ar worship as a god. Jean is being kept under observation in the X-Mansion's infirmary until it can be determined that she is not a threat to her fellow students.

anwhile, Elliot Boggs–the new X-Man known as Magician–has taken the world by storm. This popularity followed an uspicious debut–the teenager was dropped onto the X-Men's doorstep by Nick Fury (head of the superhuman defense nitiative called the Ultimates) after the first manifestation of Elliot's powers (inadvertently) killed his parents. In the time since his arrival, Elliot has become a media darling, bringing the X-Men back into the spotlight.

ut Elliot and the X-Men aren't the only people in Professor Charles Xavier's world. Some months ago, he had a rather unusual meeting with a rather unique mutant...

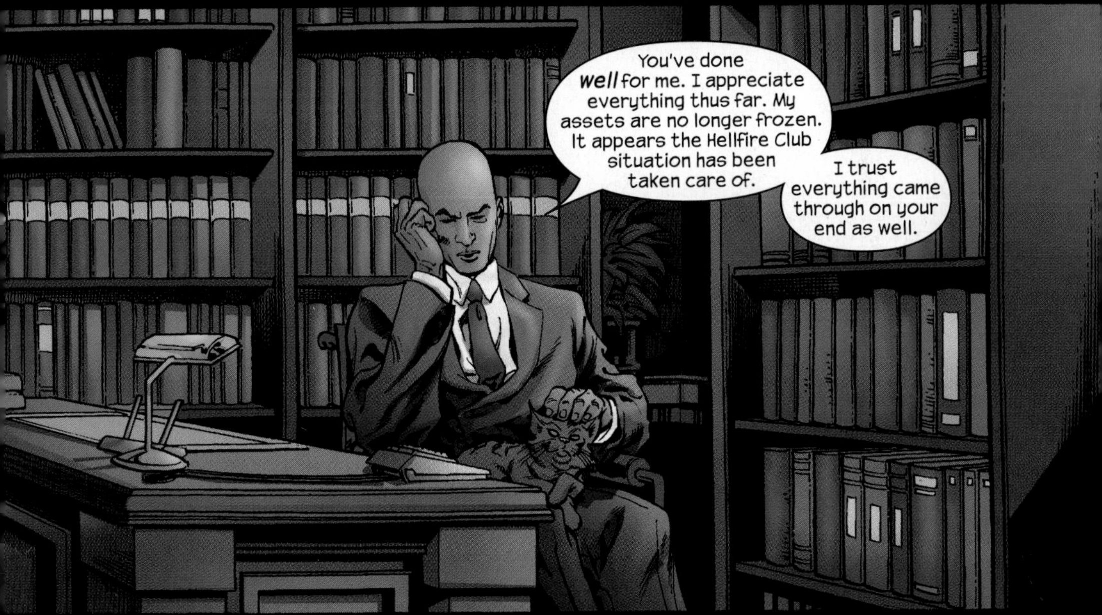
You've done *well* for me. I appreciate everything thus far. My assets are no longer frozen. It appears the Hellfire Club situation has been taken care of.
I trust everything came through on your end as well.

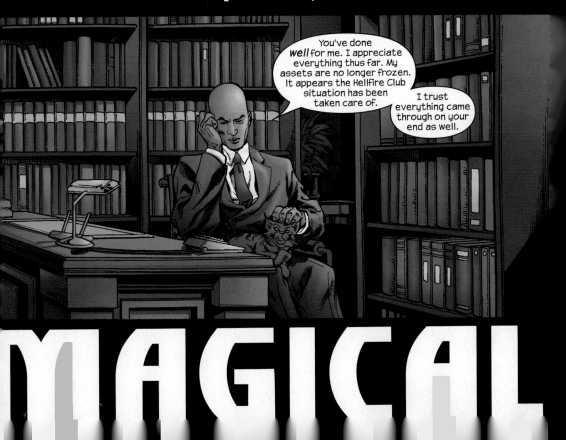

MAGICAL

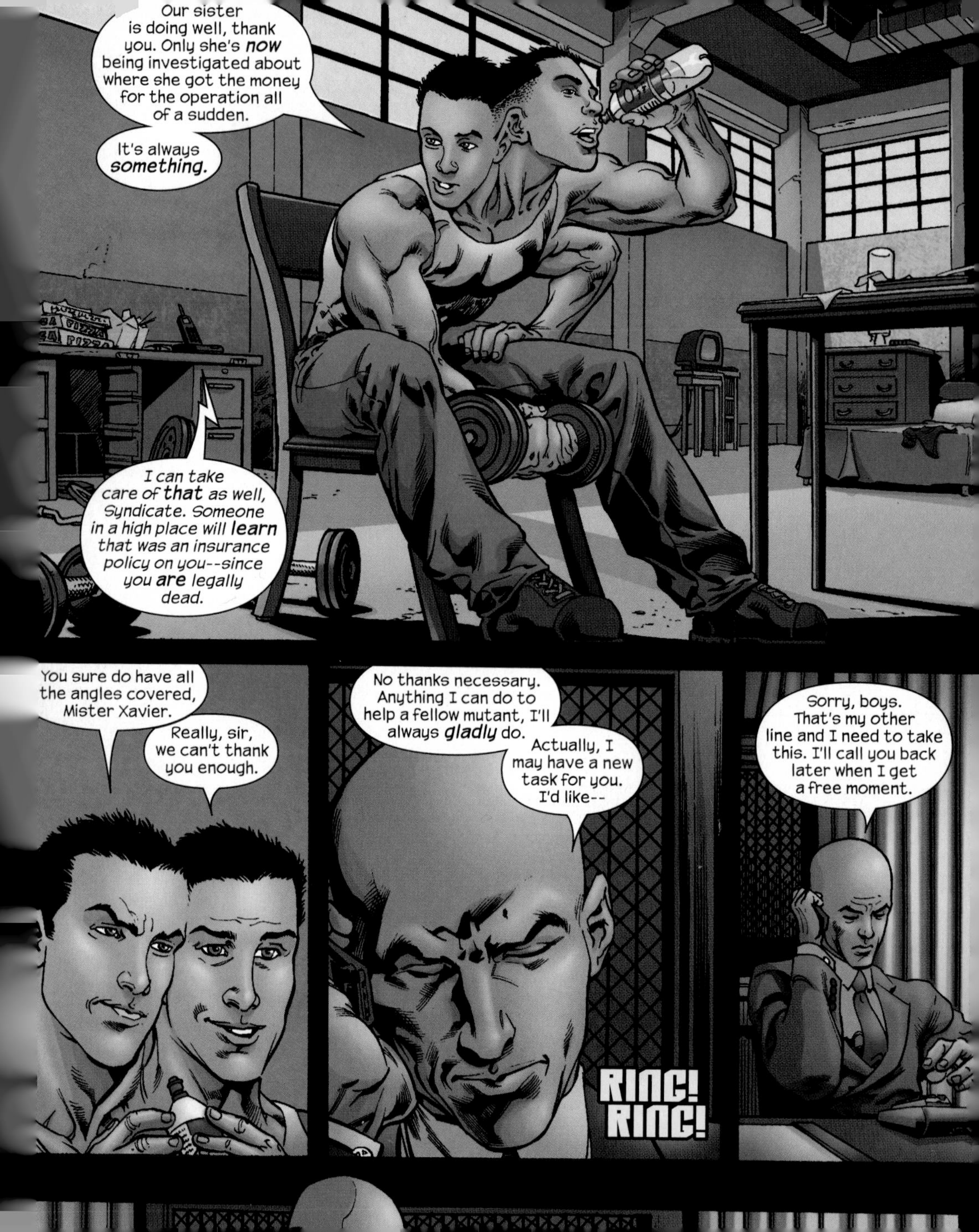
Our sister is doing well, thank you. Only she's *now* being investigated about where she got the money for the operation all of a sudden.
It's always *something.*
I can take care of **that** as well, Syndicate. Someone in a high place will **learn** that was an insurance policy on you--since you **are** legally dead.
You sure do have all the angles covered, Mister Xavier.
Really, sir, we can't thank you enough.
No thanks necessary. Anything I can do to help a fellow mutant, I'll always *gladly* do.
Actually, I may have a new task for you. I'd like--
RING! RING!
Sorry, boys. That's my other line and I need to take this. I'll call you back later when I get a free moment.

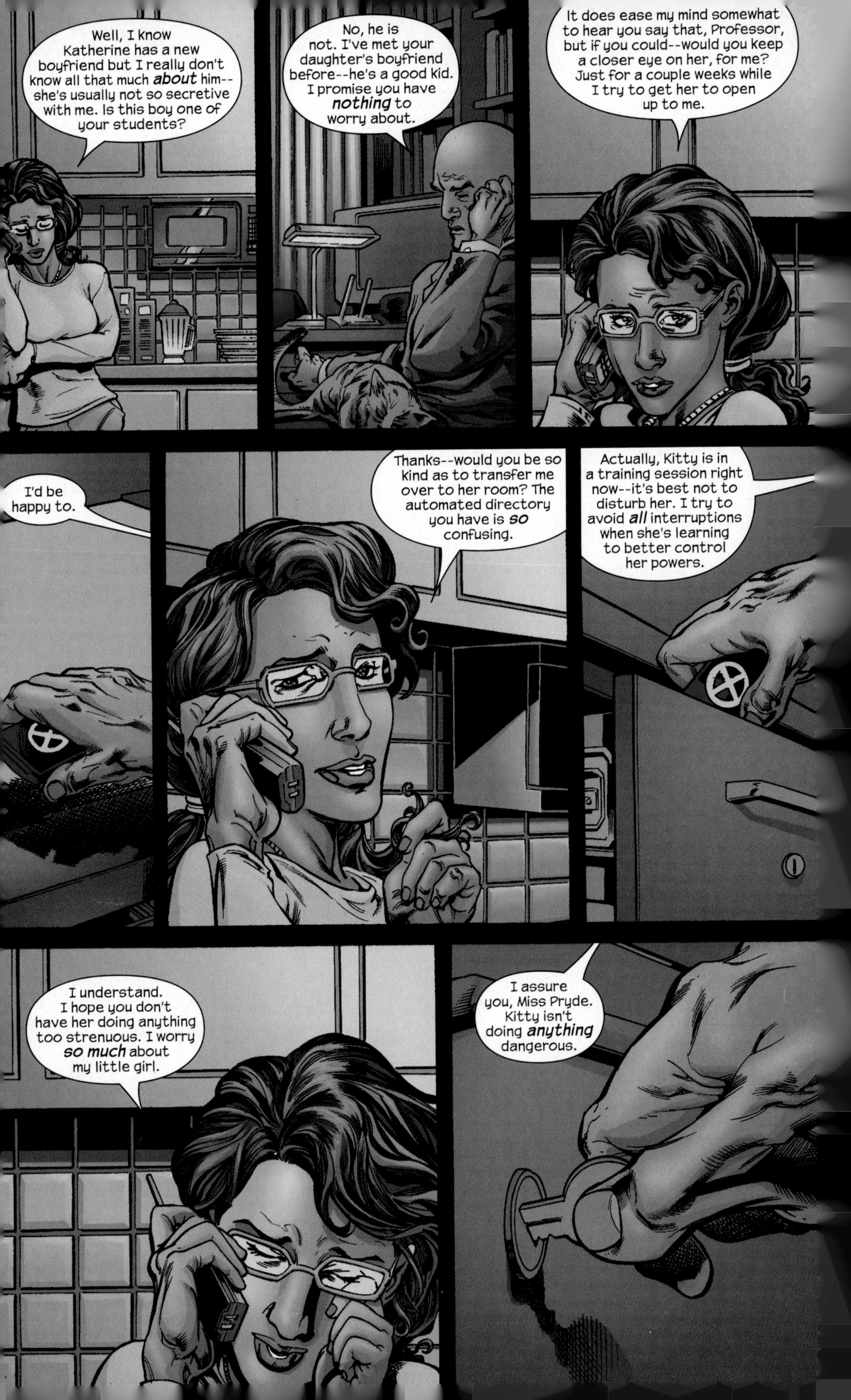
Well, I know Katherine has a new boyfriend but I really don't know all that much *about* him--she's usually not so secretive with me. Is this boy one of your students?
No, he is not. I've met your daughter's boyfriend before--he's a good kid. I promise you have *nothing* to worry about.
It does ease my mind somewhat to hear you say that, Professor, but if you could--would you keep a closer eye on her, for me? Just for a couple weeks while I try to get her to open up to me.
I'd be happy to.
Thanks--would you be so kind as to transfer me over to her room? The automated directory you have is *so* confusing.
Actually, Kitty is in a training session right now--it's best not to disturb her. I try to avoid *all* interruptions when she's learning to better control her powers.
I understand. I hope you don't have her doing anything too strenuous. I worry *so much* about my little girl.
I assure you, Miss Pryde. Kitty isn't doing *anything* dangerous.

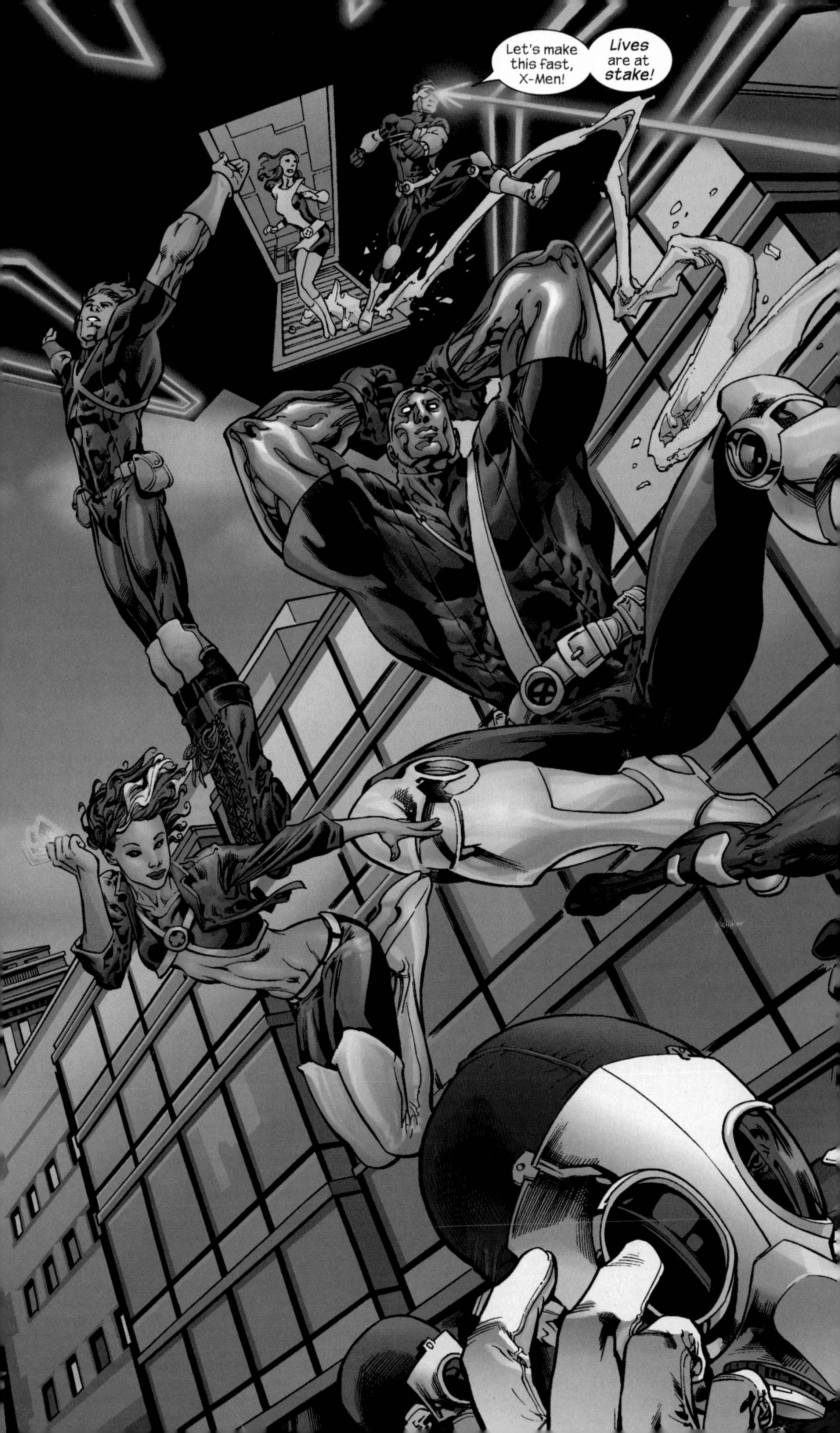
Let's make this fast, X-Men!
Lives are at stake!

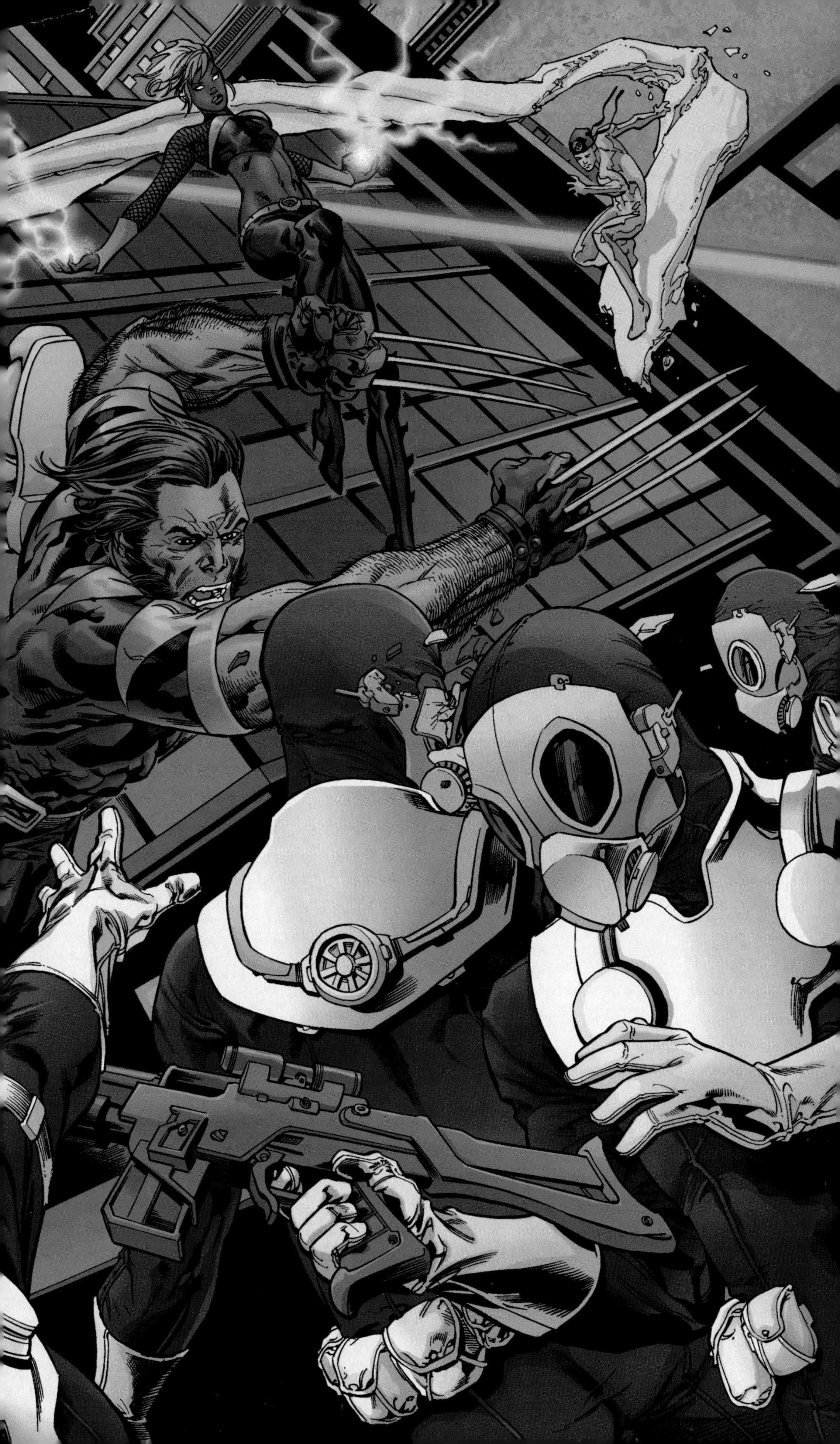

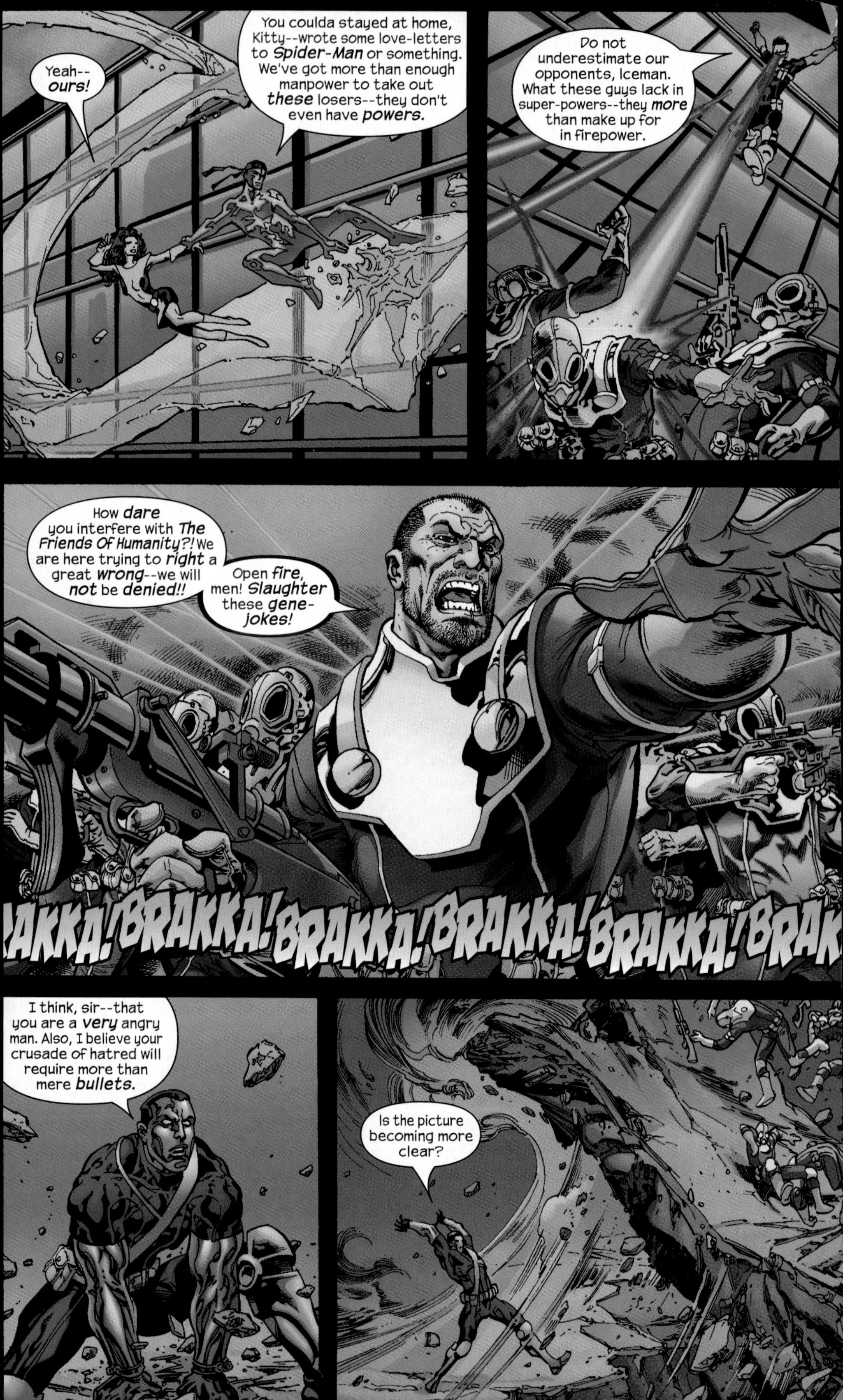

Yeah-- ours!
You coulda stayed at home, Kitty--wrote some love-letters to Spider-Man or something. We've got more than enough manpower to take out these losers--they don't even have powers.
Do not underestimate our opponents, Iceman. What these guys lack in super-powers--they more than make up for in firepower.
How dare you interfere with The Friends Of Humanity?! We are here trying to right a great wrong--we will not be denied!!
Open fire, men! Slaughter these gene-jokes!
BRAKKA! BRAKKA! BRAKKA! BRAKKA! BRAKKA!
I think, sir--that you are a very angry man. Also, I believe your crusade of hatred will require more than mere bullets.
Is the picture becoming more clear?

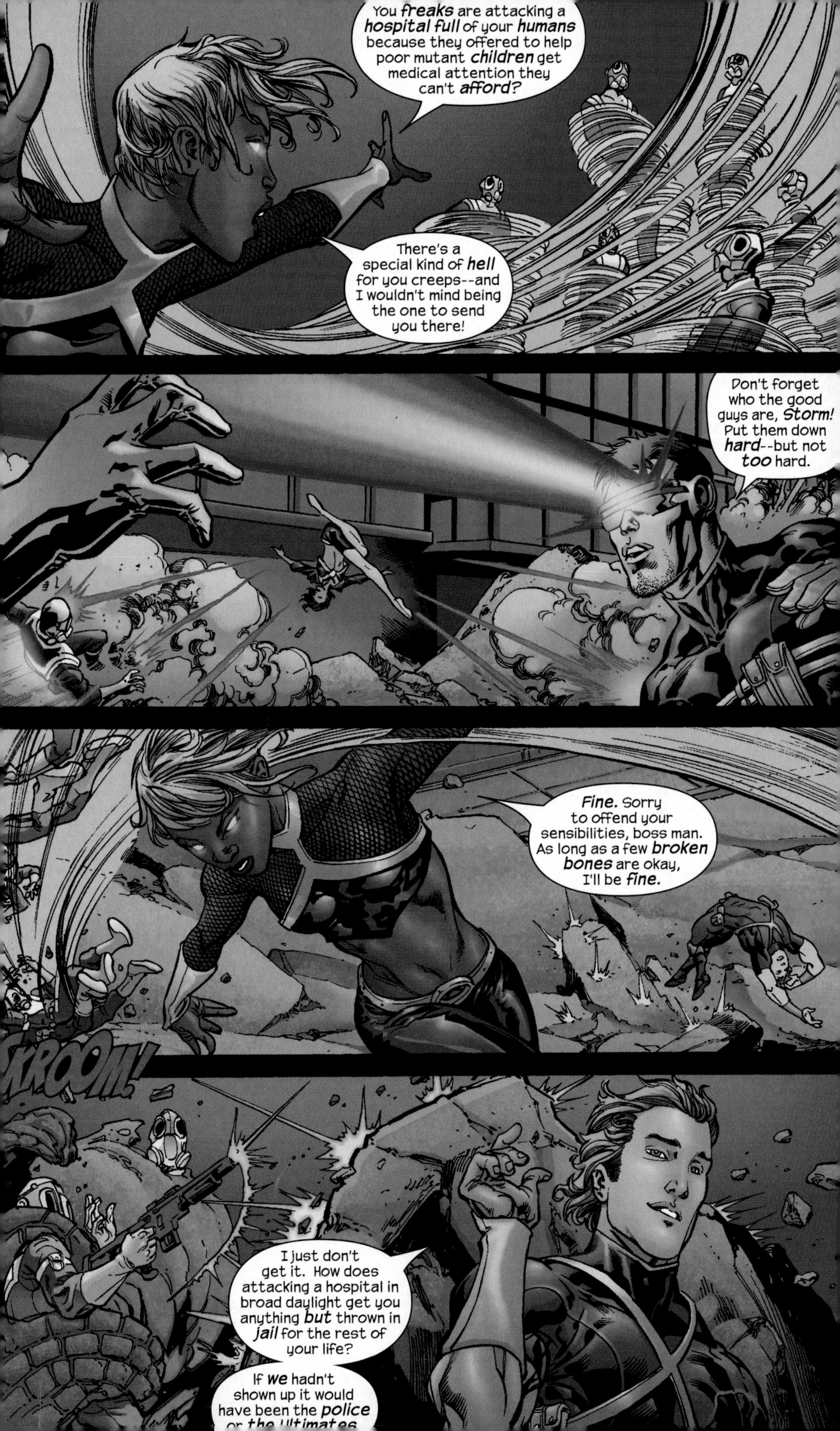
You freaks are attacking a hospital full of your humans because they offered to help poor mutant children get medical attention they can't afford?
There's a special kind of hell for you creeps--and I wouldn't mind being the one to send you there!
Don't forget who the good guys are, Storm! Put them down hard--but not too hard.
Fine. Sorry to offend your sensibilities, boss man. As long as a few broken bones are okay, I'll be fine.
KROOM!
I just don't get it. How does attacking a hospital in broad daylight get you anything but thrown in jail for the rest of your life?
If we hadn't shown up it would have been the police

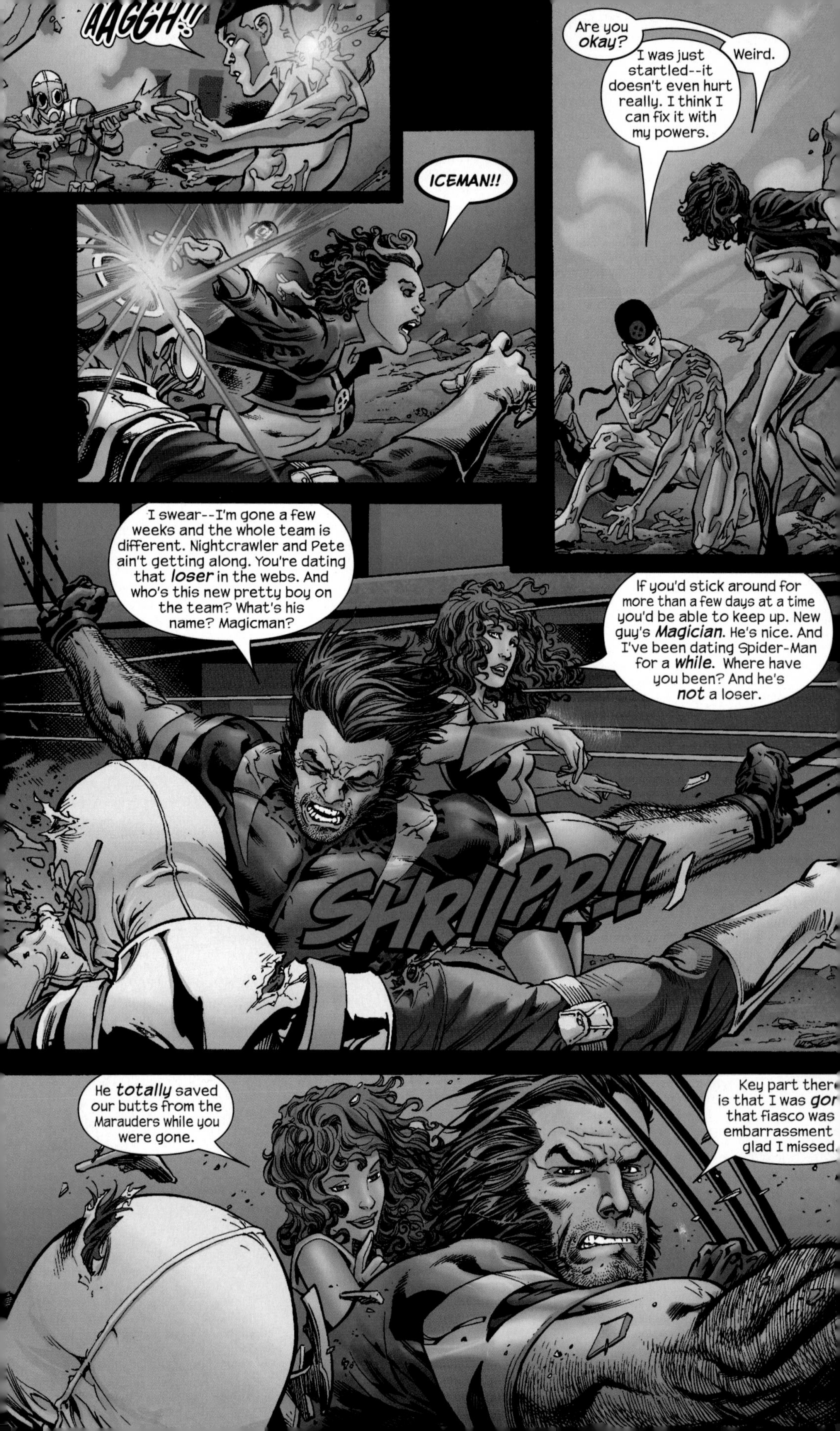
AAGGH!!
Are you okay?
Weird.
I was just startled--it doesn't even hurt really. I think I can fix it with my powers.
ICEMAN!!
I swear--I'm gone a few weeks and the whole team is different. Nightcrawler and Pete ain't getting along. You're dating that loser in the webs. And who's this new pretty boy on the team? What's his name? Magicman?
If you'd stick around for more than a few days at a time you'd be able to keep up. New guy's Magician. He's nice. And I've been dating Spider-Man for a while. Where have you been? And he's not a loser.
SHRIPP!!
He totally saved our butts from the Marauders while you were gone.
Key part ther is that I was gor that fiasco was embarrassment glad I missed.

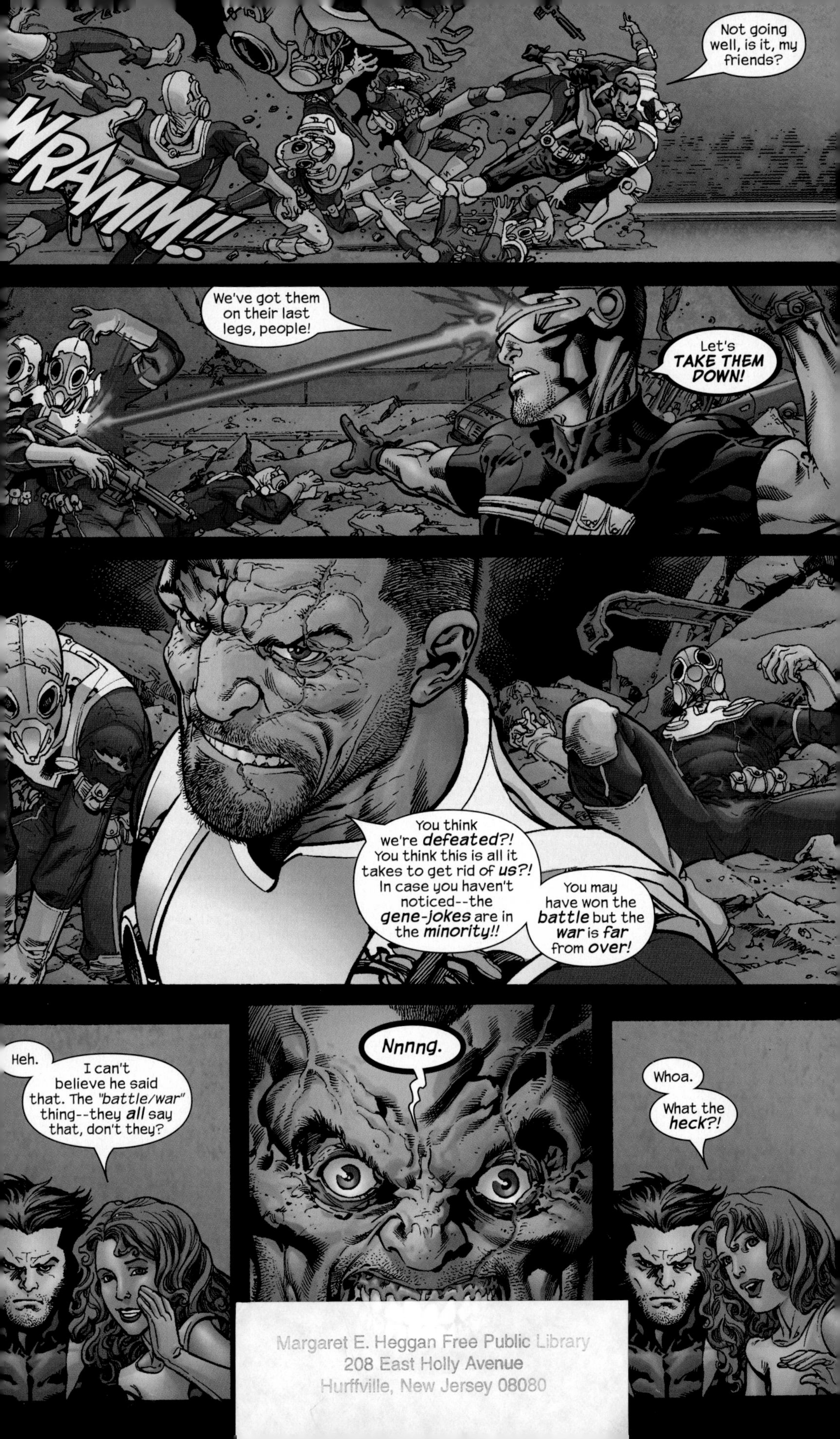
WRAMM!!
Not going well, is it, my friends?
We've got them on their last legs, people!
Let's TAKE THEM DOWN!
You think we're defeated?! You think this is all it takes to get rid of us?! In case you haven't noticed--the gene-jokes are in the minority!!
You may have won the battle but the war is far from over!
Heh.
I can't believe he said that. The "battle/war" thing--they all say that, don't they?
Nnnng.
Whoa.
What the heck?!

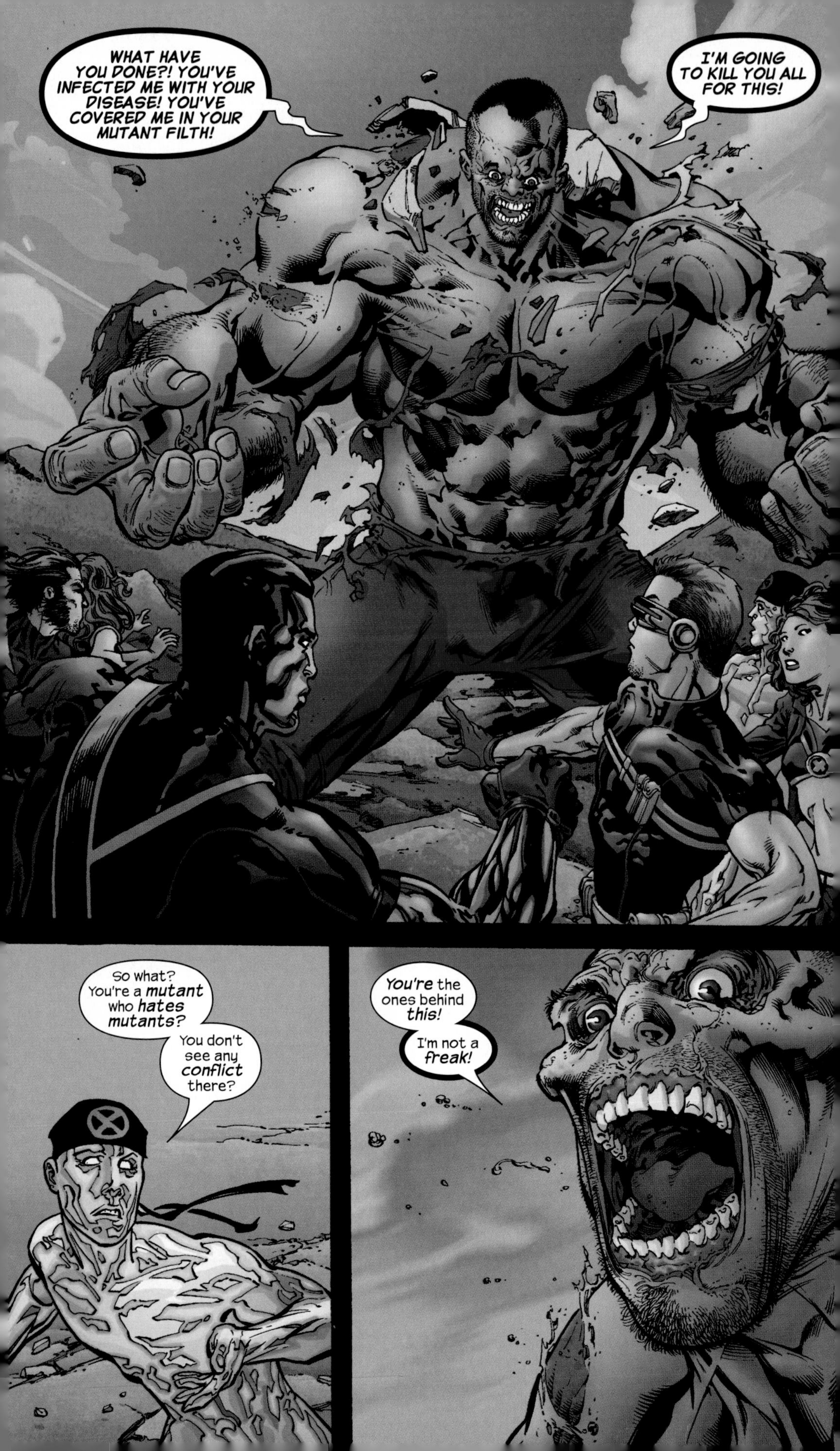
WHAT HAVE YOU DONE?! YOU'VE INFECTED ME WITH YOUR DISEASE! YOU'VE COVERED ME IN YOUR MUTANT FILTH!
I'M GOING TO KILL YOU ALL FOR THIS!
So what? You're a *mutant* who *hates mutants*?
You don't see any *conflict* there?
You're the ones behind *this!*
I'm not a *freak!*

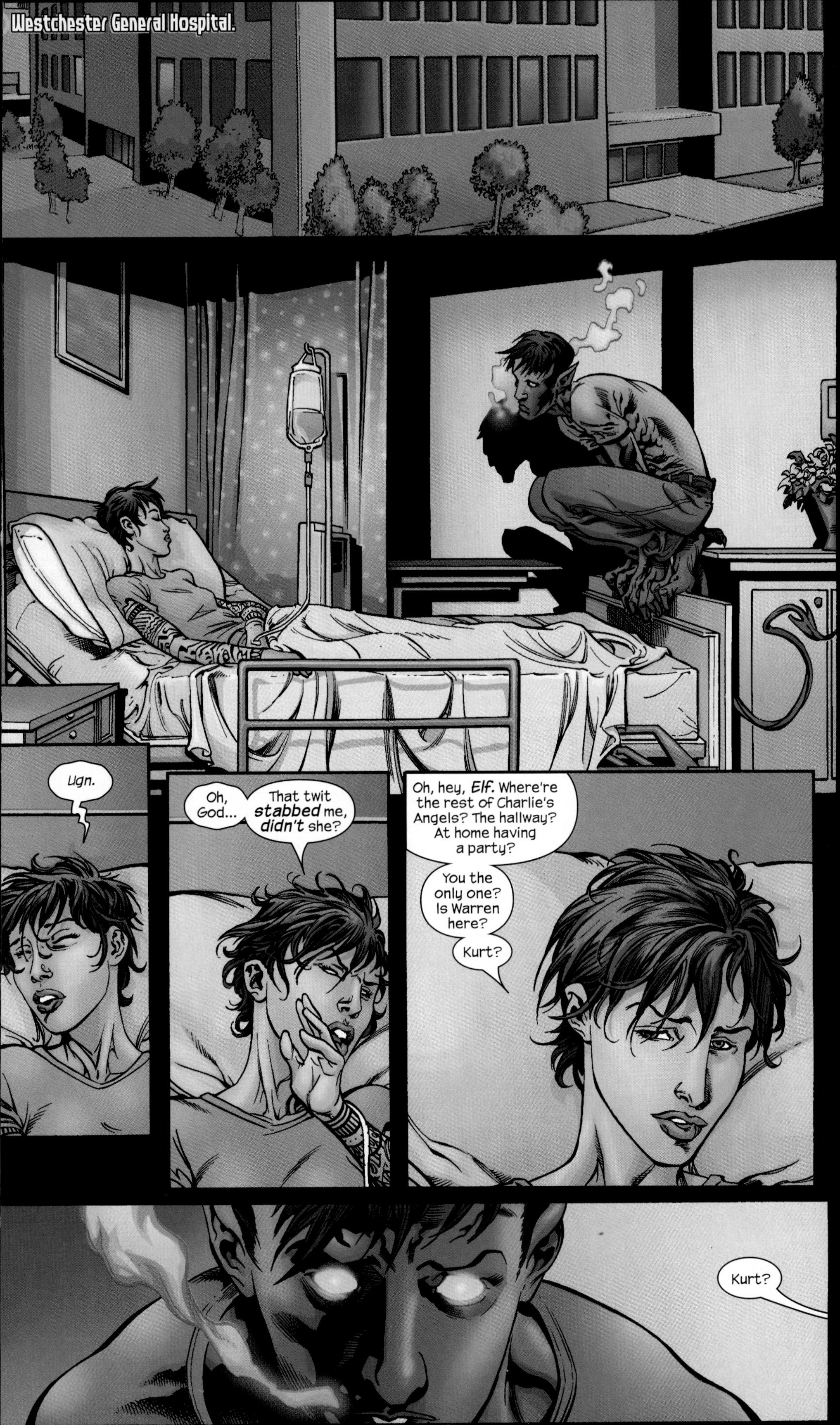
Westchester General Hospital.
Ugn.
Oh, God...
That twit stabbed me, didn't she?
Oh, hey, Elf. Where're the rest of Charlie's Angels? The hallway? At home having a party?
You the only one? Is Warren here?
Kurt?
Kurt?

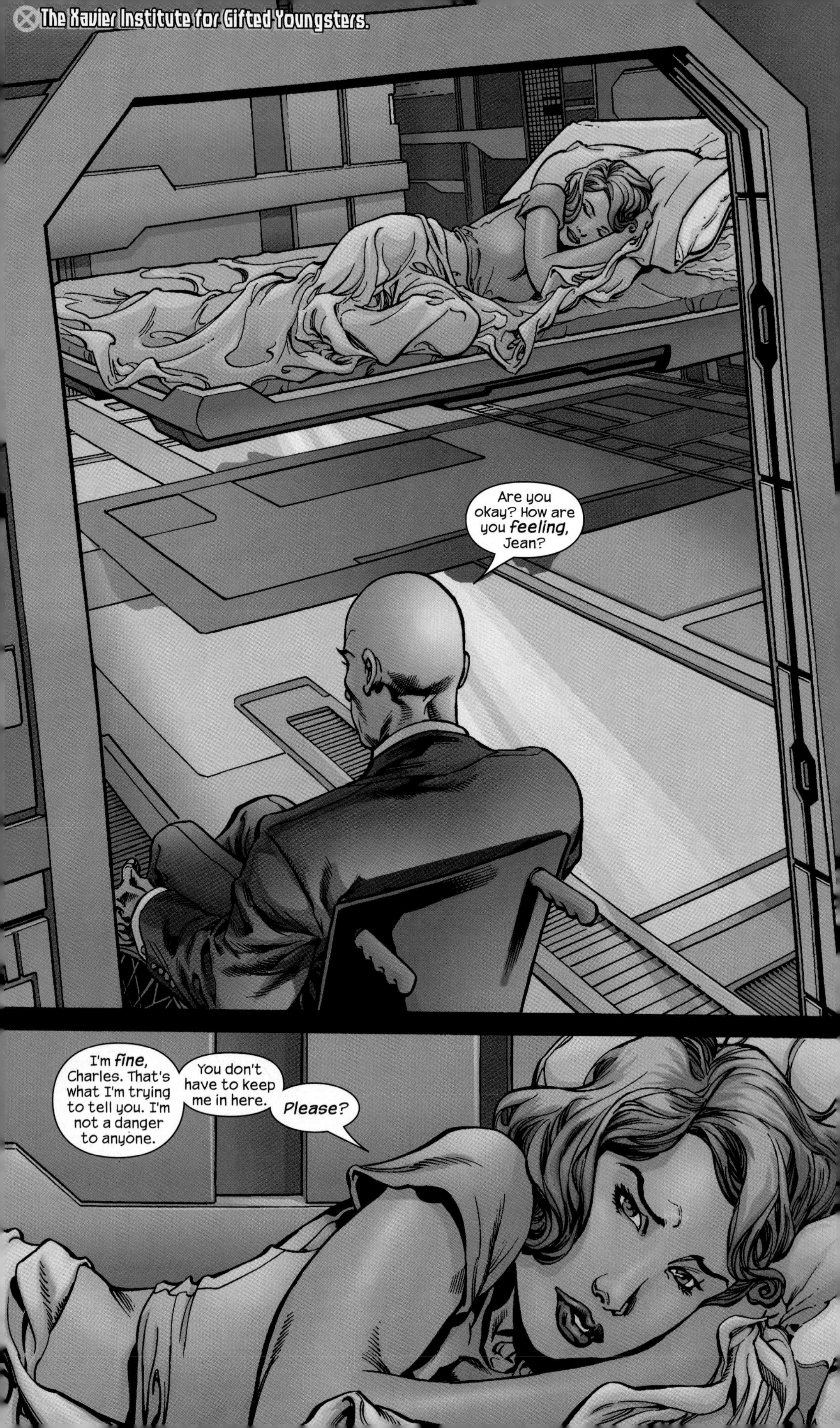
The Xavier Institute for Gifted Youngsters.
Are you okay? How are you *feeling*, Jean?
I'm *fine*, Charles. That's what I'm trying to tell you. I'm not a danger to anyone.
You don't have to keep me in here.
Please?

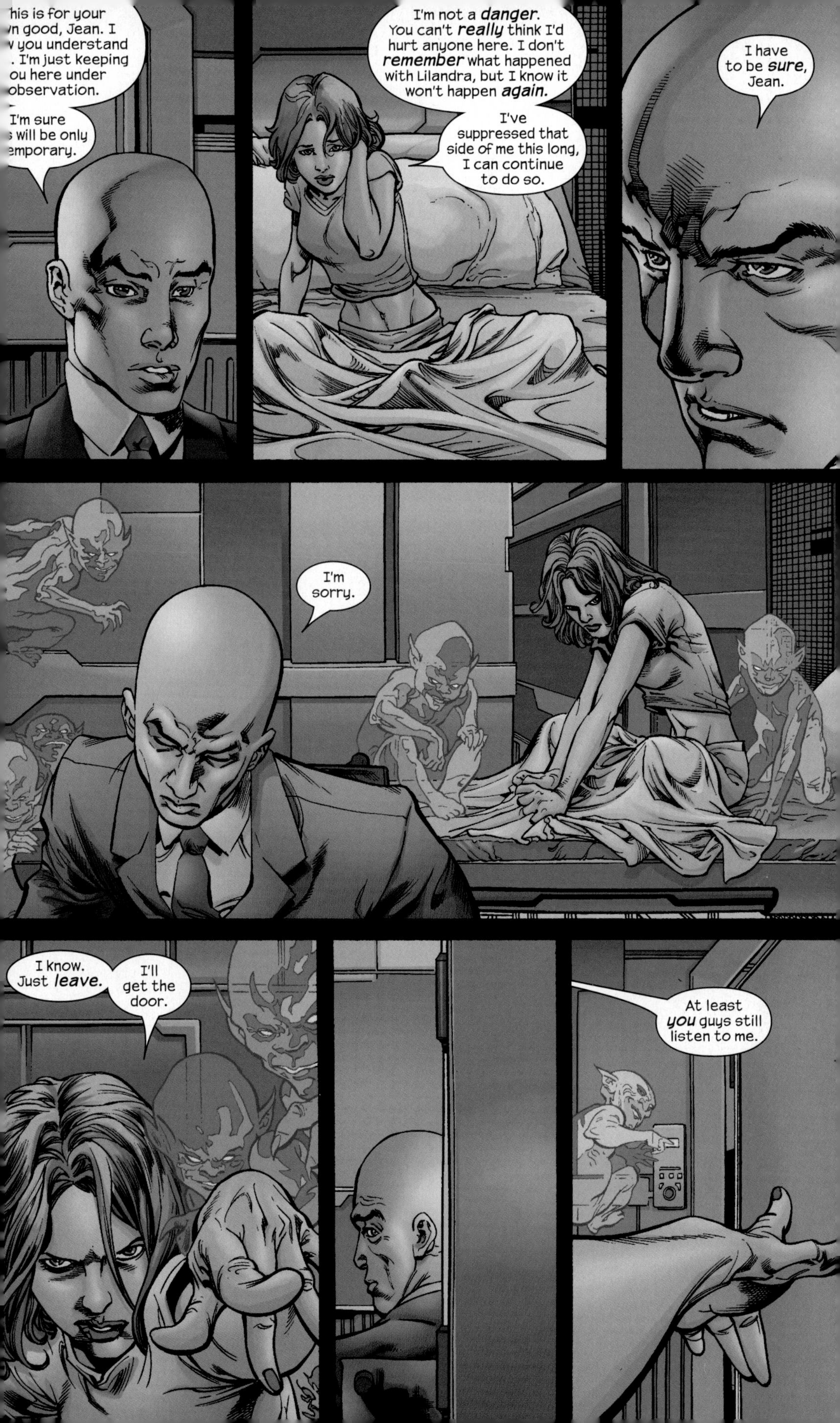

his is for your
n good, Jean. I
v you understand
. I'm just keeping
ou here under
observation.
I'm sure
s will be only
emporary.
I'm not a danger. You can't really think I'd hurt anyone here. I don't remember what happened with Lilandra, but I know it won't happen again.
I've suppressed that side of me this long, I can continue to do so.
I have to be sure, Jean.
I'm sorry.
I know. Just leave.
I'll get the door.
At least you guys still listen to me.

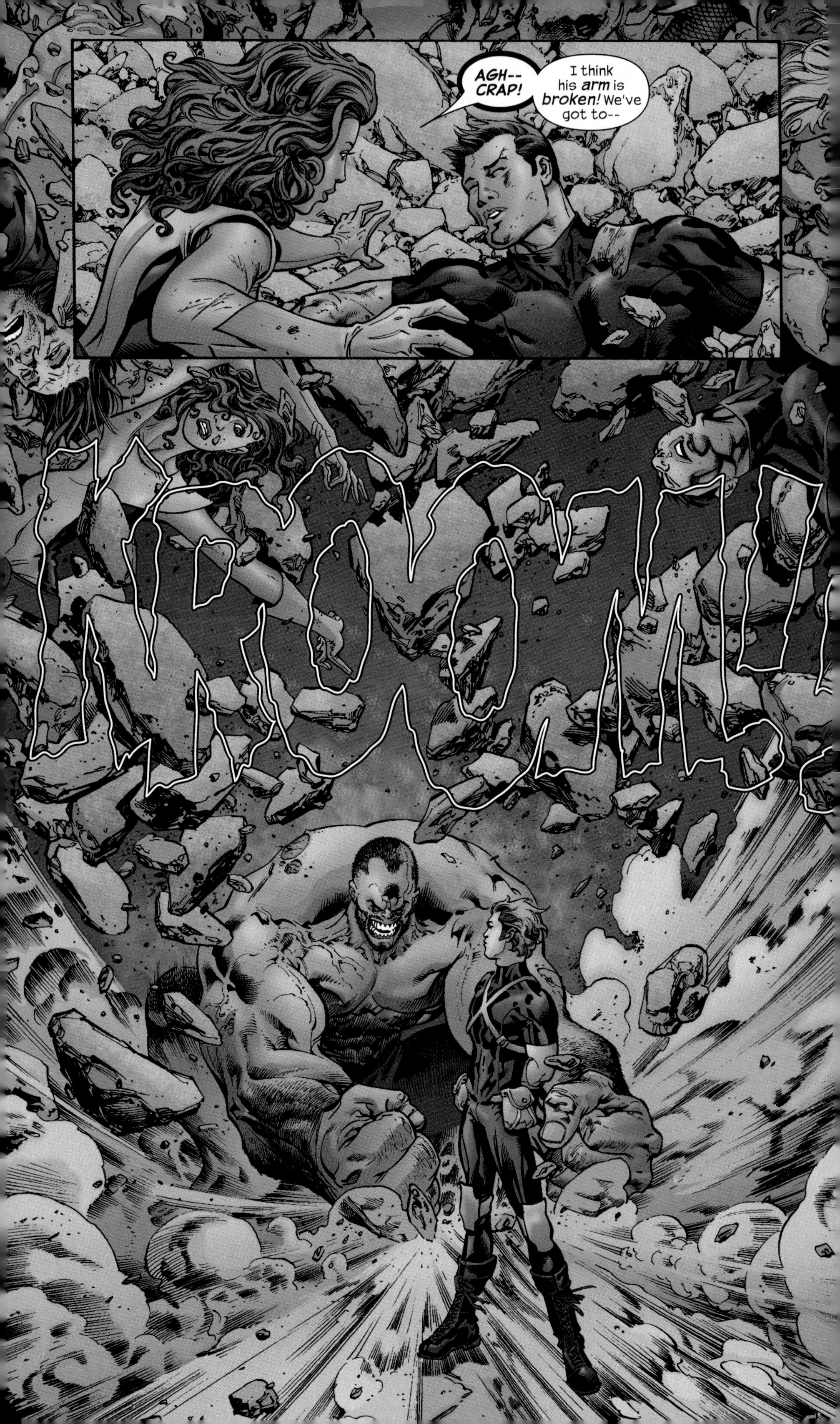
AGH-- CRAP!
I think his arm is broken! We've got to--

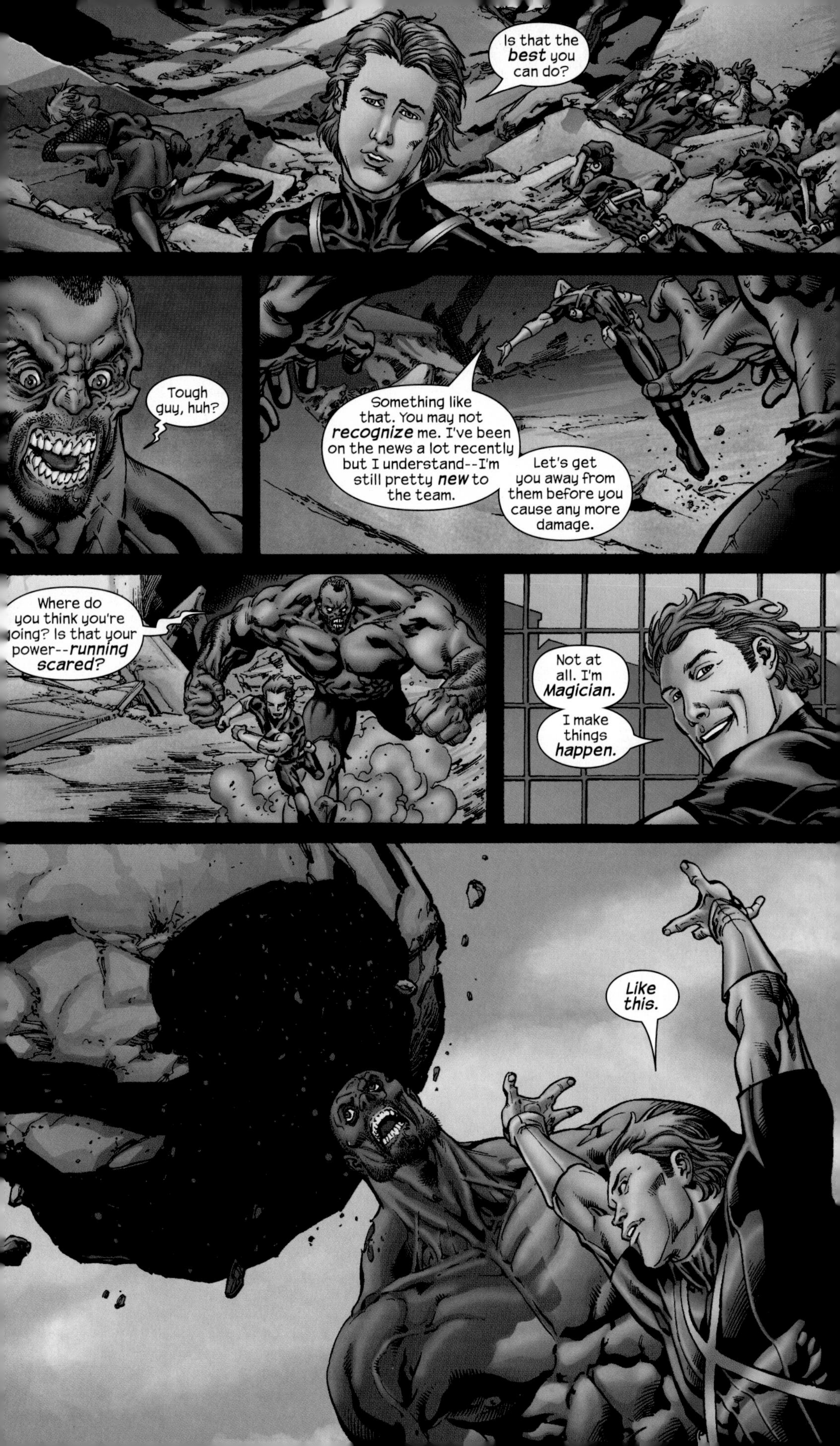
Is that the best you can do?
Tough guy, huh?
Something like that. You may not recognize me. I've been on the news a lot recently but I understand--I'm still pretty new to the team.
Let's get you away from them before you cause any more damage.
Where do you think you're going? Is that your power--running scared?
Not at all. I'm Magician.
I make things happen.
Like this.

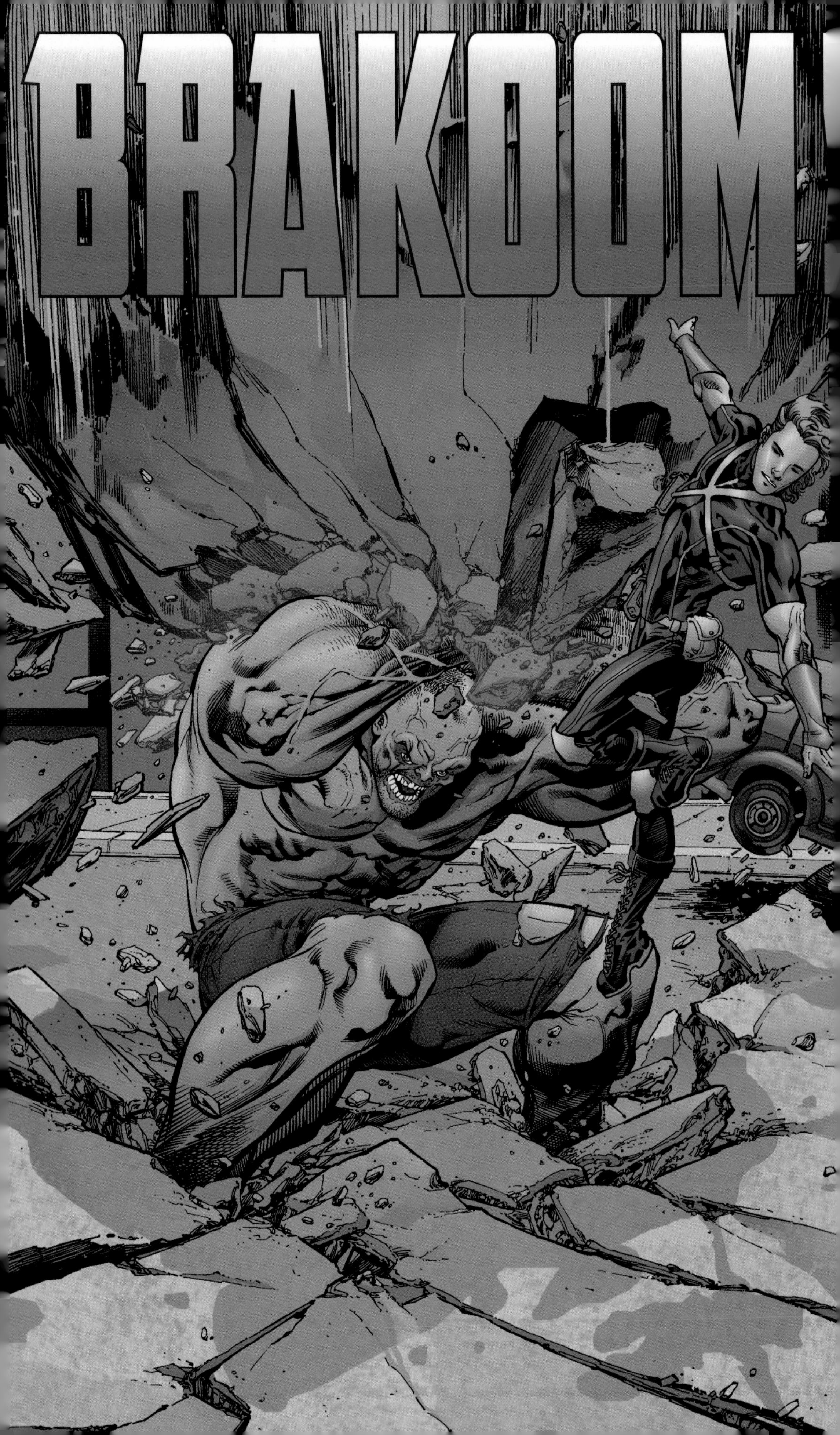
BRAKOOM!

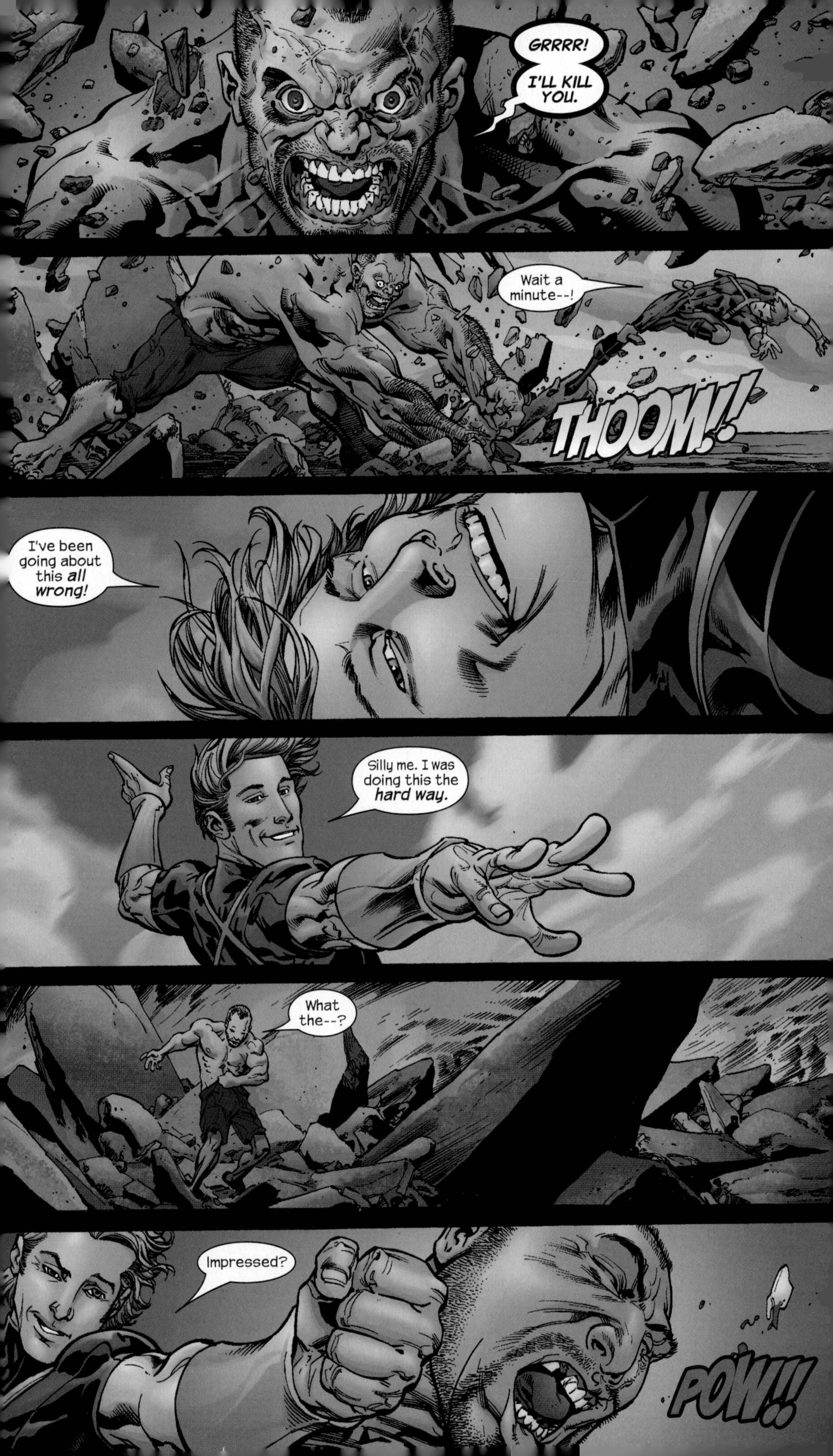
GRRRR!
I'LL KILL YOU.
Wait a minute--!
THOOM!!
I've been going about this *all wrong!*
Silly me. I was doing this the *hard way.*
What the--?
Impressed?
POW!!

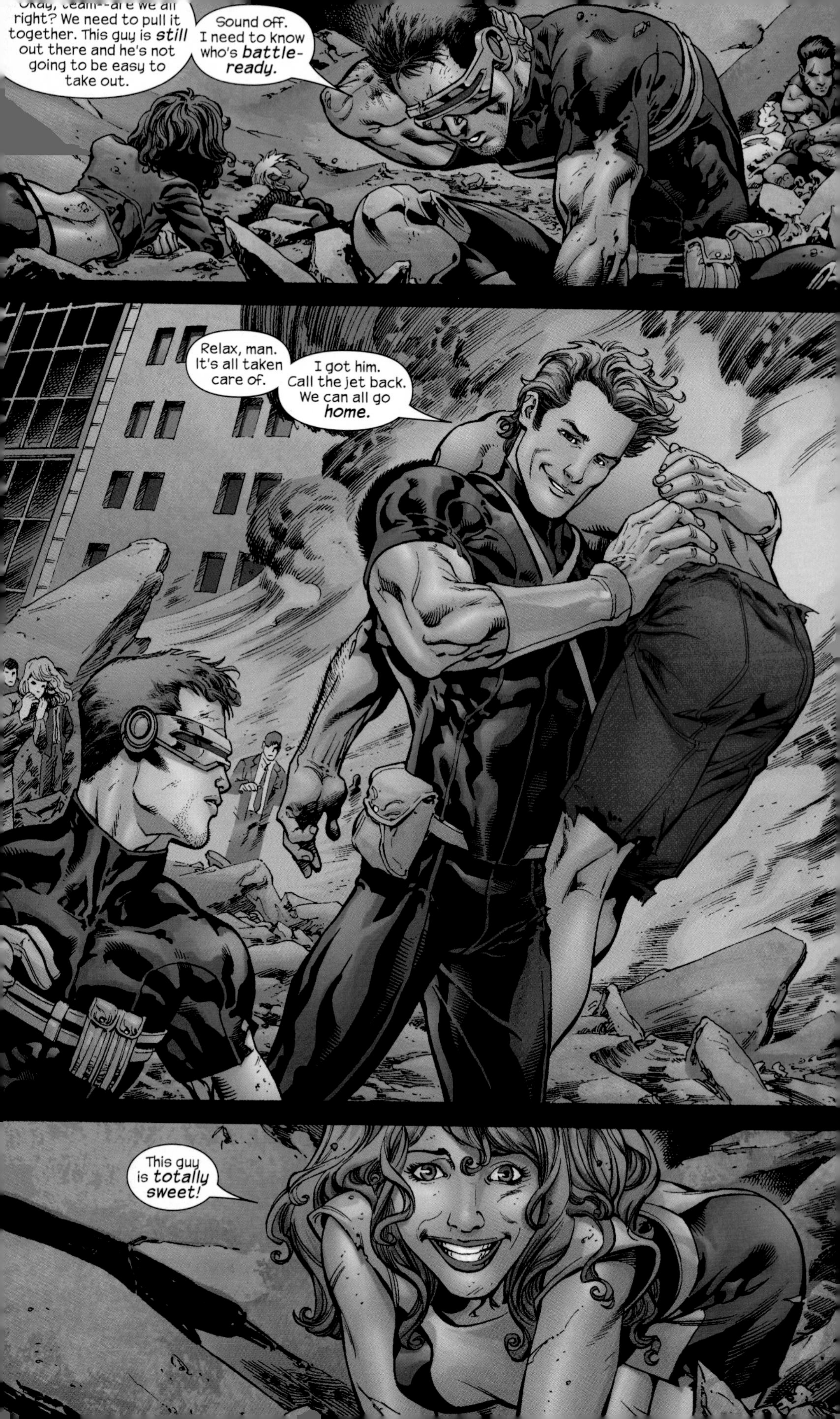
Okay, team--are we all right? We need to pull it together. This guy is *still* out there and he's not going to be easy to take out.
Sound off. I need to know who's *battle-ready.*
Relax, man. It's all taken care of.
I got him. Call the jet back. We can all go *home.*
This guy is *totally sweet!*

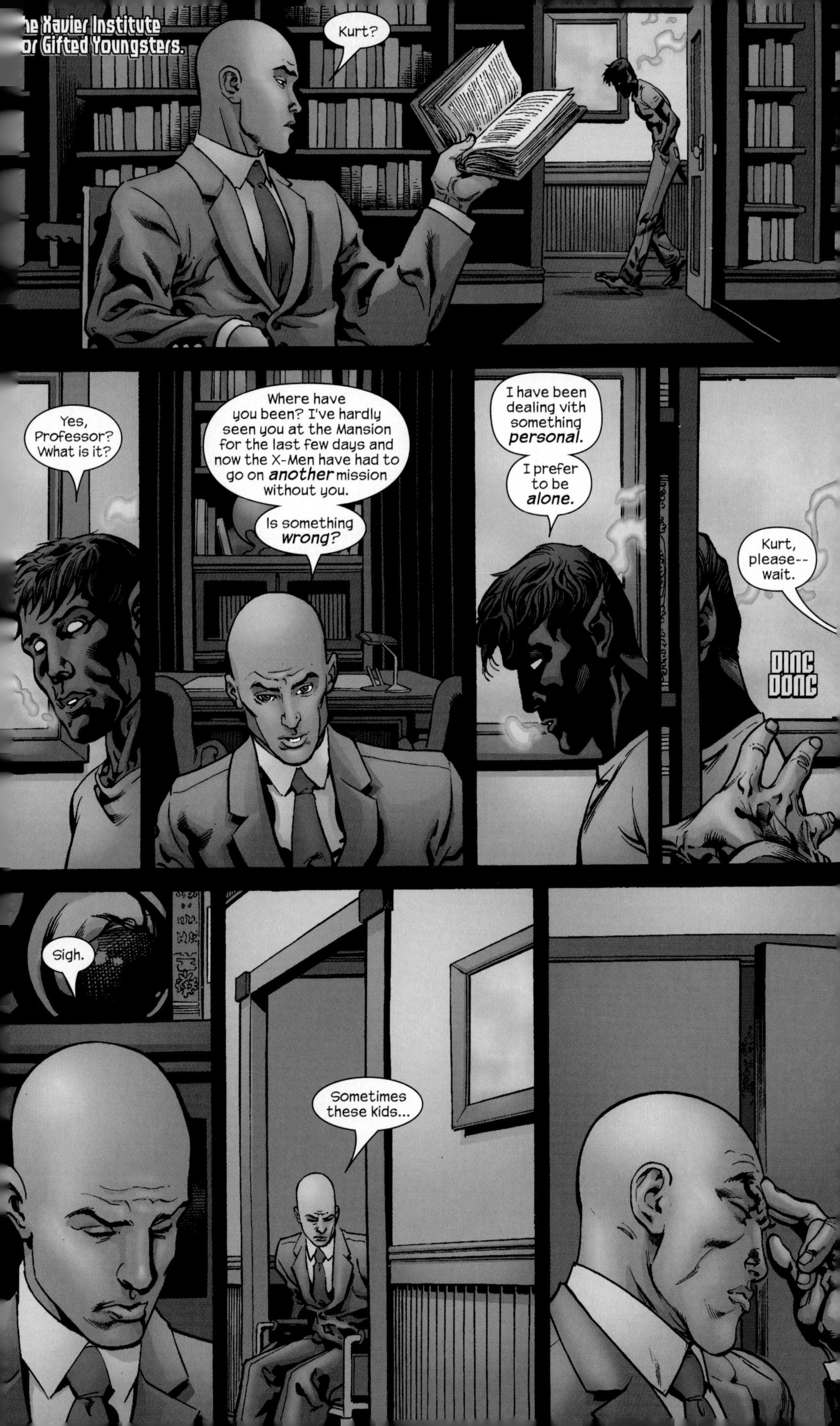

The Xavier Institute for Gifted Youngsters.
Kurt?
Yes, Professor? What is it?
Where have you been? I've hardly seen you at the Mansion for the last few days and now the X-Men have had to go on *another* mission without you.
Is something *wrong*?
I have been dealing vith something *personal.*
I prefer to be *alone.*
Kurt, please-- wait.
DING DONG
Sigh.
Sometimes these kids...

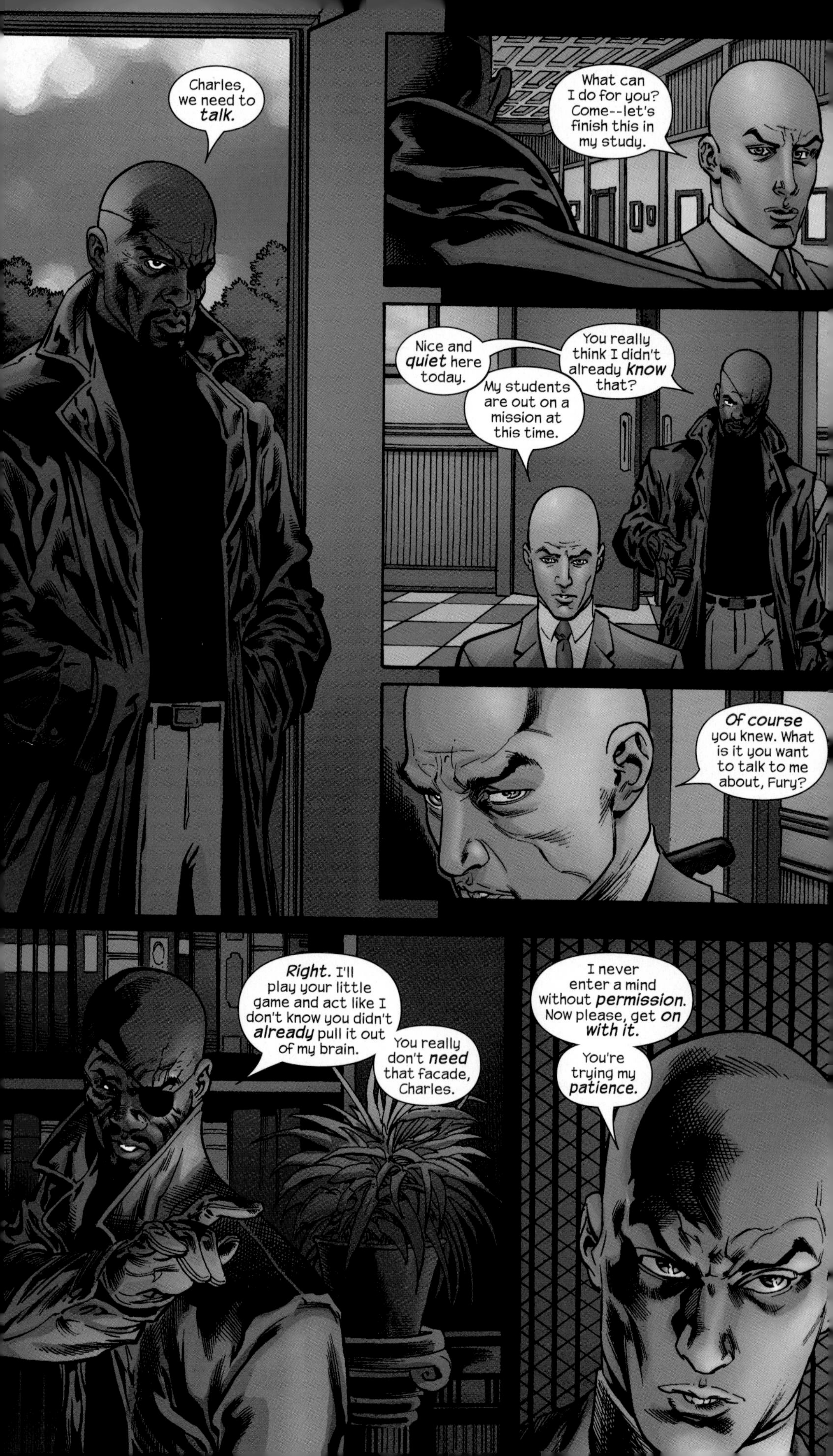

Charles, we need to *talk.*
What can I do for you? Come--let's finish this in my study.
Nice and *quiet* here today.
You really think I didn't already *know* that?
My students are out on a mission at this time.
Of course you knew. What is it you want to talk to me about, Fury?
Right. I'll play your little game and act like I don't know you didn't *already* pull it out of my brain.
You really don't *need* that facade, Charles.
I never enter a mind without *permission.* Now please, get *on with it.*
You're trying my *patience.*

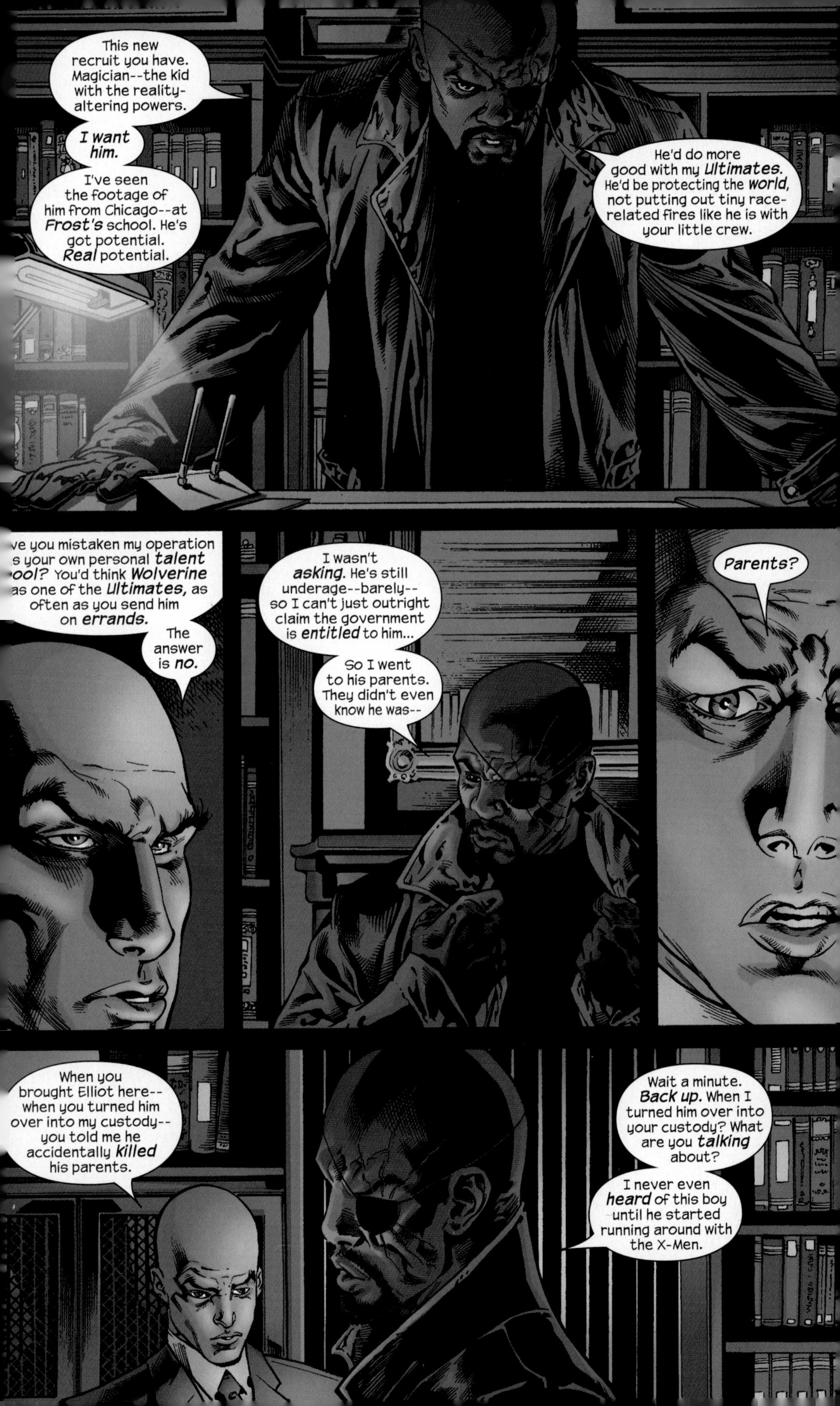
This new recruit you have. Magician--the kid with the reality-altering powers.
I want him.
I've seen the footage of him from Chicago--at Frost's school. He's got potential. Real potential.
He'd do more good with my Ultimates. He'd be protecting the world, not putting out tiny race-related fires like he is with your little crew.
ve you mistaken my operation s your own personal talent ool? You'd think Wolverine as one of the Ultimates, as often as you send him on errands.
The answer is no.
I wasn't asking. He's still underage--barely--so I can't just outright claim the government is entitled to him...
So I went to his parents. They didn't even know he was--
Parents?
When you brought Elliot here--when you turned him over into my custody--you told me he accidentally killed his parents.
Wait a minute. Back up. When I turned him over into your custody? What are you talking about?
I never even heard of this boy until he started running around with the X-Men.

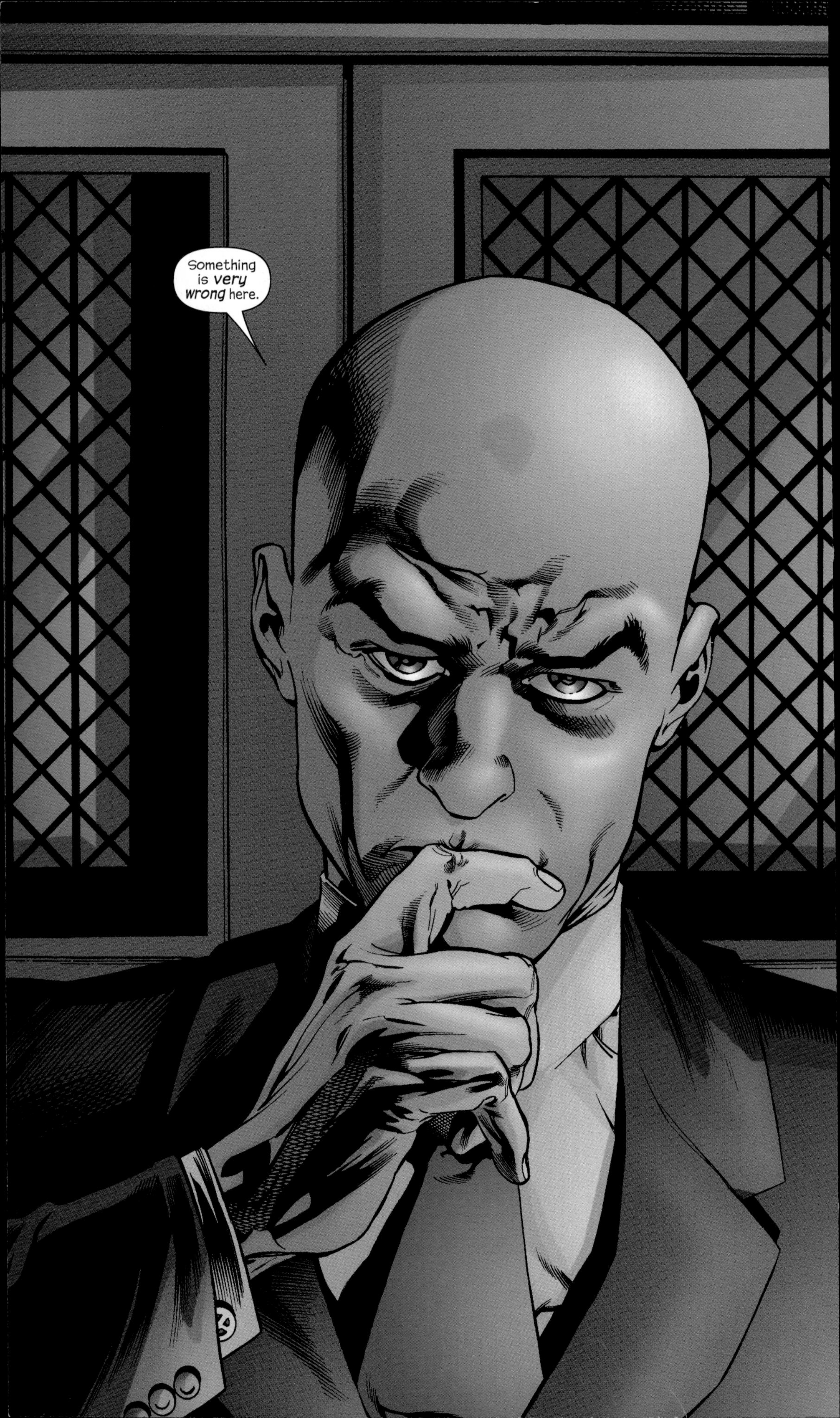
Something is *very* *wrong* here.

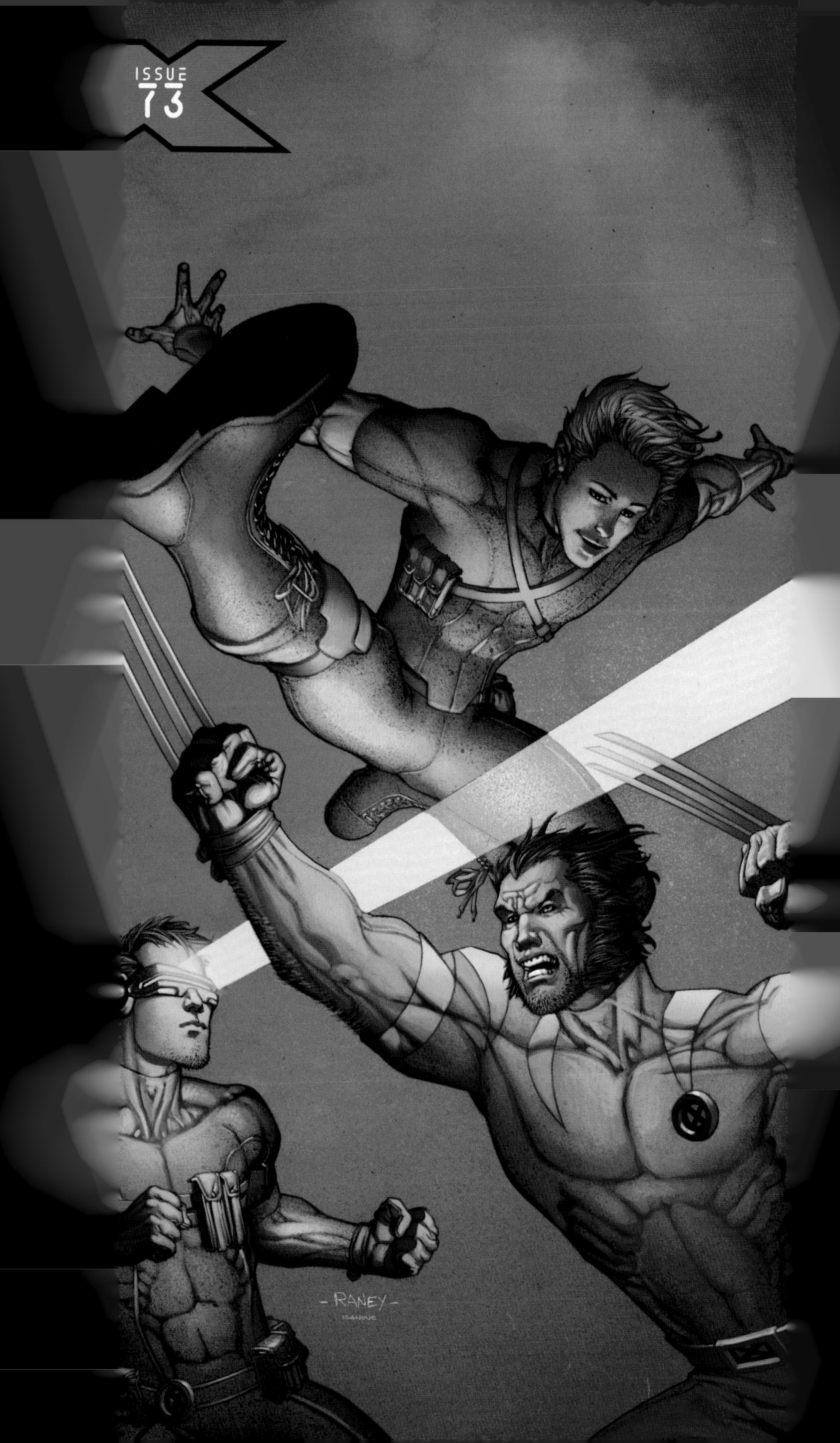
ISSUE
73
- RANEY -

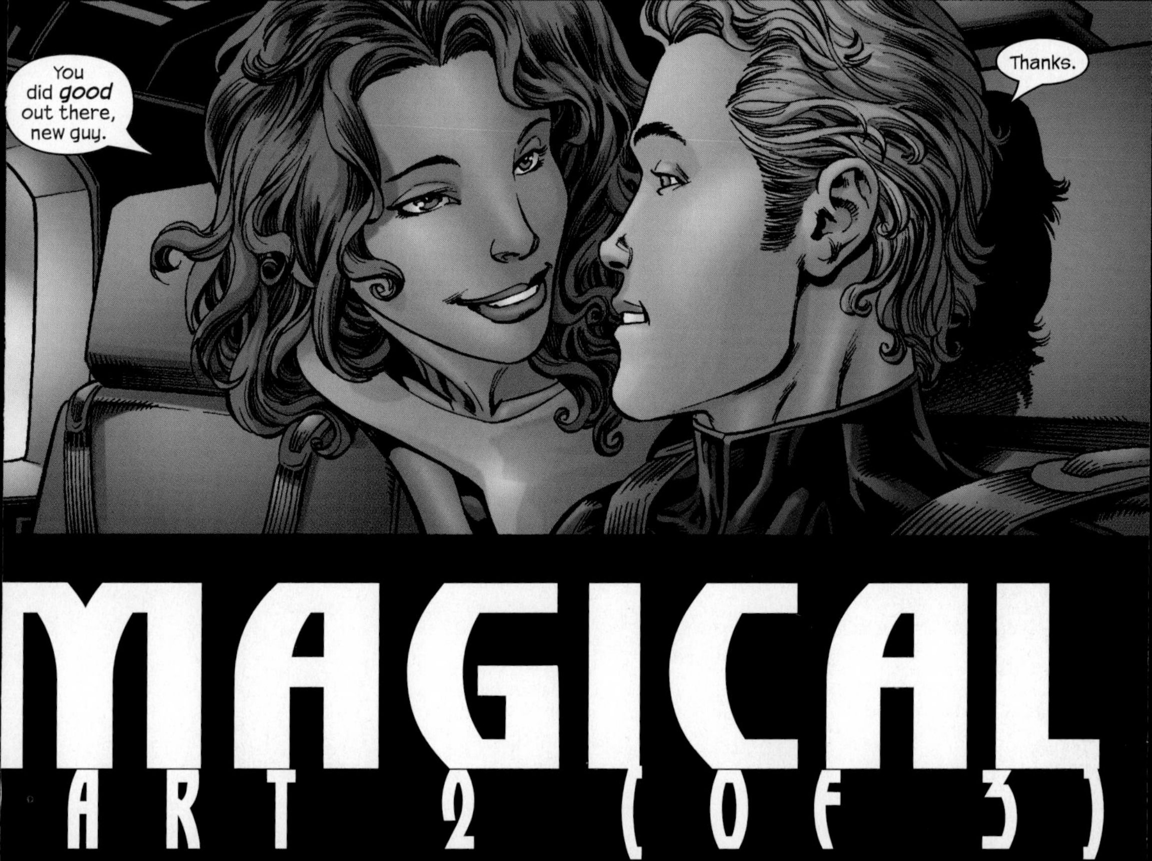
You did *good* out there, new guy.
Thanks.
MAGICAL
ART 2 (OF 3)

Panel 1: Maybe you could show *me* a few of those moves sometime. Lord knows I could *use* some improvement in my fighting. What do you say?

Panel 2: You've twisted my arm.

Panel 3: Anytime, Kitty. Just say the word.

Panel 4: Don't you *have* a boyfriend already?

Panel 5: Shut up.

Panel 6: Are you *okay*? You seem preoccupied.

Panel 7: It's nothing, really.

Thinking about *Jean*.

BEEP BEEP

Yes? It's done. We're on our way back to the Mansion now. Yes, sir. At present speed? No more than ten minutes. Yes, sir.

What was *that* about?

The Professor, seeing when we'll be back at the Mansion. That's odd, he *never* checks up on us like that.

Maybe something is wrong.

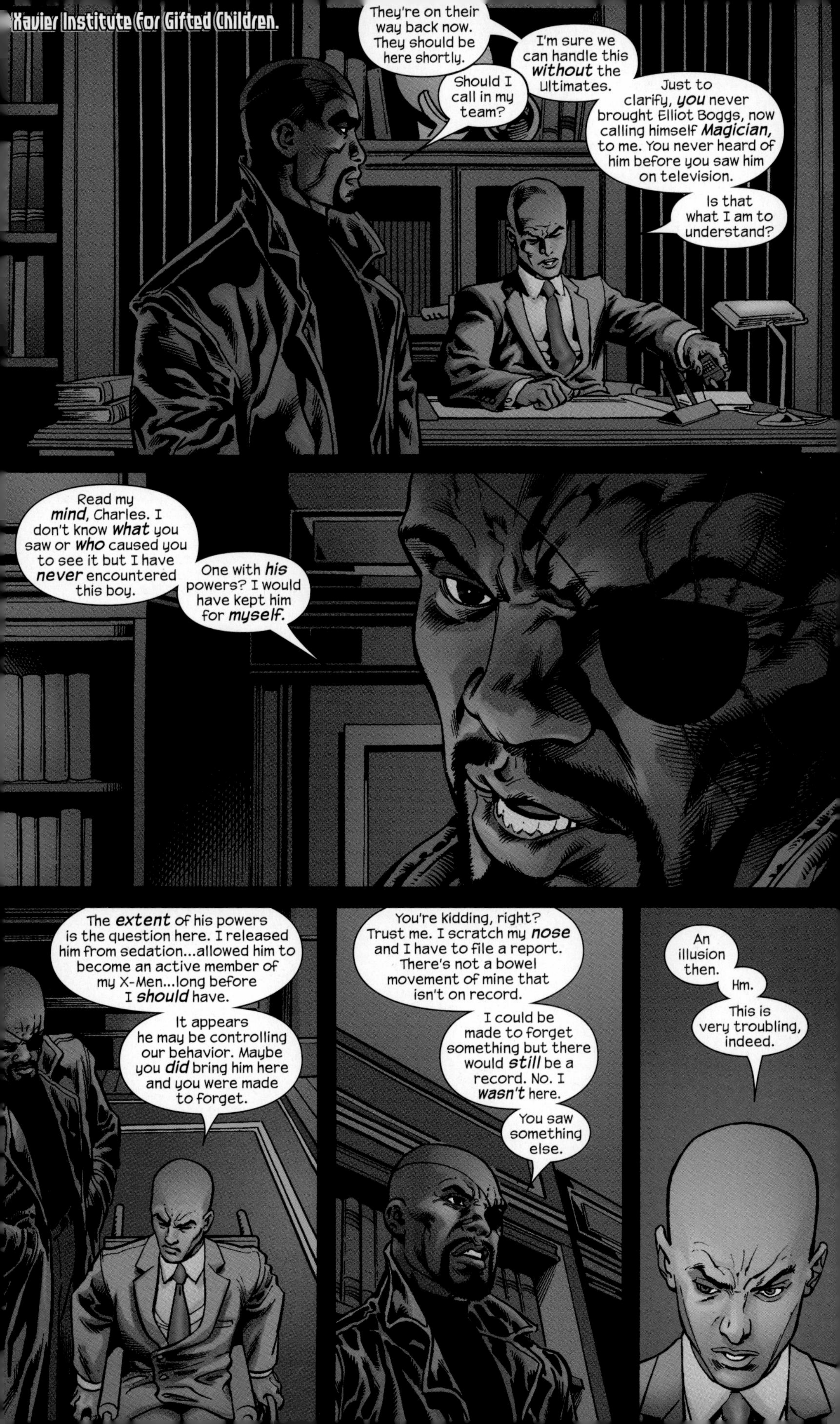
Xavier Institute For Gifted Children.
They're on their way back now. They should be here shortly.
Should I call in my team?
I'm sure we can handle this without the Ultimates.
Just to clarify, you never brought Elliot Boggs, now calling himself Magician, to me. You never heard of him before you saw him on television.
Is that what I am to understand?
Read my mind, Charles. I don't know what you saw or who caused you to see it but I have never encountered this boy.
One with his powers? I would have kept him for myself.
The extent of his powers is the question here. I released him from sedation...allowed him to become an active member of my X-Men...long before I should have.
It appears he may be controlling our behavior. Maybe you did bring him here and you were made to forget.
You're kidding, right? Trust me. I scratch my nose and I have to file a report. There's not a bowel movement of mine that isn't on record.
I could be made to forget something but there would still be a record. No. I wasn't here.
You saw something else.
An illusion then.
Hm.
This is very troubling, indeed.

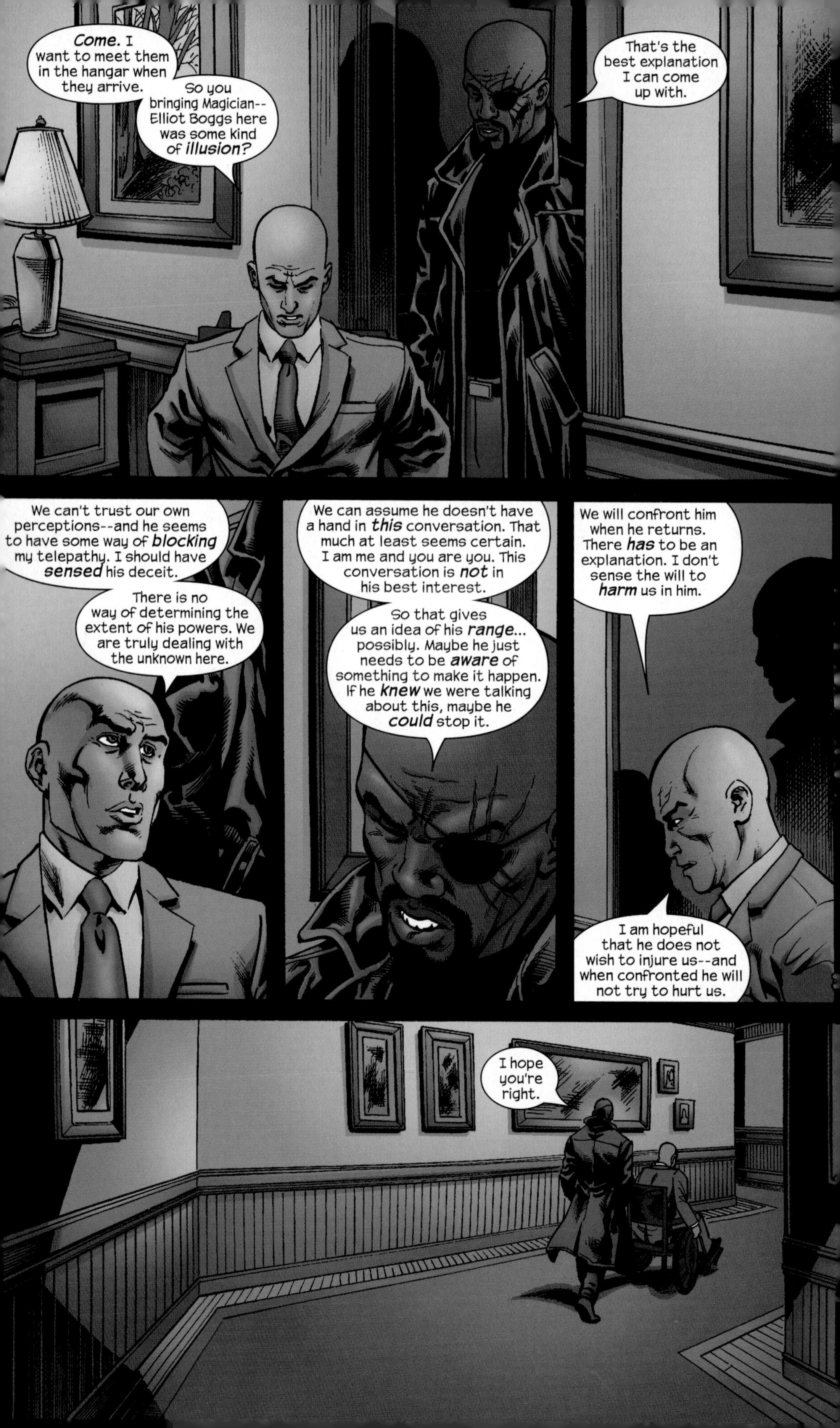

Come. I want to meet them in the hangar when they arrive.
So you bringing Magician-- Elliot Boggs here was some kind of illusion?
That's the best explanation I can come up with.
We can't trust our own perceptions--and he seems to have some way of blocking my telepathy. I should have sensed his deceit.
There is no way of determining the extent of his powers. We are truly dealing with the unknown here.
We can assume he doesn't have a hand in this conversation. That much at least seems certain. I am me and you are you. This conversation is not in his best interest.
So that gives us an idea of his range... possibly. Maybe he just needs to be aware of something to make it happen. If he knew we were talking about this, maybe he could stop it.
We will confront him when he returns. There has to be an explanation. I don't sense the will to harm us in him.
I am hopeful that he does not wish to injure us--and when confronted he will not try to hurt us.
I hope you're right.

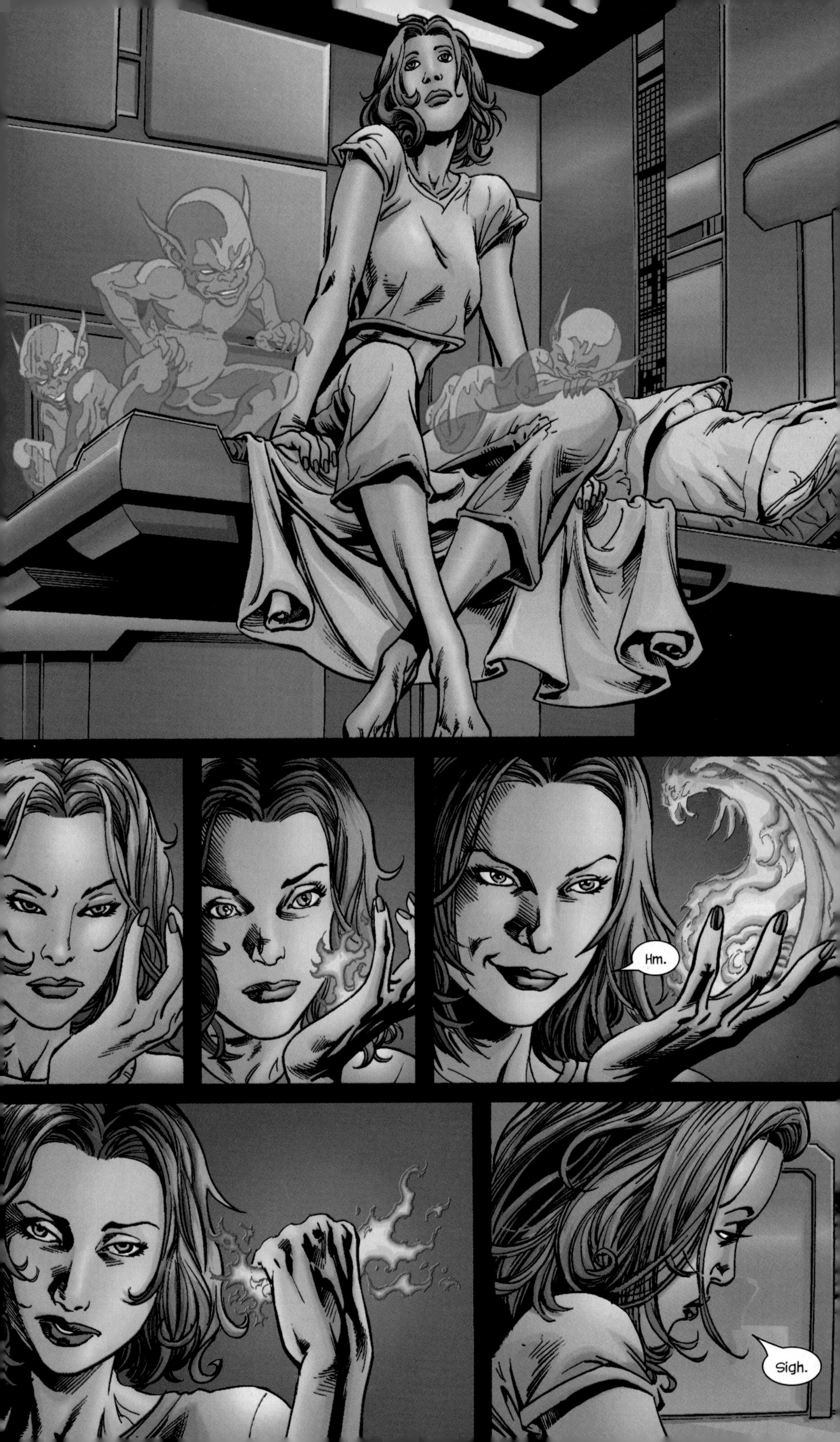
Hm.
Sigh.

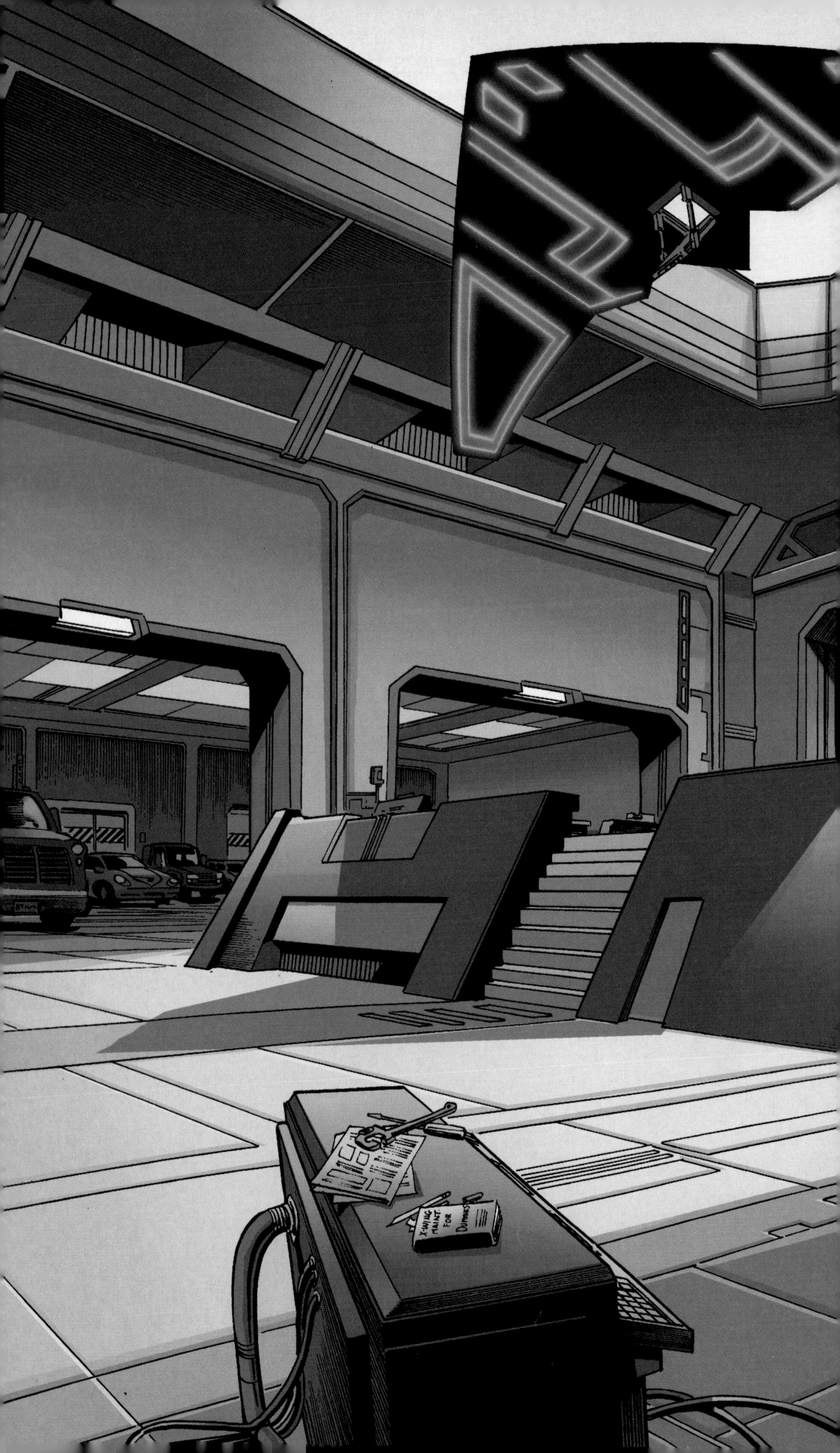
X-WING MAINT. FOR DUMMIES

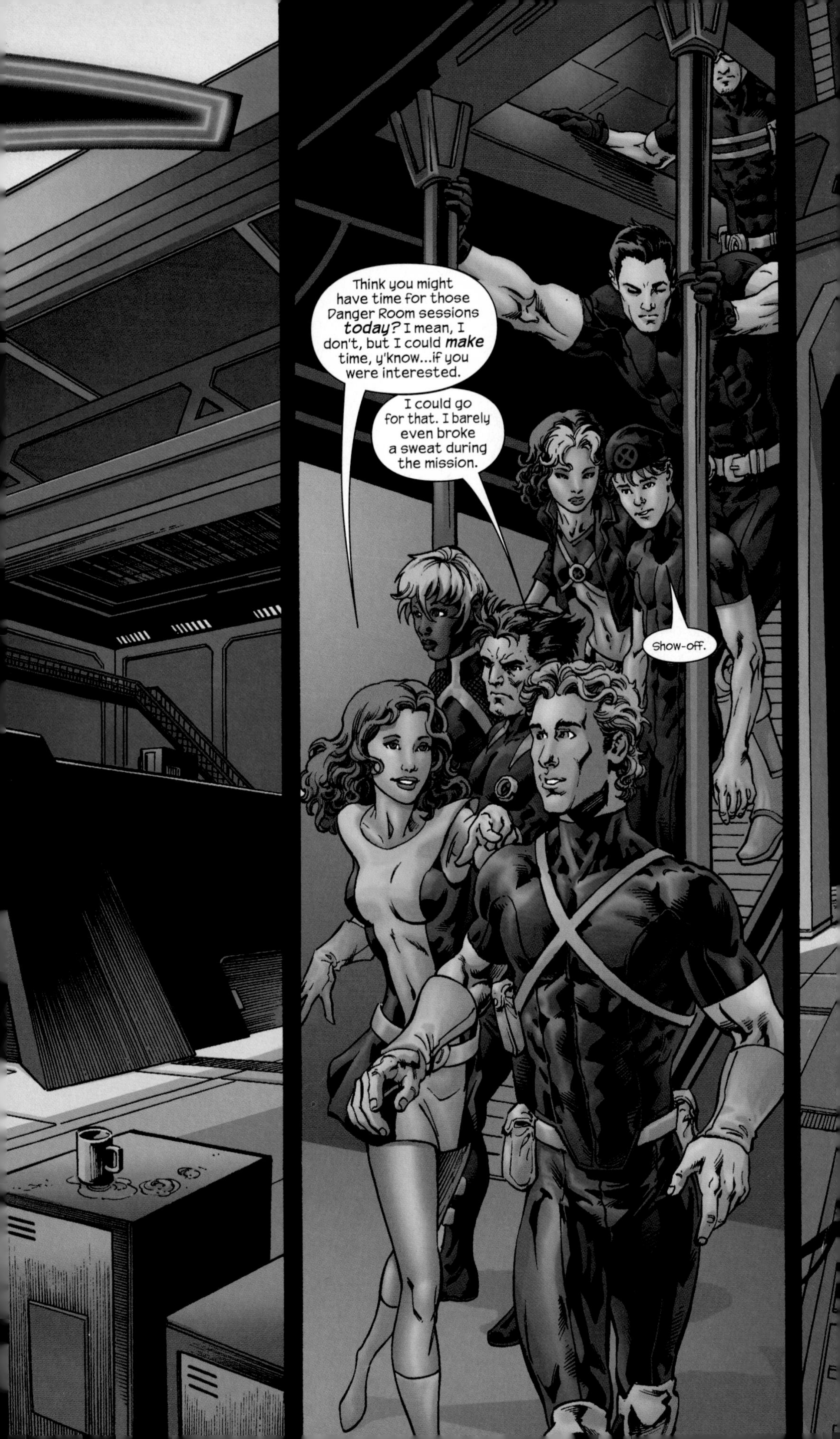
Think you might have time for those Danger Room sessions today? I mean, I don't, but I could make time, y'know...if you were interested.
I could go for that. I barely even broke a sweat during the mission.
Show-off.

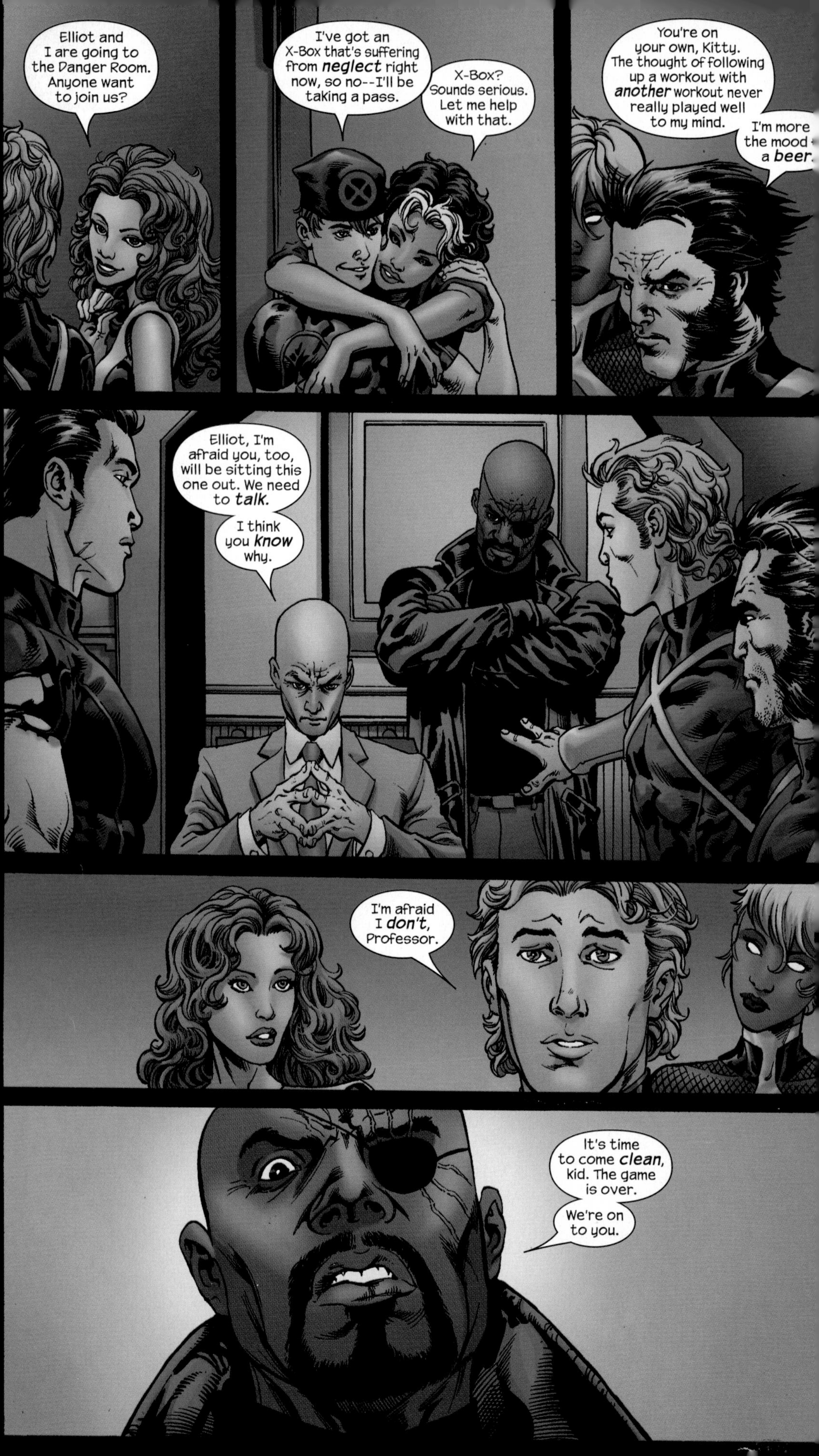
Elliot and I are going to the Danger Room. Anyone want to join us?
I've got an X-Box that's suffering from neglect right now, so no--I'll be taking a pass.
X-Box? Sounds serious. Let me help with that.
You're on your own, Kitty. The thought of following up a workout with another workout never really played well to my mind.
I'm more the mood a beer.
Elliot, I'm afraid you, too, will be sitting this one out. We need to talk.
I think you know why.
I'm afraid I don't, Professor.
It's time to come clean, kid. The game is over.
We're on to you.

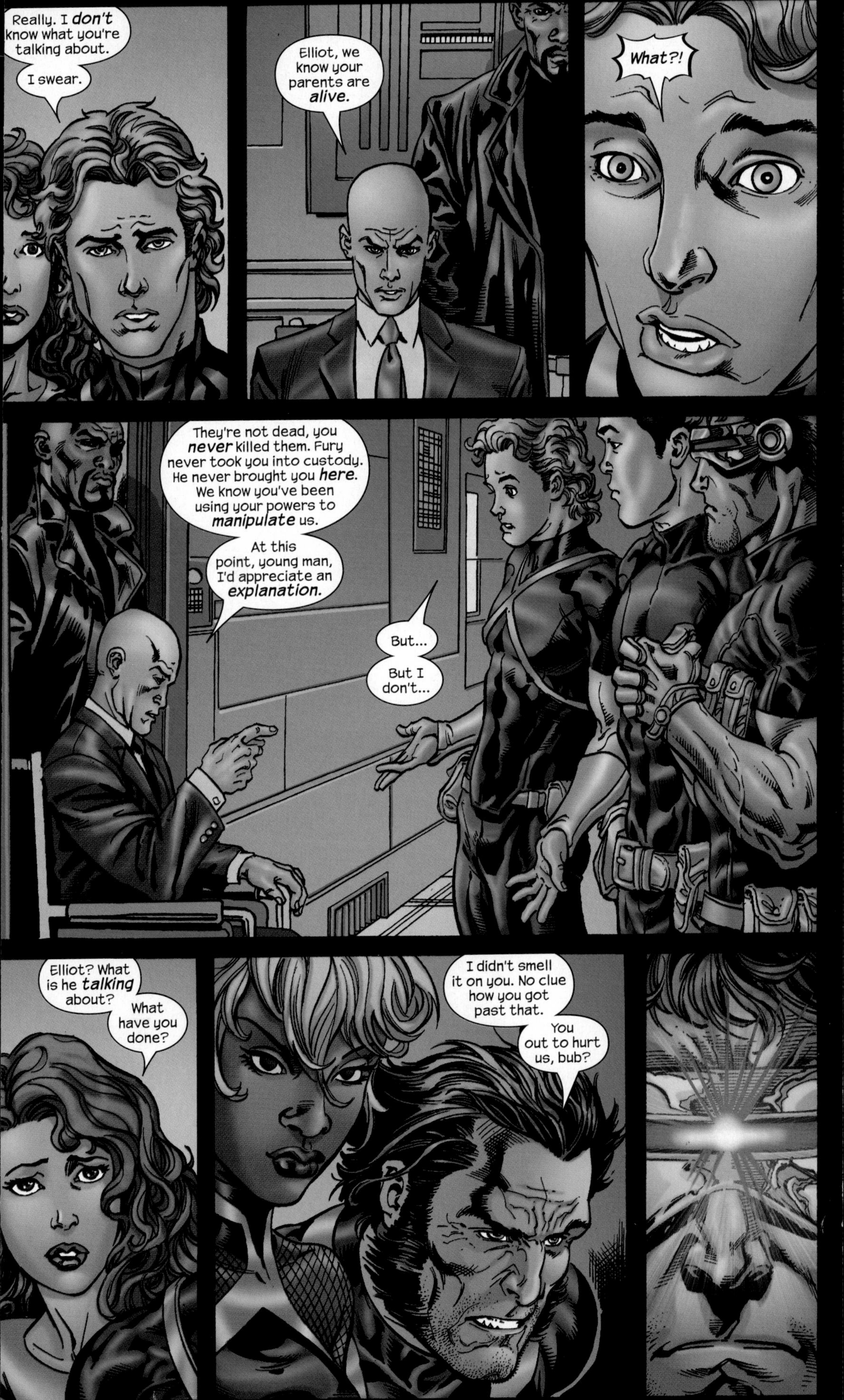
Really. I don't know what you're talking about.
I swear.
Elliot, we know your parents are alive.
What?!
They're not dead, you never killed them. Fury never took you into custody. He never brought you here. We know you've been using your powers to manipulate us.
At this point, young man, I'd appreciate an explanation.
But...
But I don't...
Elliot? What is he talking about?
What have you done?
I didn't smell it on you. No clue how you got past that.
You out to hurt us, bub?

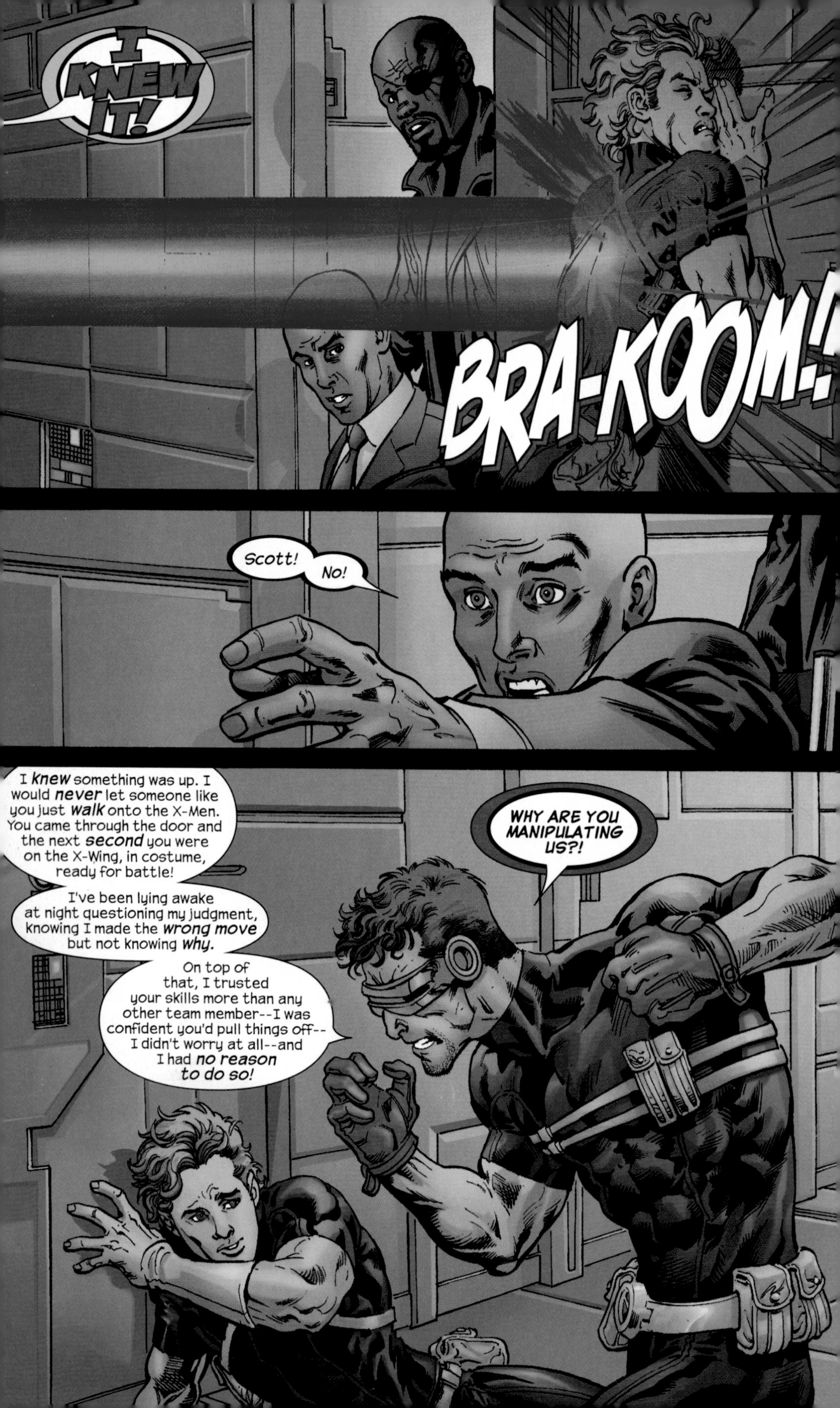
I KNEW IT!
BRA-KOOM!!
Scott!
No!
I knew something was up. I would never let someone like you just walk onto the X-Men. You came through the door and the next second you were on the X-Wing, in costume, ready for battle!
WHY ARE YOU MANIPULATING US?!
I've been lying awake at night questioning my judgment, knowing I made the wrong move but not knowing why.
On top of that, I trusted your skills more than any other team member--I was confident you'd pull things off--I didn't worry at all--and I had no reason to do so!

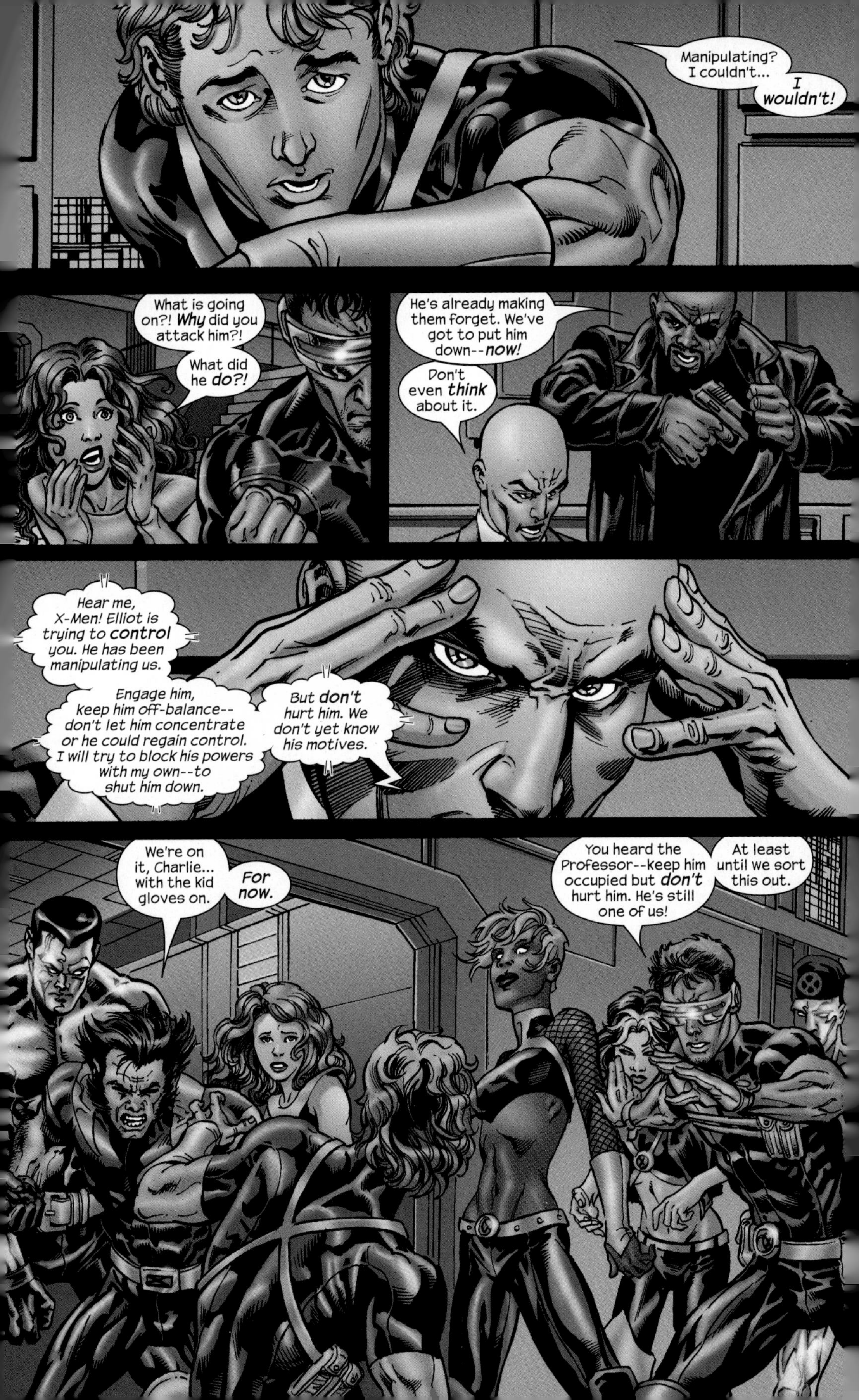
Manipulating? I couldn't... I wouldn't!
What is going on?! Why did you attack him?!
What did he do?!
He's already making them forget. We've got to put him down--now!
Don't even think about it.
Hear me, X-Men! Elliot is trying to control you. He has been manipulating us.
Engage him, keep him off-balance--don't let him concentrate or he could regain control. I will try to block his powers with my own--to shut him down.
But don't hurt him. We don't yet know his motives.
We're on it, Charlie... with the kid gloves on.
For now.
You heard the Professor--keep him occupied but don't hurt him. He's still one of us!
At least until we sort this out.

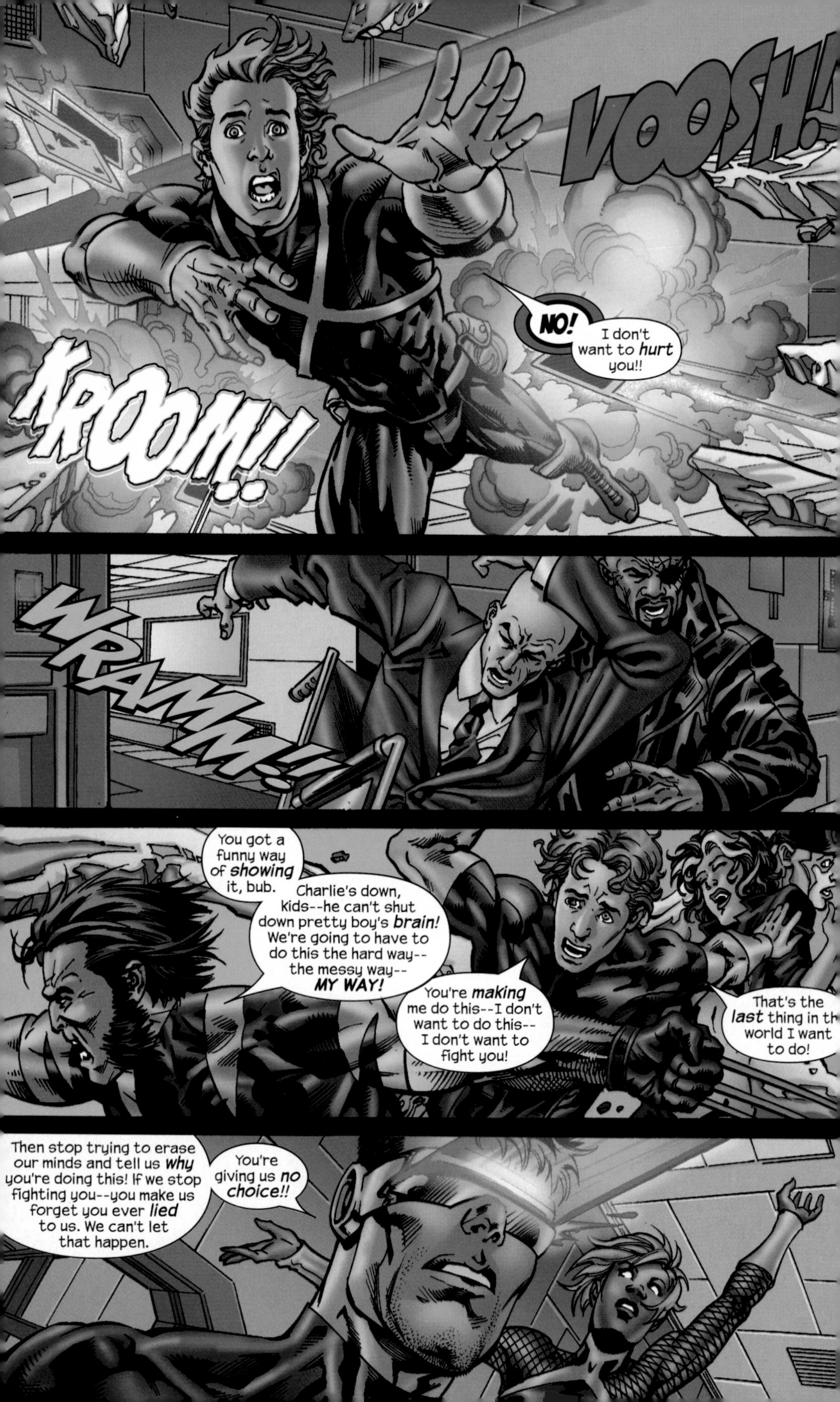
VOOSH!!
NO! I don't want to hurt you!!
KROOM!!
WRAMM!!
You got a funny way of showing it, bub.
Charlie's down, kids--he can't shut down pretty boy's brain! We're going to have to do this the hard way--the messy way--MY WAY!
You're making me do this--I don't want to do this--I don't want to fight you!
That's the last thing in th world I want to do!
Then stop trying to erase our minds and tell us why you're doing this! If we stop fighting you--you make us forget you ever lied to us. We can't let that happen.
You're giving us no choice!!

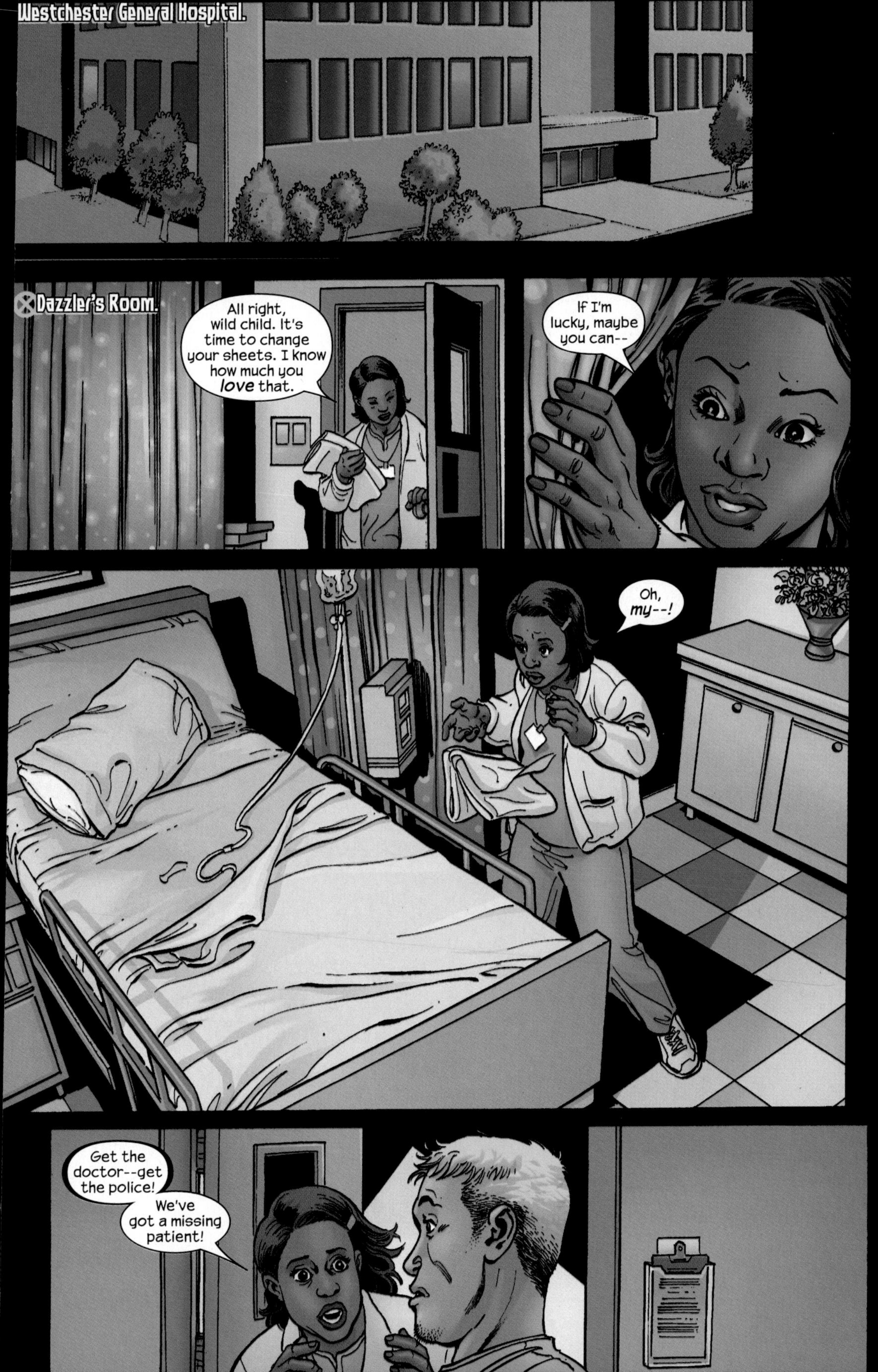
Westchester General Hospital.
Dazzler's Room.
All right, wild child. It's time to change your sheets. I know how much you *love* that.
If I'm lucky, maybe you can--
Oh, *my*--!
Get the doctor--get the police!
We've got a missing patient!

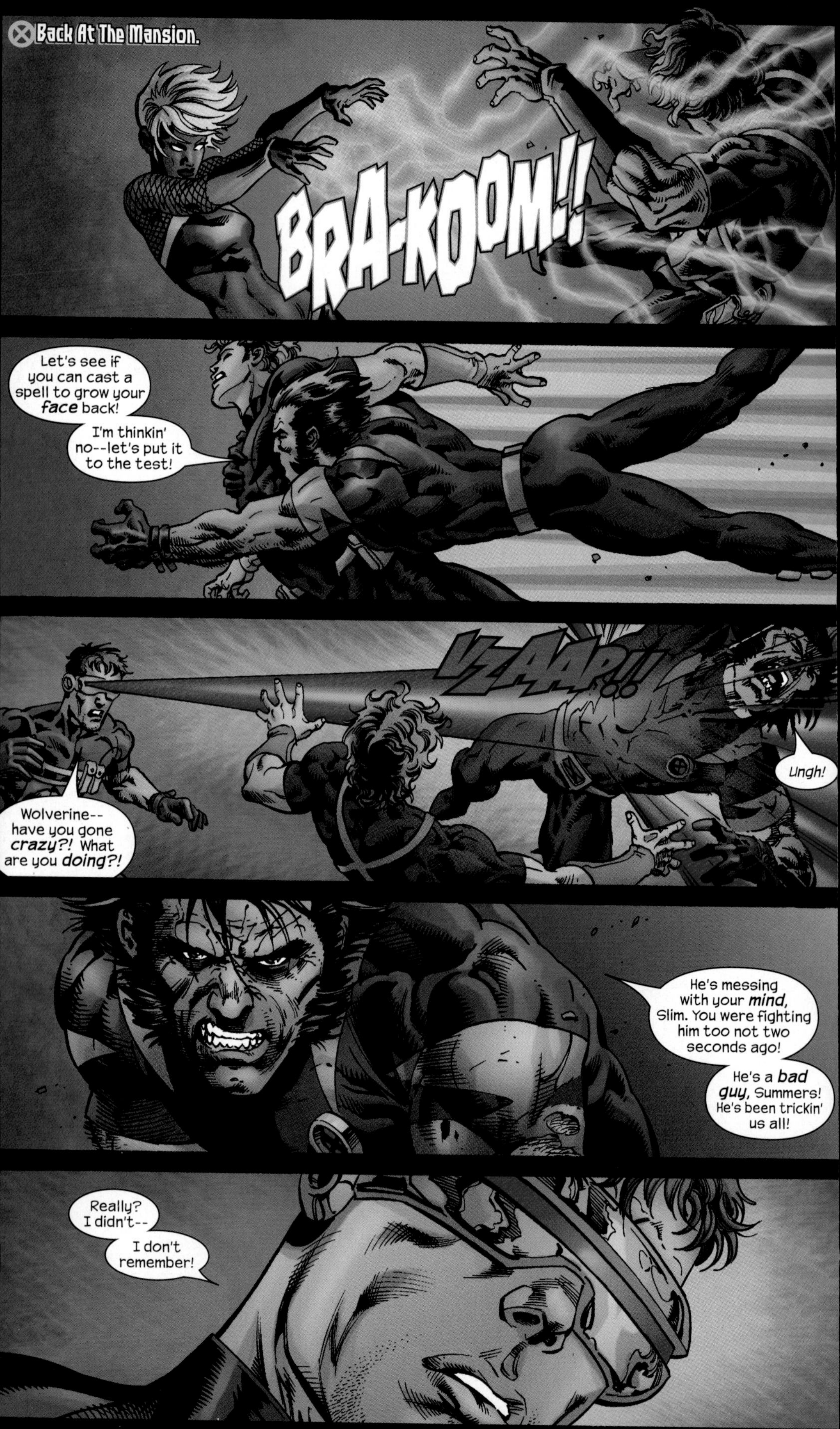
Back At The Mansion.
BRA-KOOM!!
Let's see if you can cast a spell to grow your *face* back!
I'm thinkin' no--let's put it to the test!
VZAAP!!
Ungh!
Wolverine-- have you gone *crazy?!* What are you *doing?!*
He's messing with your *mind*, Slim. You were fighting him too not two seconds ago!
He's a *bad guy*, Summers! He's been trickin' us all!
Really? I didn't--
I don't remember!

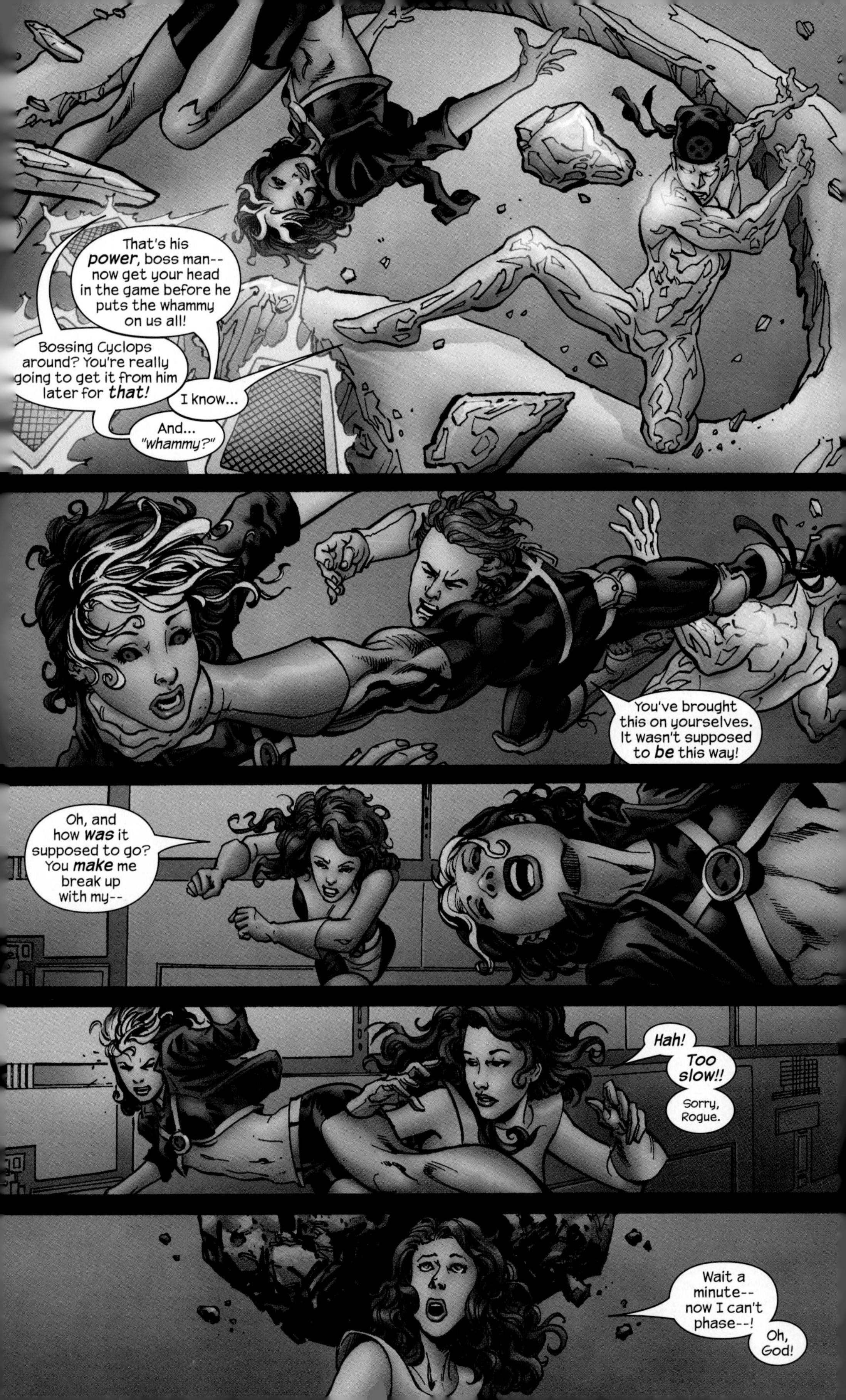

That's his power, boss man--now get your head in the game before he puts the whammy on us all!
Bossing Cyclops around? You're really going to get it from him later for that!
I know...
And... "whammy?"
You've brought this on yourselves. It wasn't supposed to be this way!
Oh, and how was it supposed to go? You make me break up with my--
Hah!
Too slow!!
Sorry, Rogue.
Wait a minute--now I can't phase--!
Oh, God!

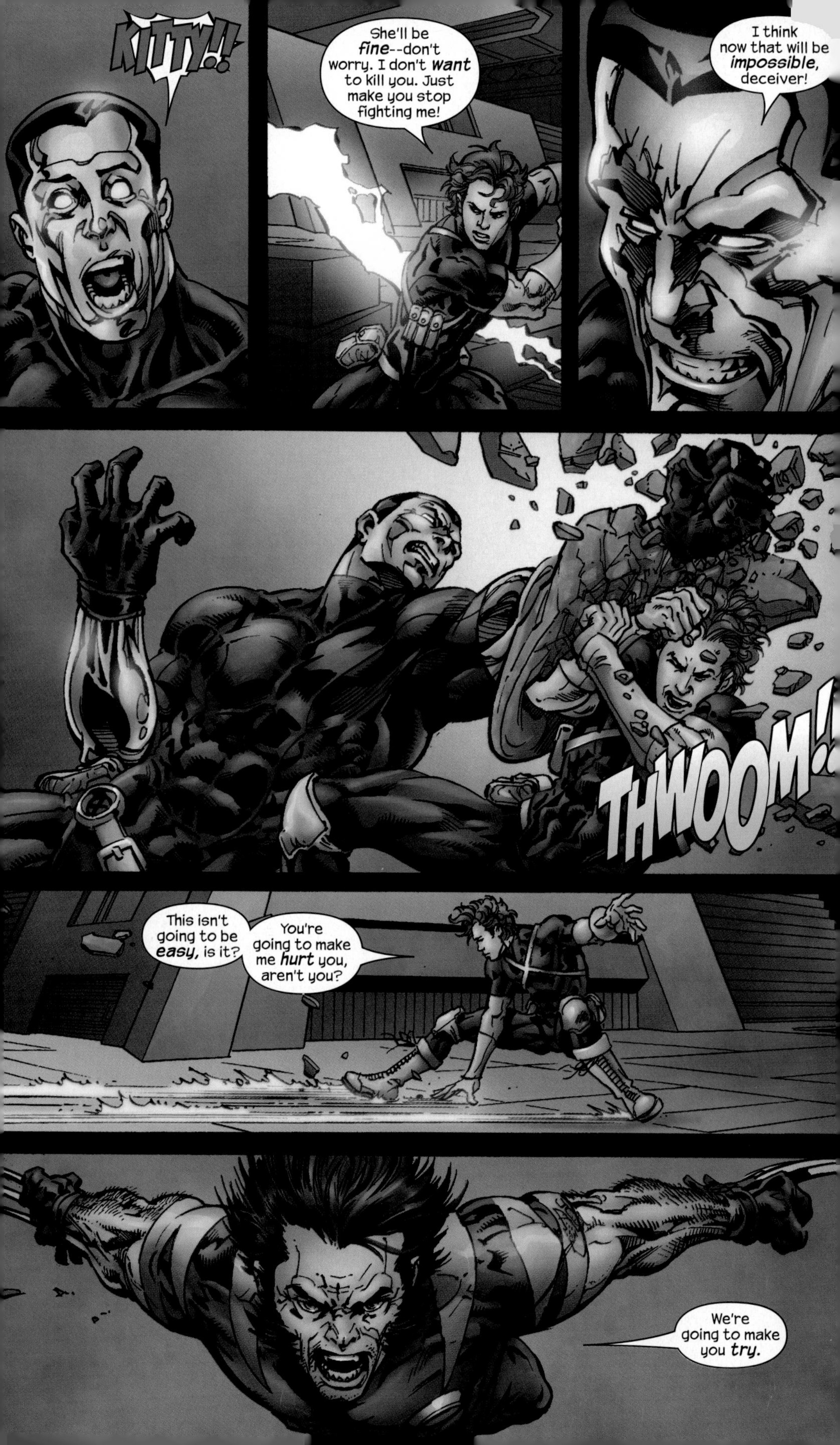
KITTY!!
She'll be fine--don't worry. I don't want to kill you. Just make you stop fighting me!
I think now that will be impossible, deceiver!
THWOOM!!
This isn't going to be easy, is it?
You're going to make me hurt you, aren't you?
We're going to make you try.

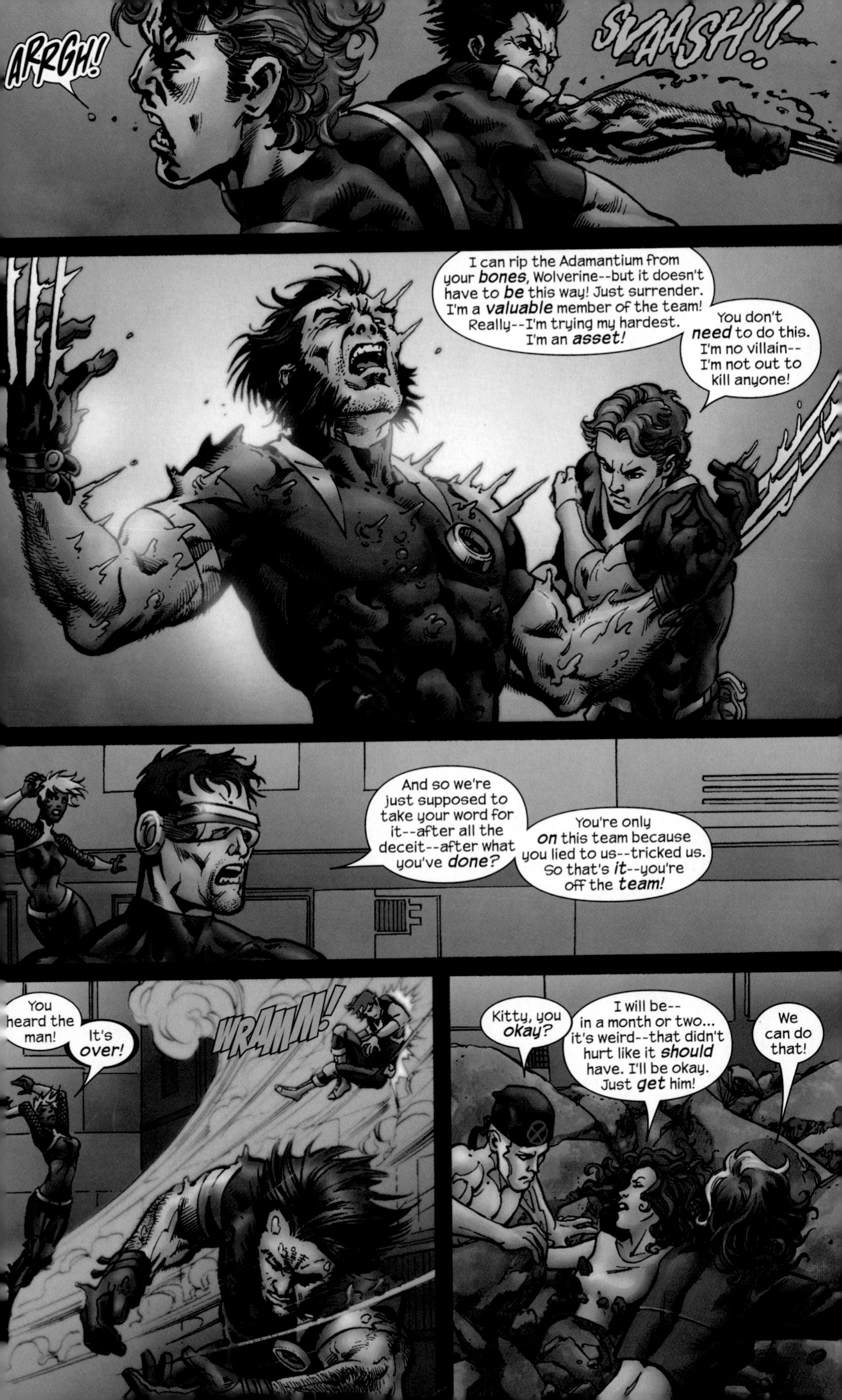

ARRGH!
SVAASH!!
I can rip the Adamantium from your bones, Wolverine--but it doesn't have to be this way! Just surrender. I'm a valuable member of the team! Really--I'm trying my hardest. I'm an asset!
You don't need to do this. I'm no villain-- I'm not out to kill anyone!
And so we're just supposed to take your word for it--after all the deceit--after what you've done?
You're only on this team because you lied to us--tricked us. So that's it--you're off the team!
You heard the man!
It's over!
WRAMM!
Kitty, you okay?
I will be-- in a month or two... it's weird--that didn't hurt like it should have. I'll be okay. Just get him!
We can do that!

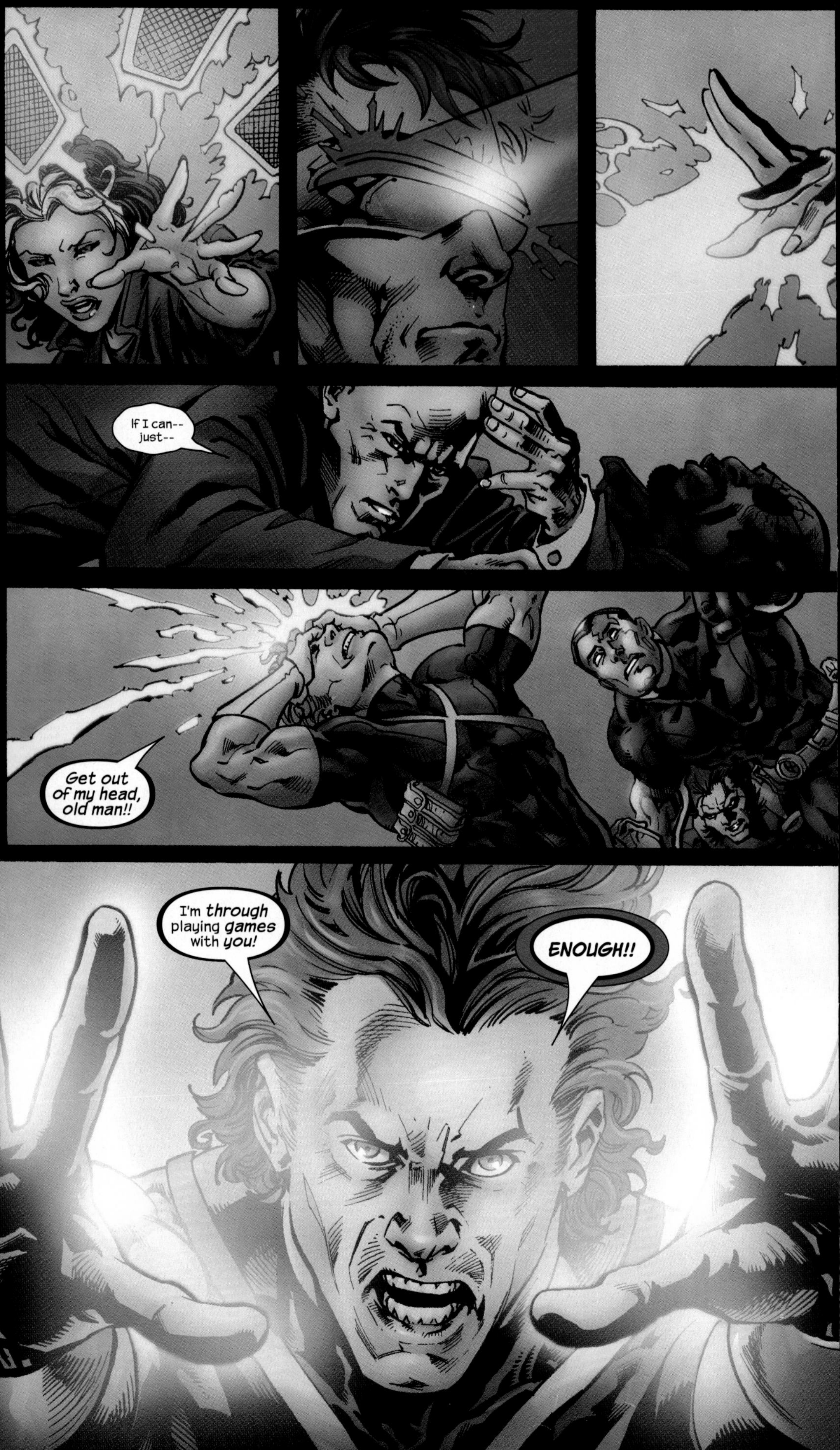
If I can-- just--
Get out of my head, old man!!
I'm through playing games with you!
ENOUGH!!

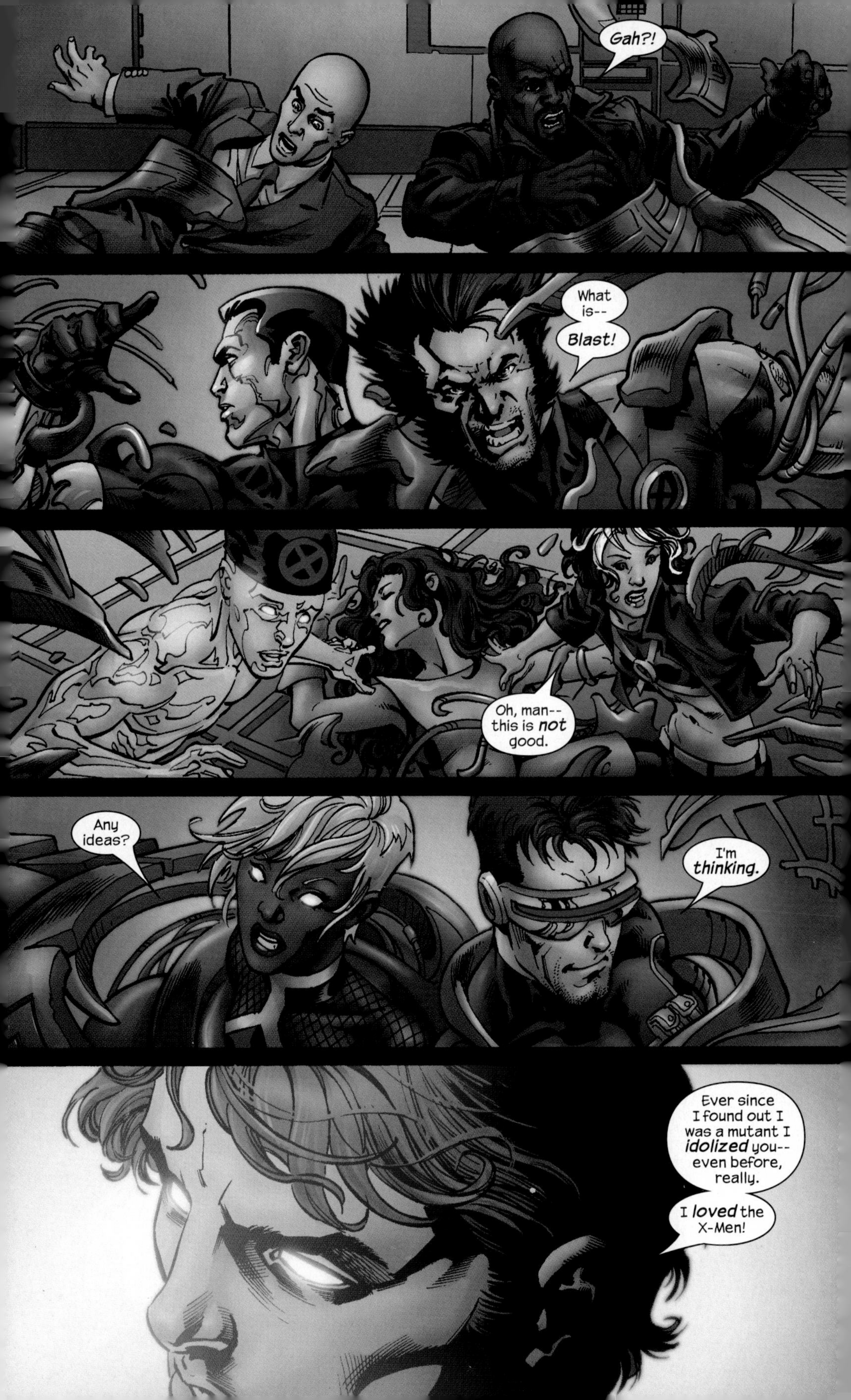
Gah?!
What is--
Blast!
Oh, man--
this is *not*
good.
Any ideas?
I'm *thinking.*
Ever since I found out I was a mutant I *idolized* you--even before, really.
I *loved* the X-Men!

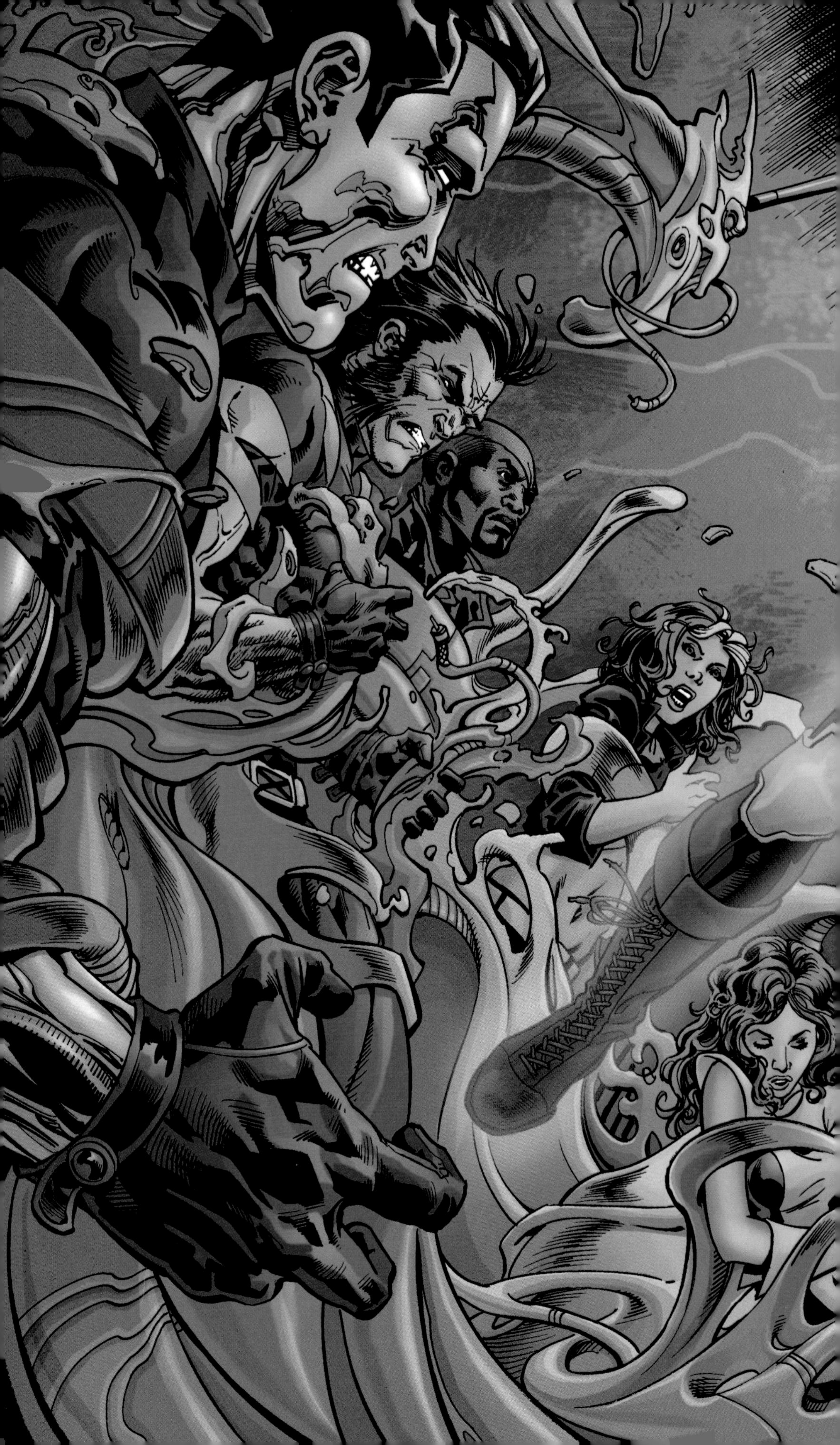

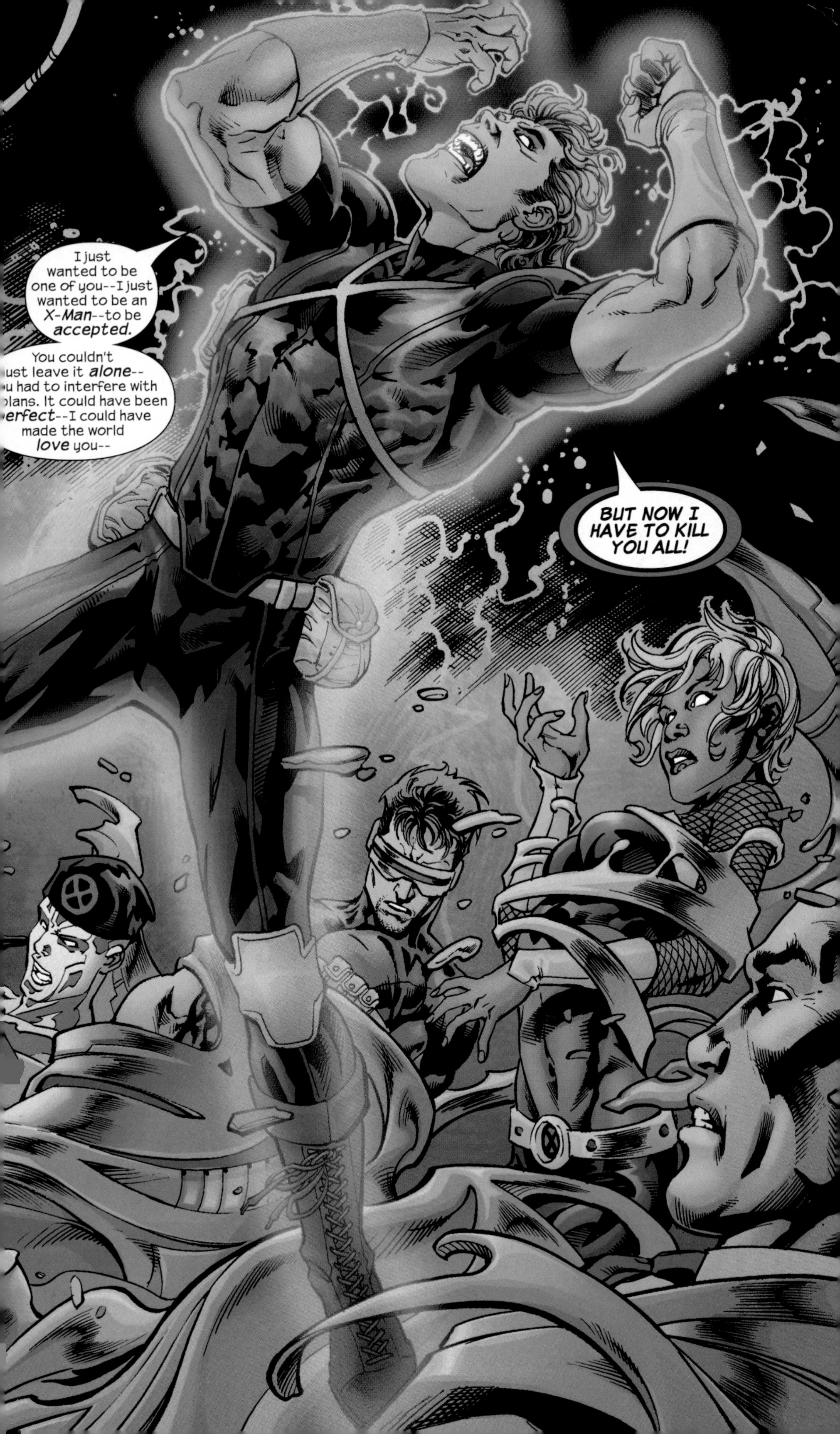
I just wanted to be one of you--I just wanted to be an X-Man--to be accepted.
You couldn't ust leave it alone-- u had to interfere with lans. It could have been erfect--I could have made the world love you--
BUT NOW I HAVE TO KILL YOU ALL!

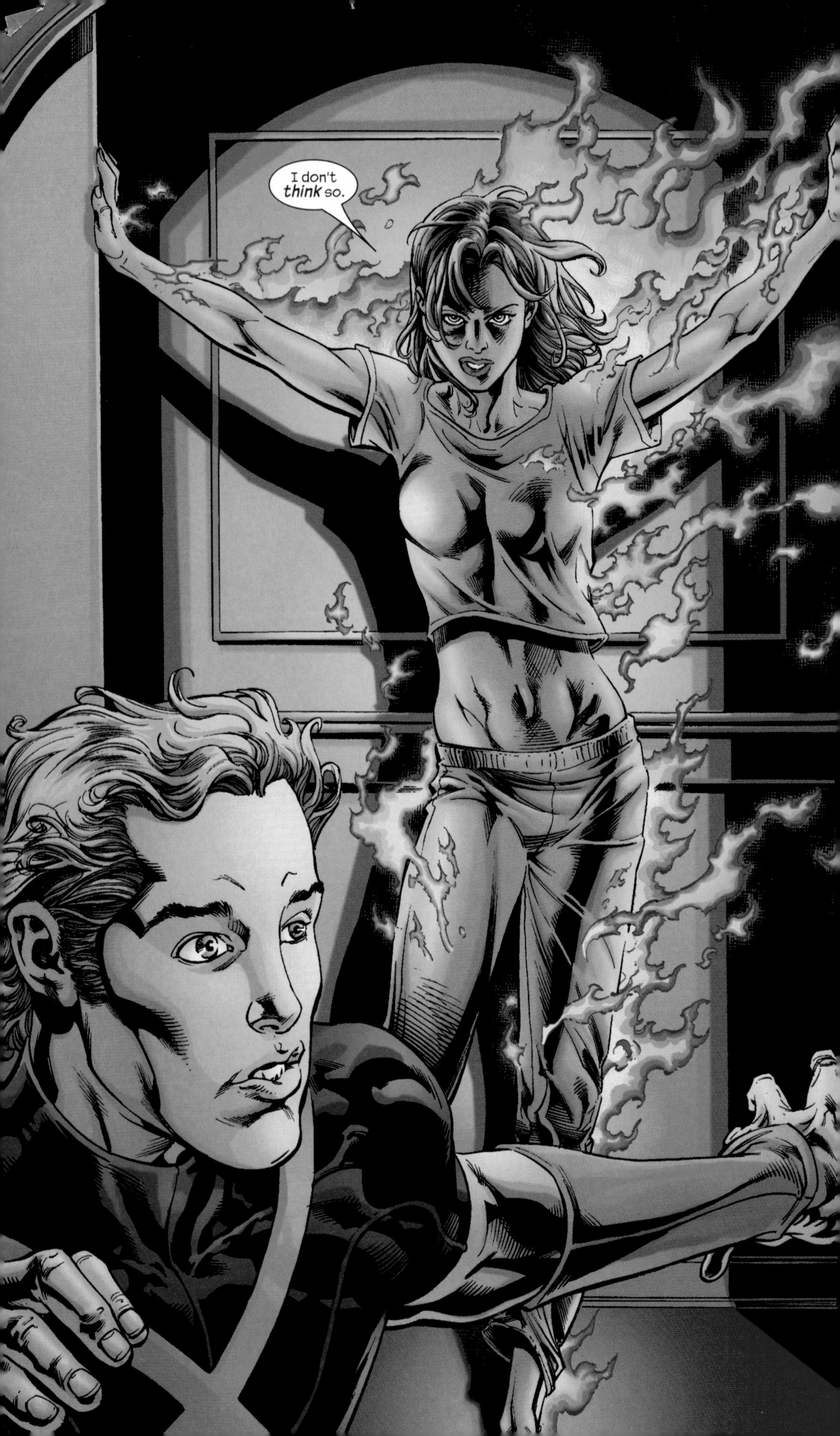
I don't *think* so.

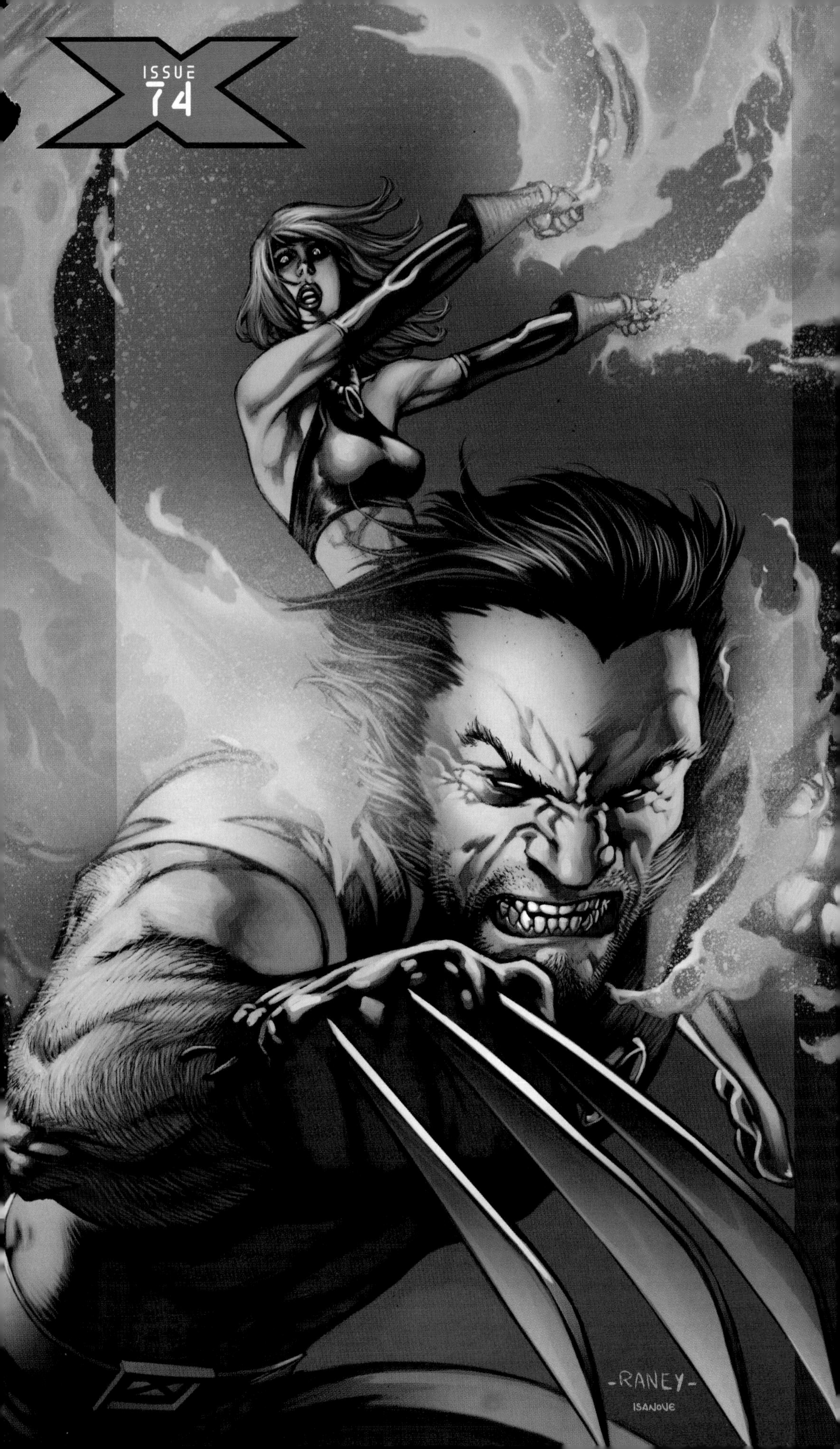
ISSUE
74
-RANEY-
ISANOVE

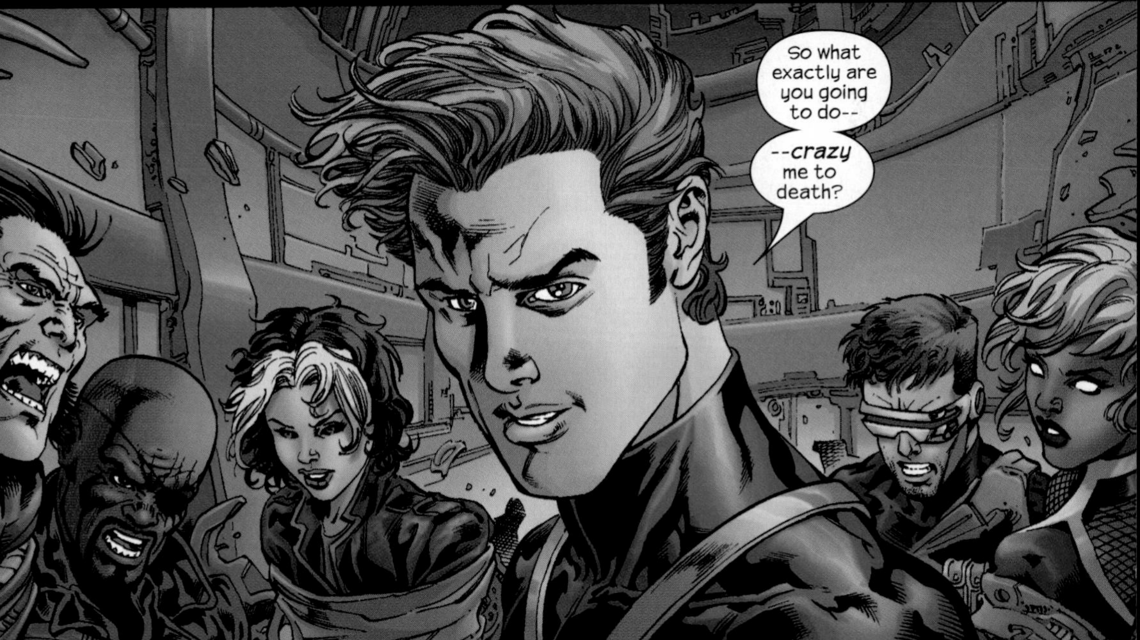
So what exactly are you going to do--
--crazy me to death?

MAGICAL
CONCLUSION

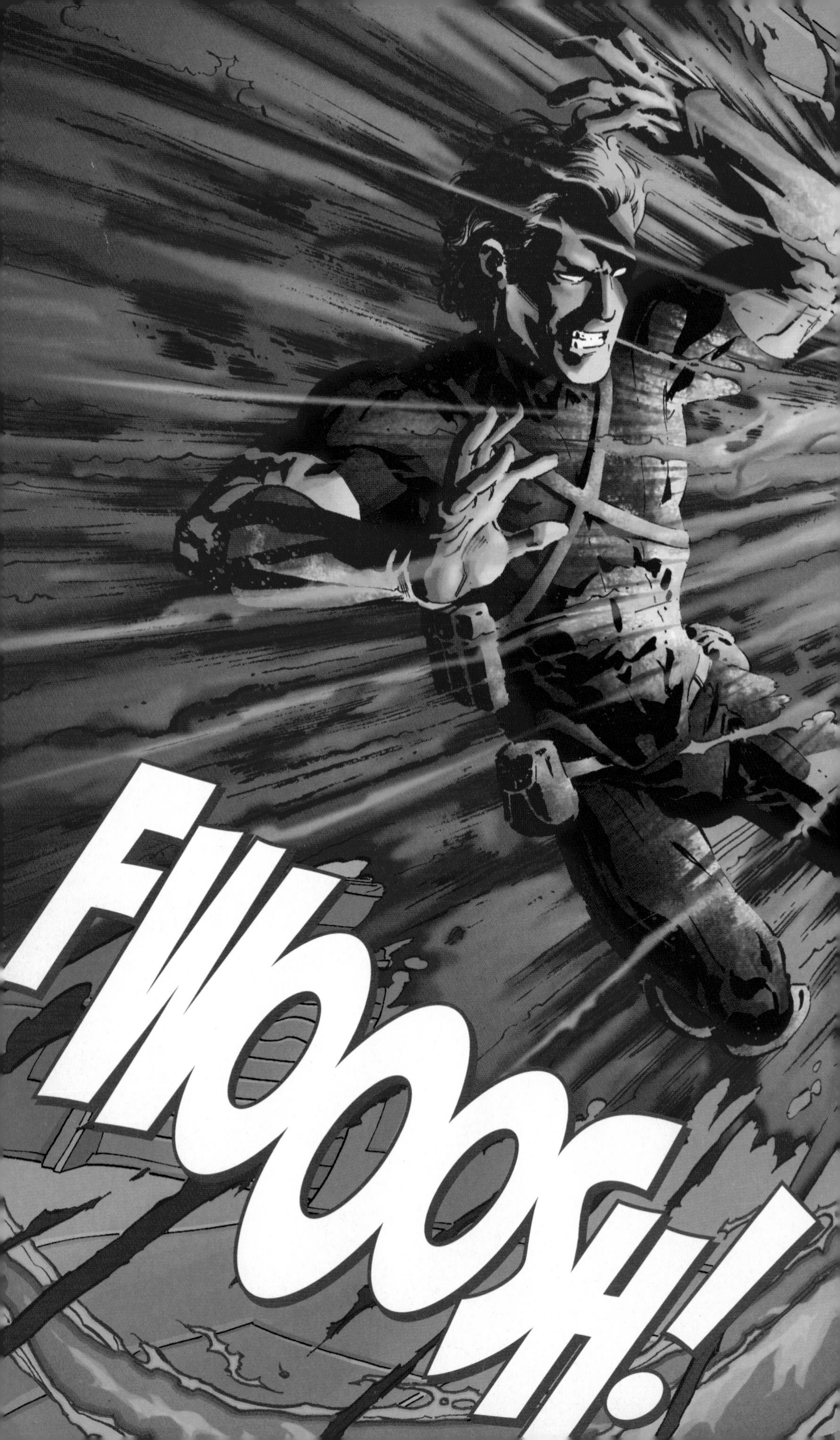
FWOOOSH!

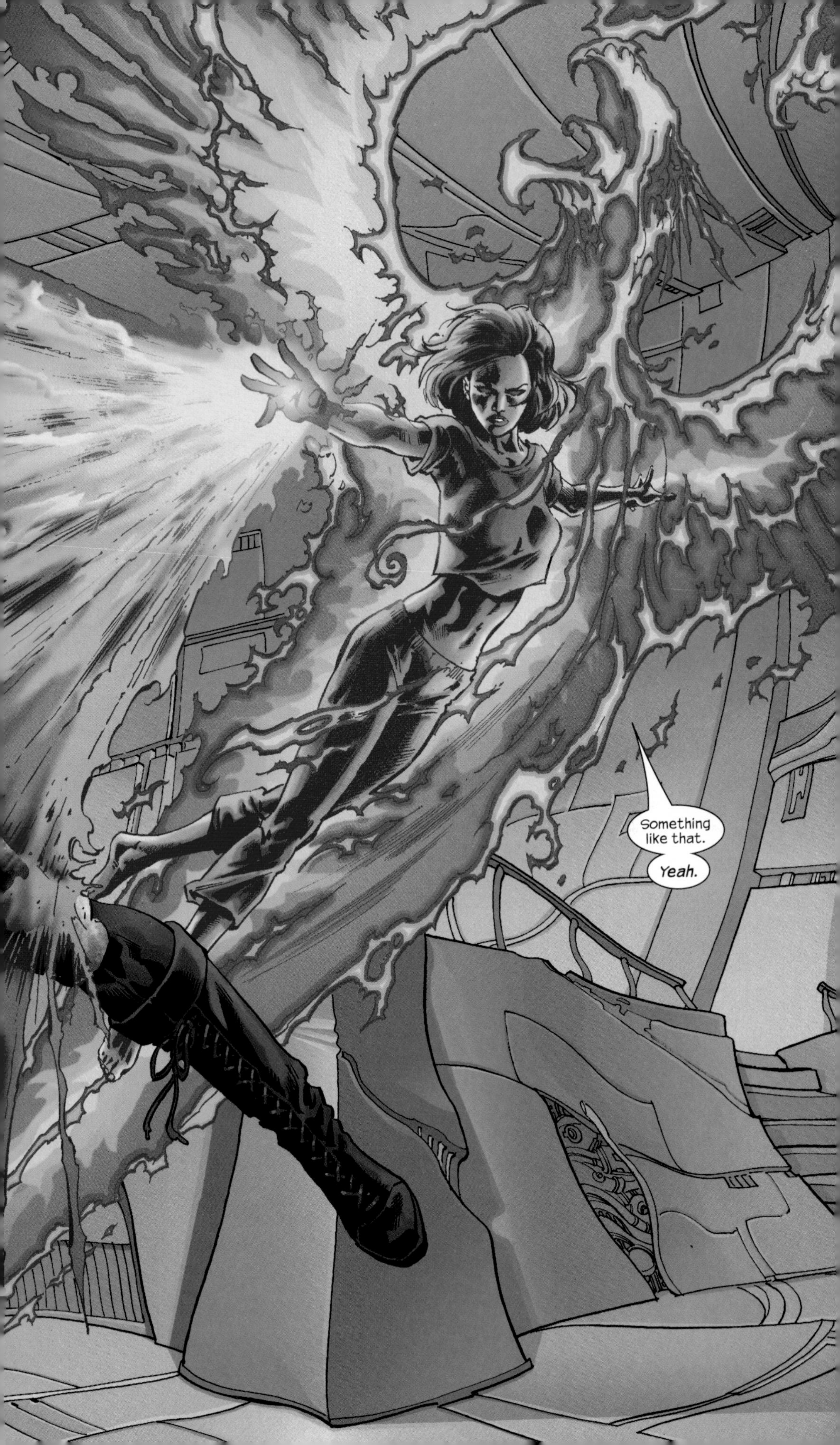
Something like that.
Yeah.

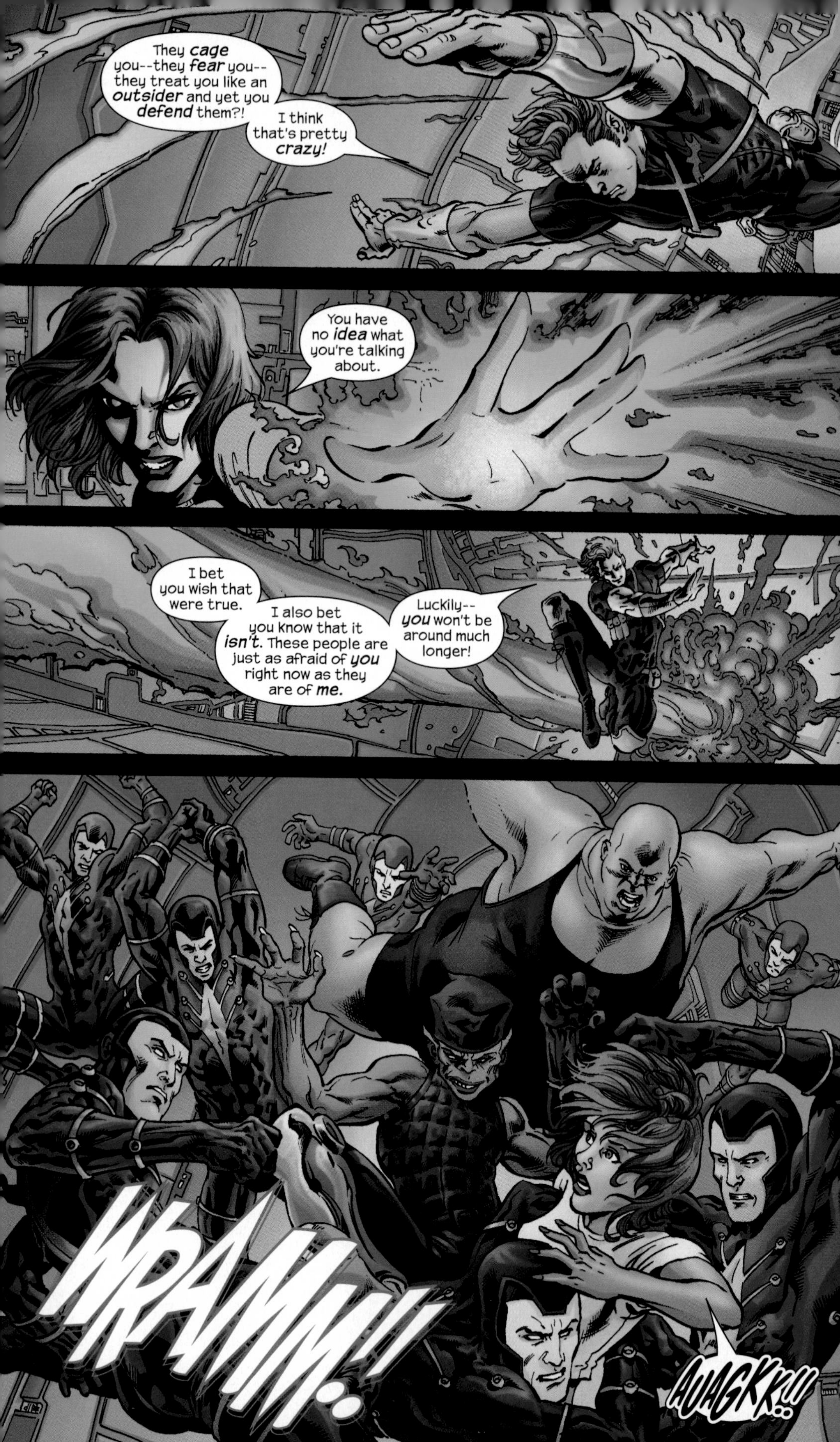
They cage you--they fear you--they treat you like an outsider and yet you defend them?!
I think that's pretty crazy!
You have no idea what you're talking about.
I bet you wish that were true.
I also bet you know that it isn't. These people are just as afraid of you right now as they are of me.
Luckily--you won't be around much longer!
WRAMM!!
AUAGKK!!

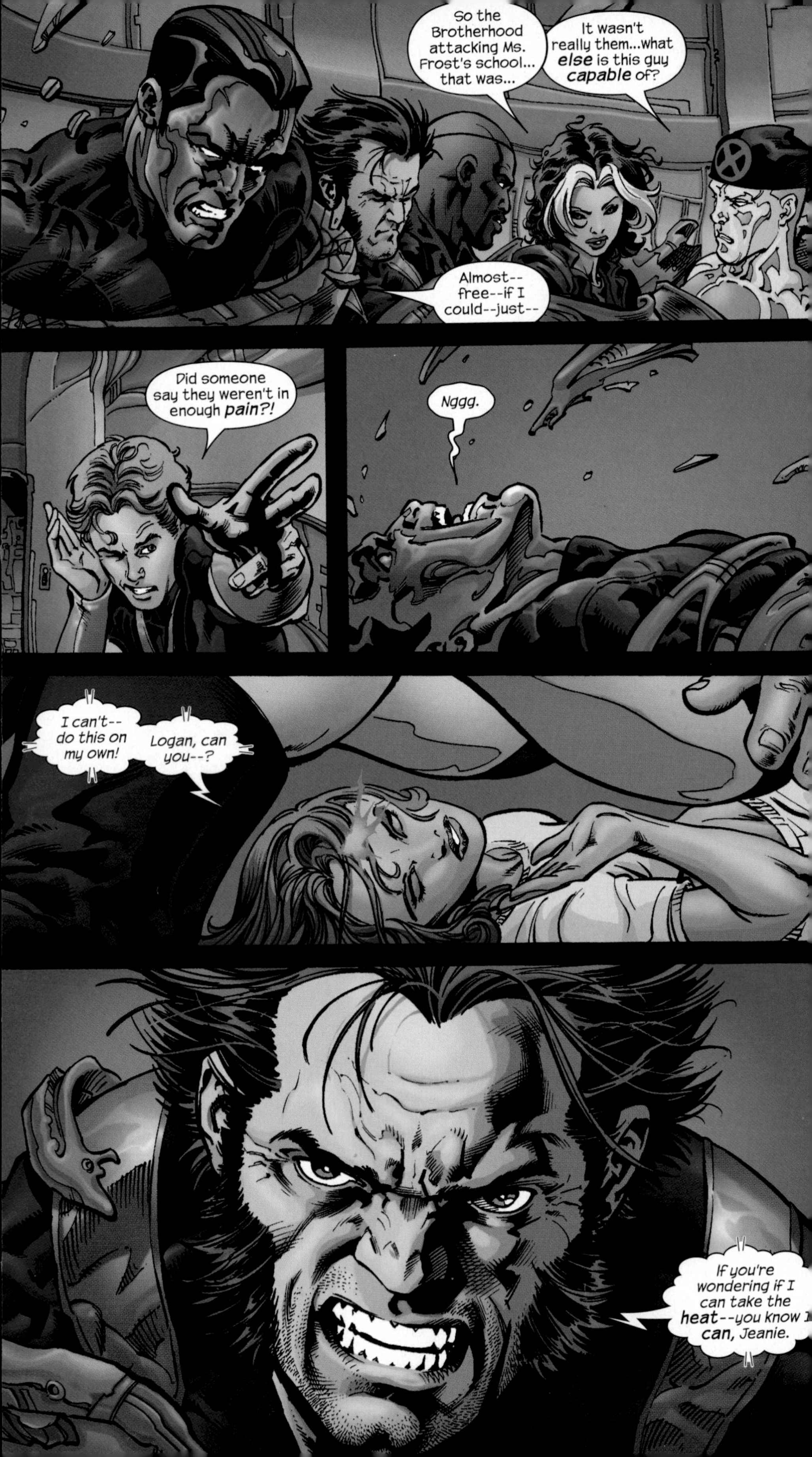
So the Brotherhood attacking Ms. Frost's school... that was...
It wasn't really them...what else is this guy capable of?
Almost--free--if I could--just--
Did someone say they weren't in enough pain?!
Nggg.
I can't--do this on my own!
Logan, can you--?
If you're wondering if I can take the heat--you know I can, Jeanie.

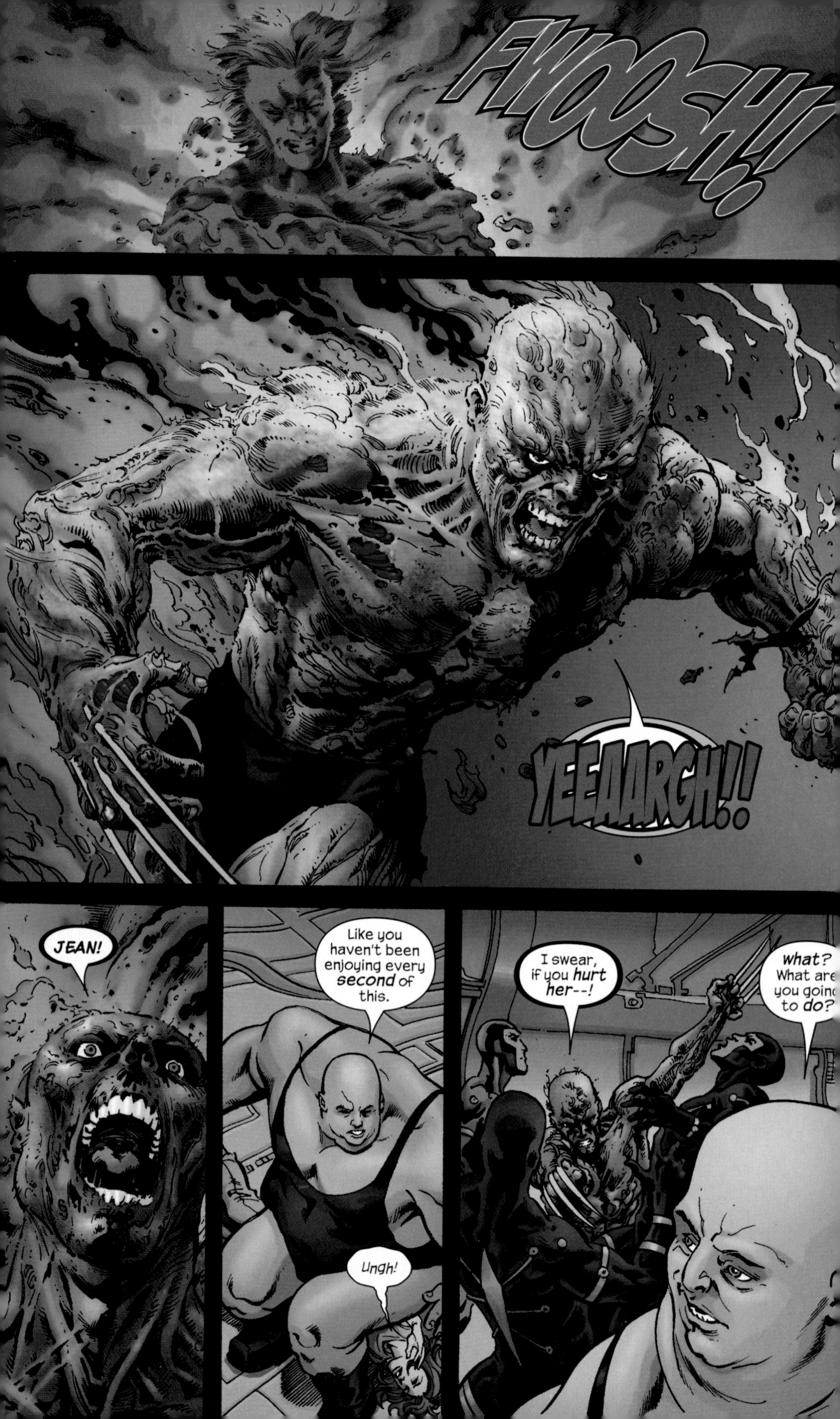
FWOOSH!!
YEEAARGH!!
JEAN!
Like you haven't been enjoying every second of this.
Ungh!
I swear, if you hurt her--!
What? What are you going to do?

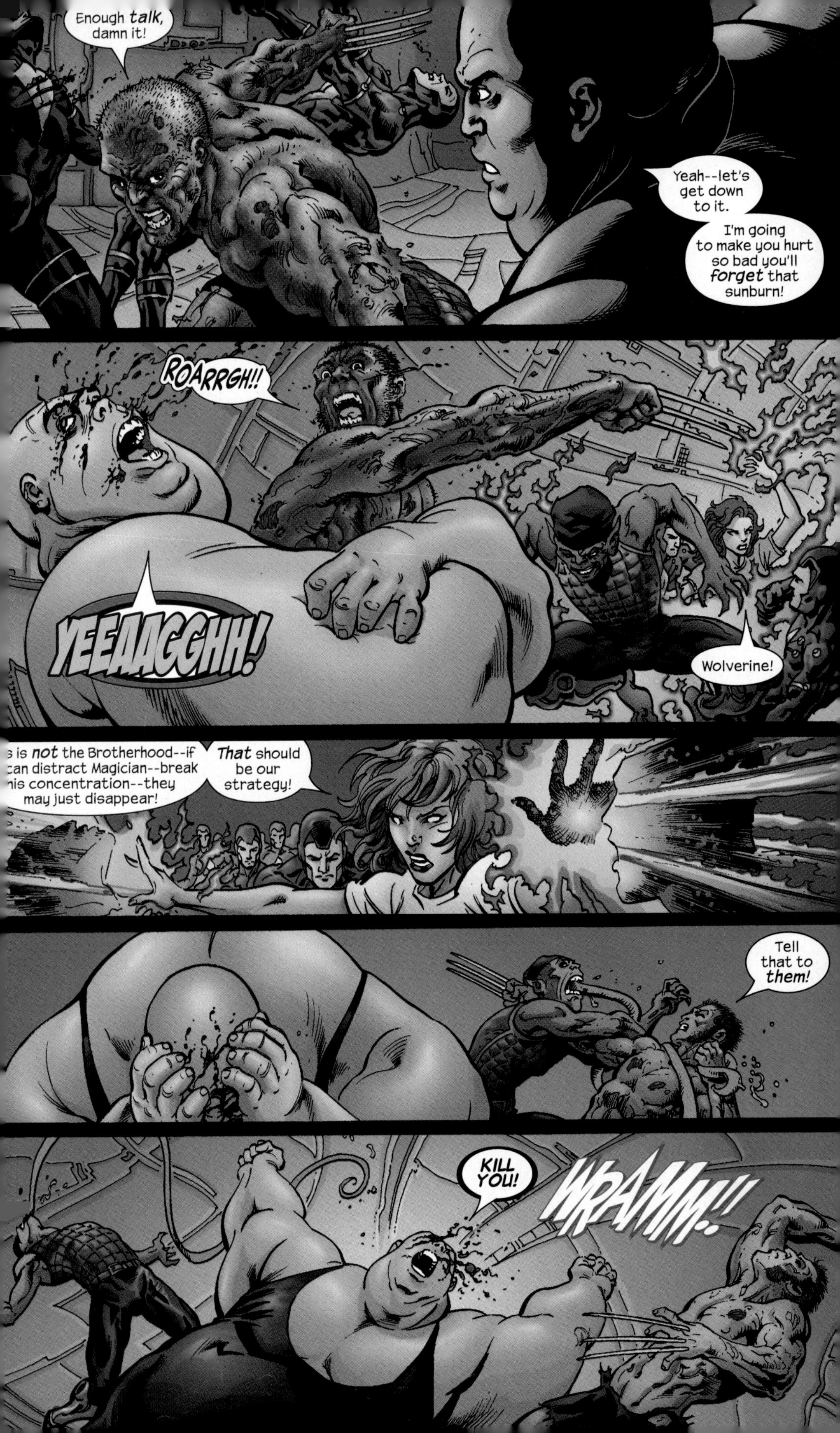

Enough *talk*, damn it!
Yeah--let's get down to it.
I'm going to make you hurt so bad you'll *forget* that sunburn!
ROARRGH!!
YEEAAGGHH!
Wolverine!
s is *not* the Brotherhood--if can distract Magician--break his concentration--they may just disappear!
That should be our strategy!
Tell that to *them!*
KILL YOU!
WRAMM!!

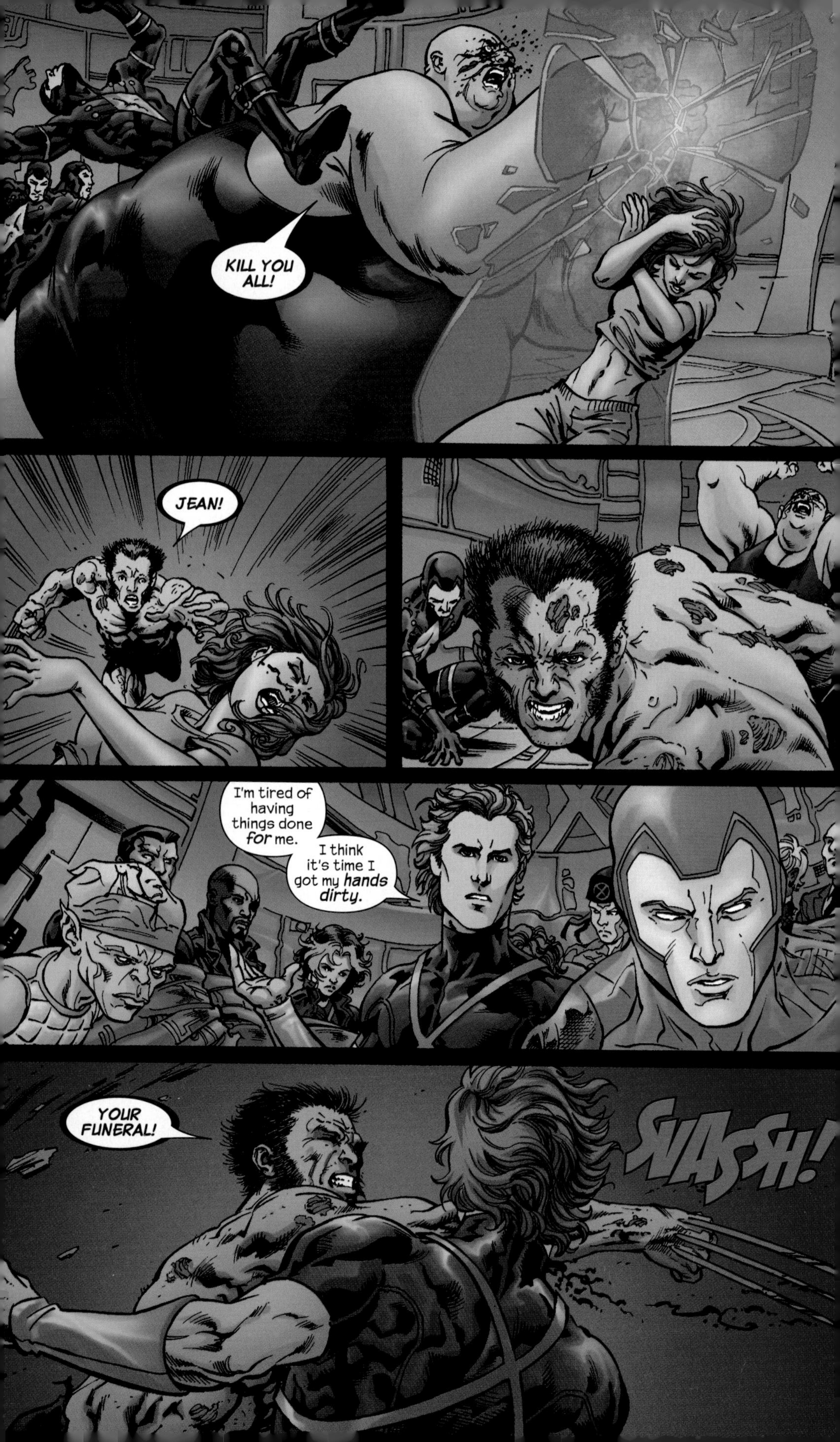
KILL YOU ALL!
JEAN!
I'm tired of having things done for me.
I think it's time I got my hands dirty.
YOUR FUNERAL!
SLASH!

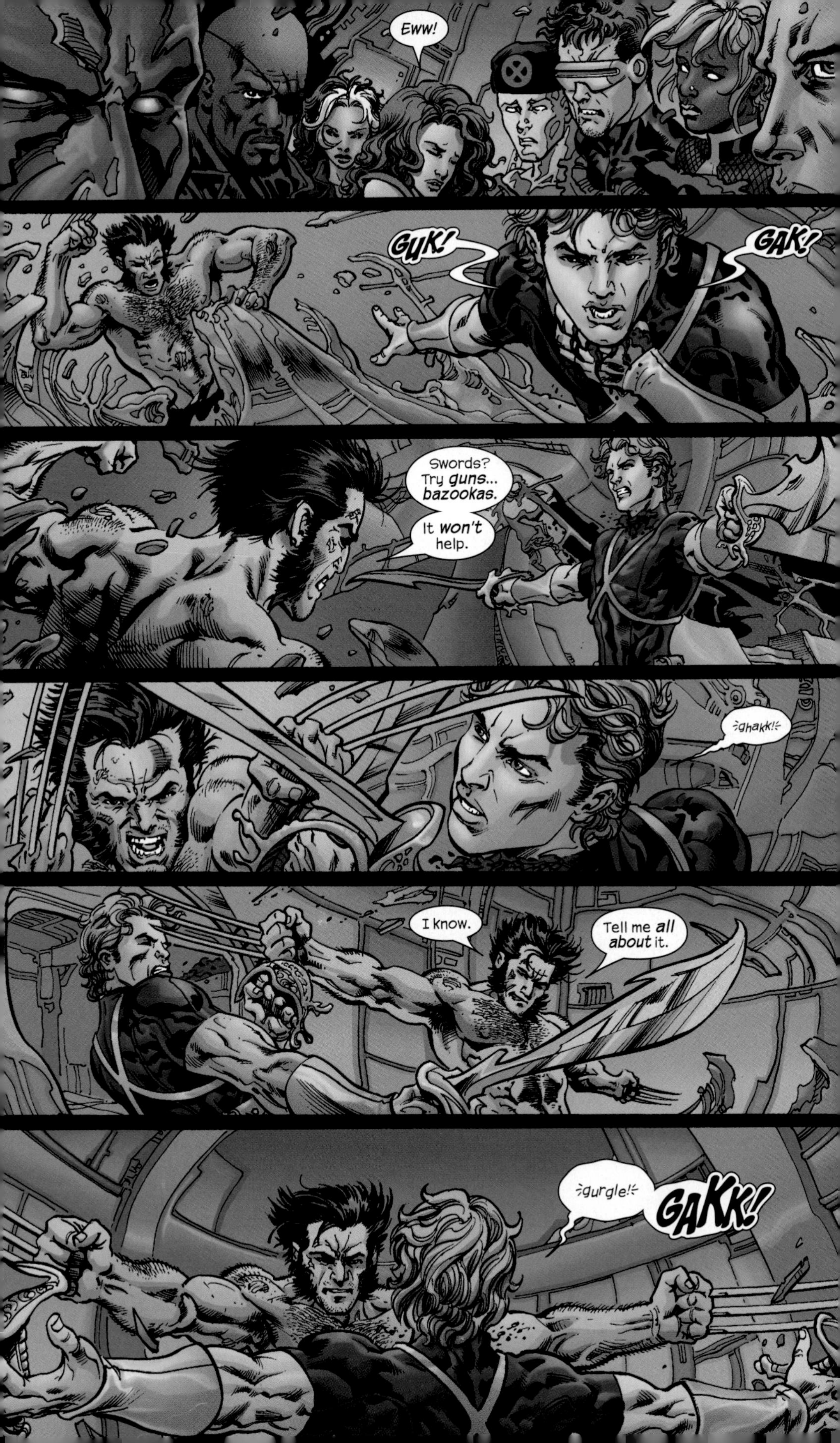
Eww!
GUK!
GAK!
Swords? Try guns... bazookas.
It won't help.
ghakk!
I know.
Tell me all about it.
gurgle!
GAKK!

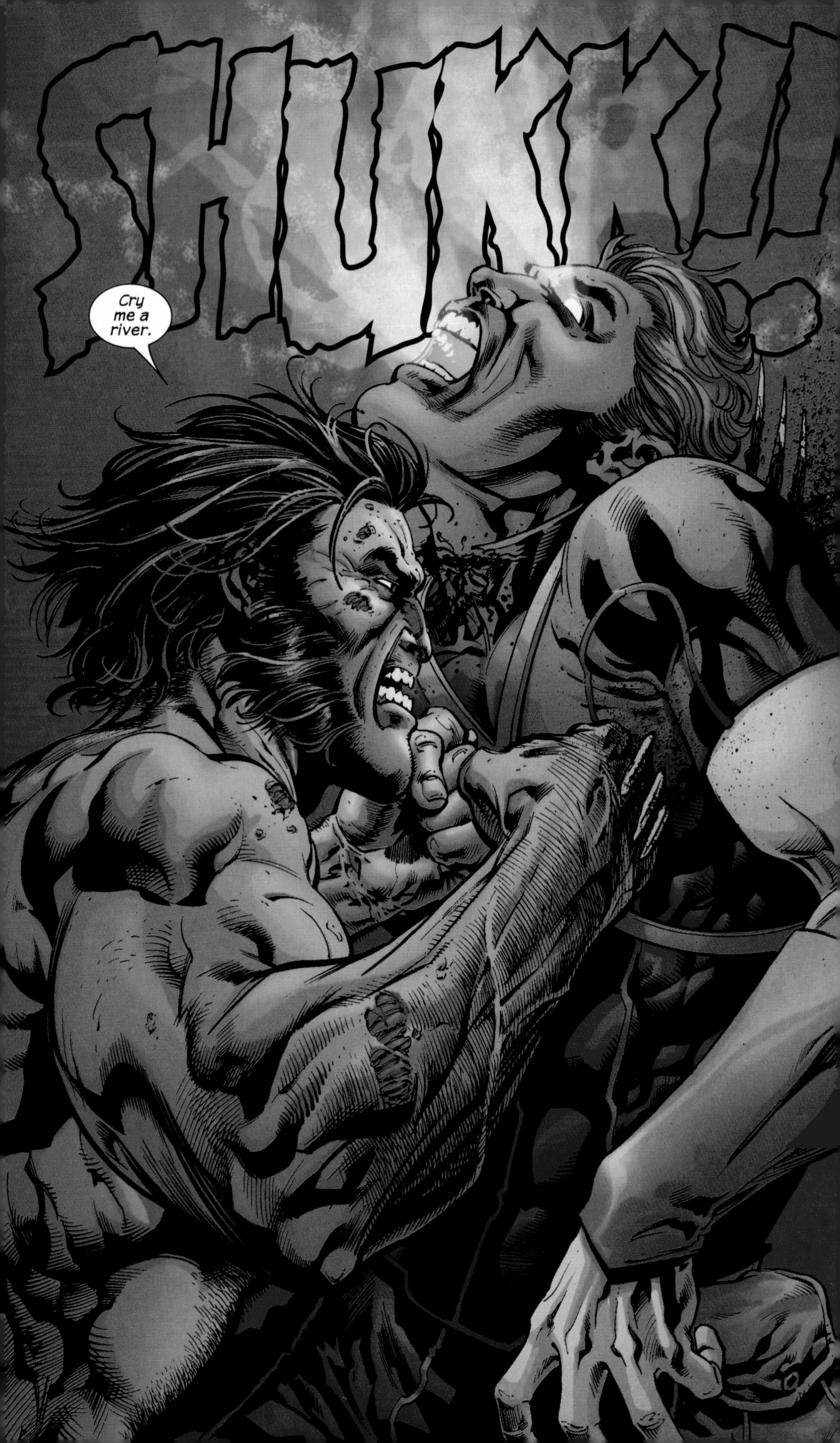
SHUNK!
Cry me a river.

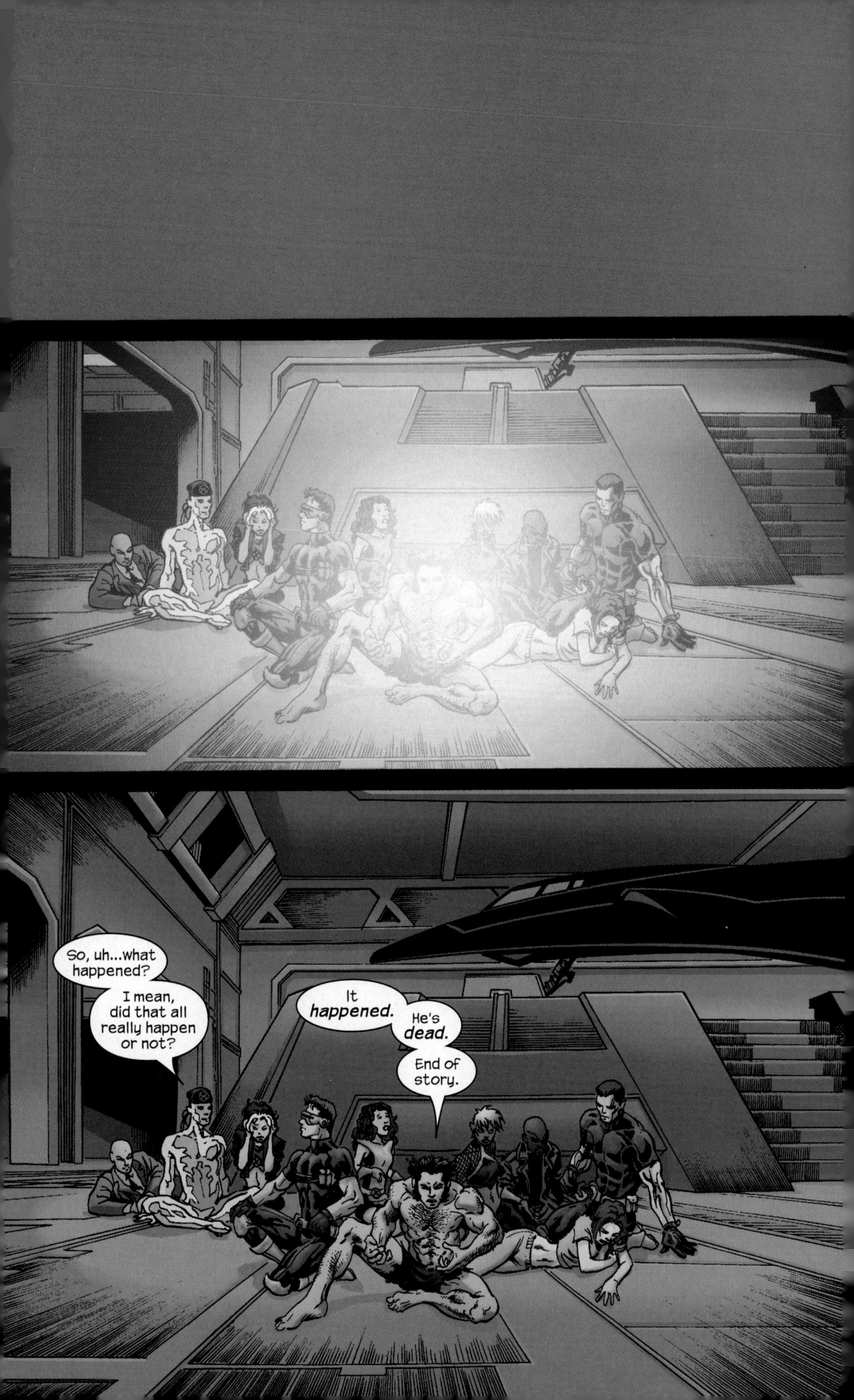
So, uh...what happened?
I mean, did that all really happen or not?
It *happened.*
He's *dead.*
End of story.

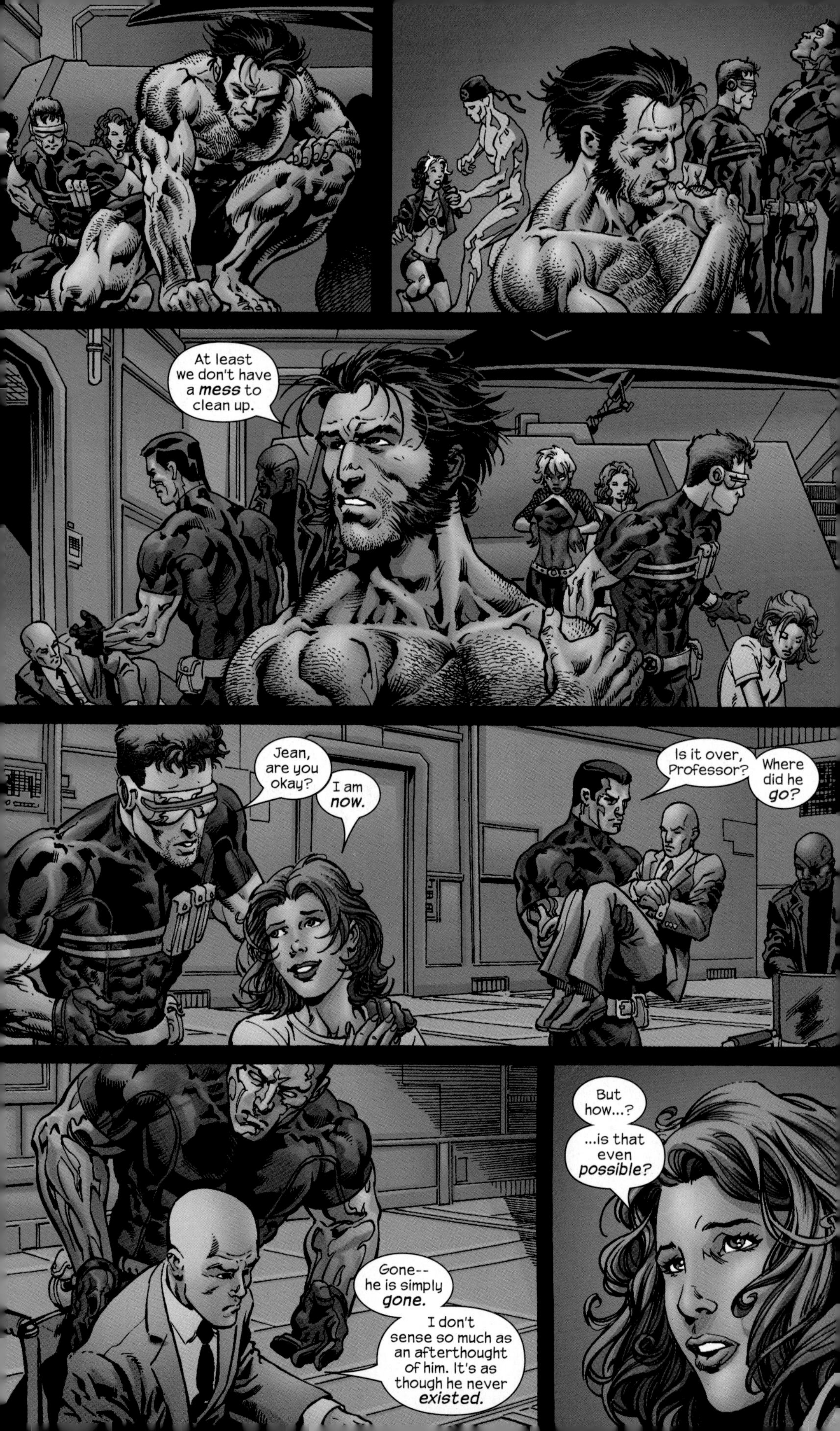

At least we don't have a *mess* to clean up.
Jean, are you okay?
I am *now.*
Is it over, Professor?
Where did he *go?*
Gone-- he is simply *gone.*
I don't sense so much as an afterthought of him. It's as though he never *existed.*
But how...?
...is that even *possible?*

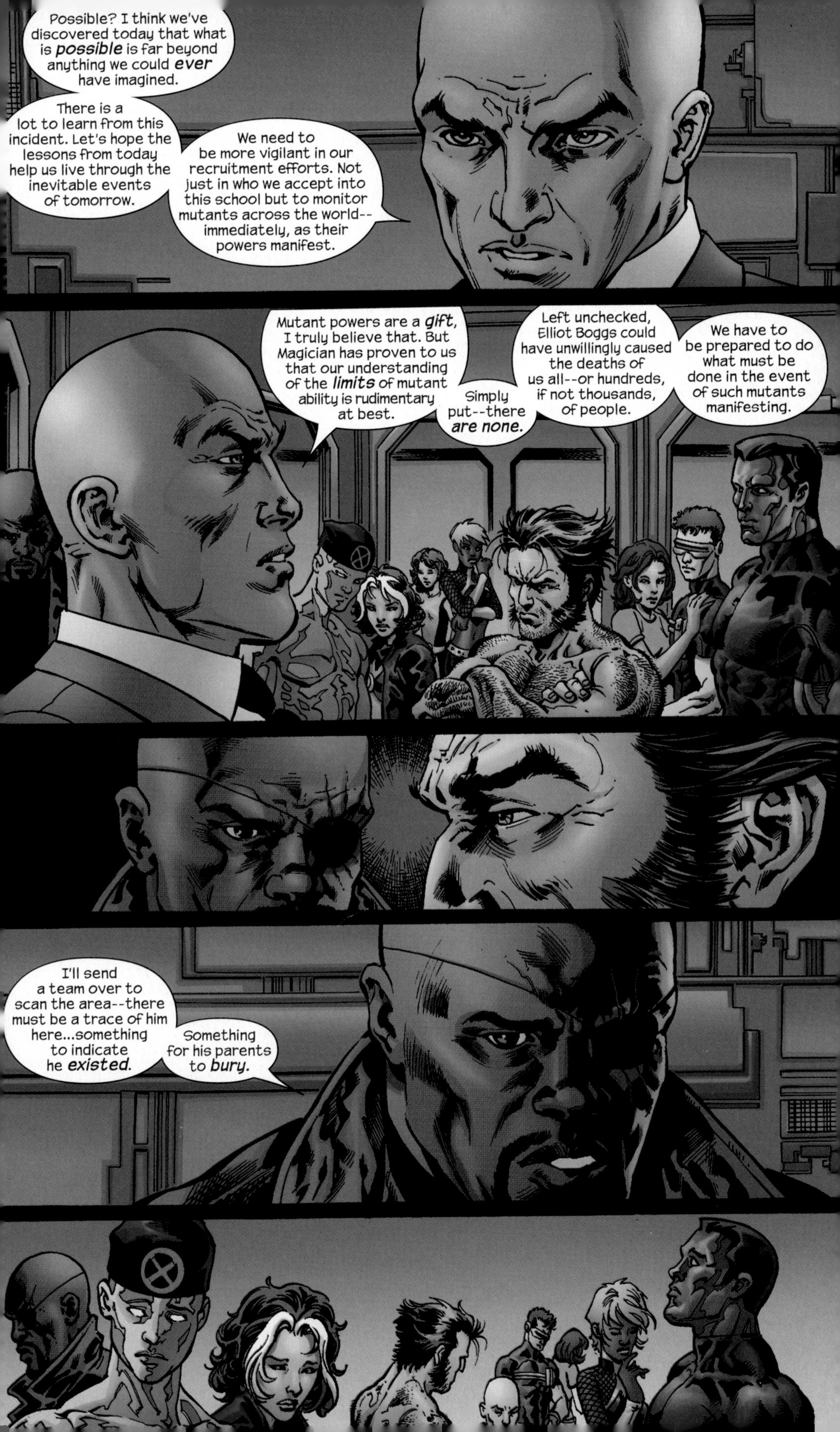
Possible? I think we've discovered today that what is possible is far beyond anything we could ever have imagined.
There is a lot to learn from this incident. Let's hope the lessons from today help us live through the inevitable events of tomorrow.
We need to be more vigilant in our recruitment efforts. Not just in who we accept into this school but to monitor mutants across the world--immediately, as their powers manifest.
Mutant powers are a gift, I truly believe that. But Magician has proven to us that our understanding of the limits of mutant ability is rudimentary at best.
Simply put--there are none.
Left unchecked, Elliot Boggs could have unwillingly caused the deaths of us all--or hundreds, if not thousands, of people.
We have to be prepared to do what must be done in the event of such mutants manifesting.
I'll send a team over to scan the area--there must be a trace of him here...something to indicate he existed.
Something for his parents to bury.

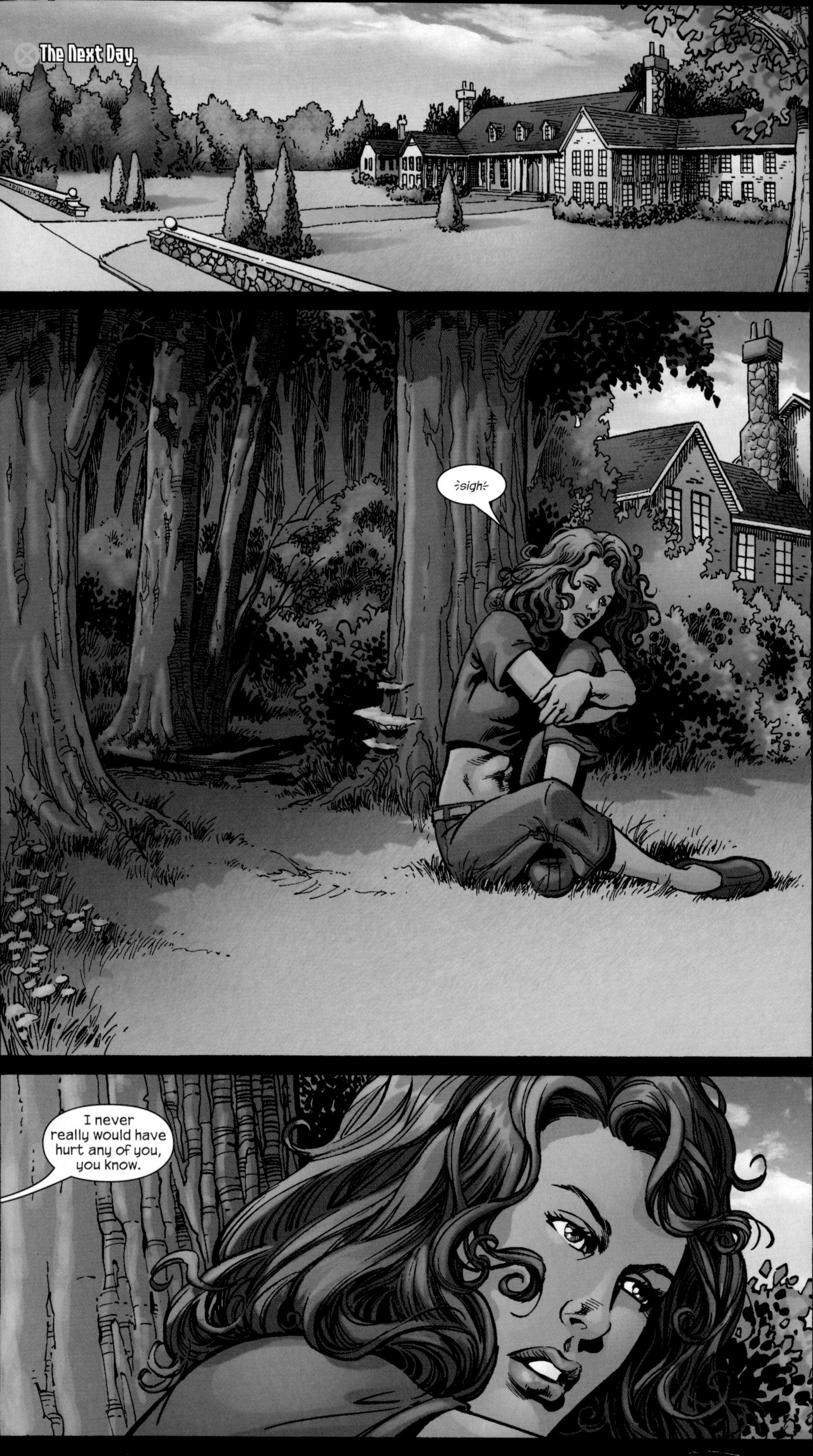
The Next Day.
sigh
I never really would have hurt any of you, you know.

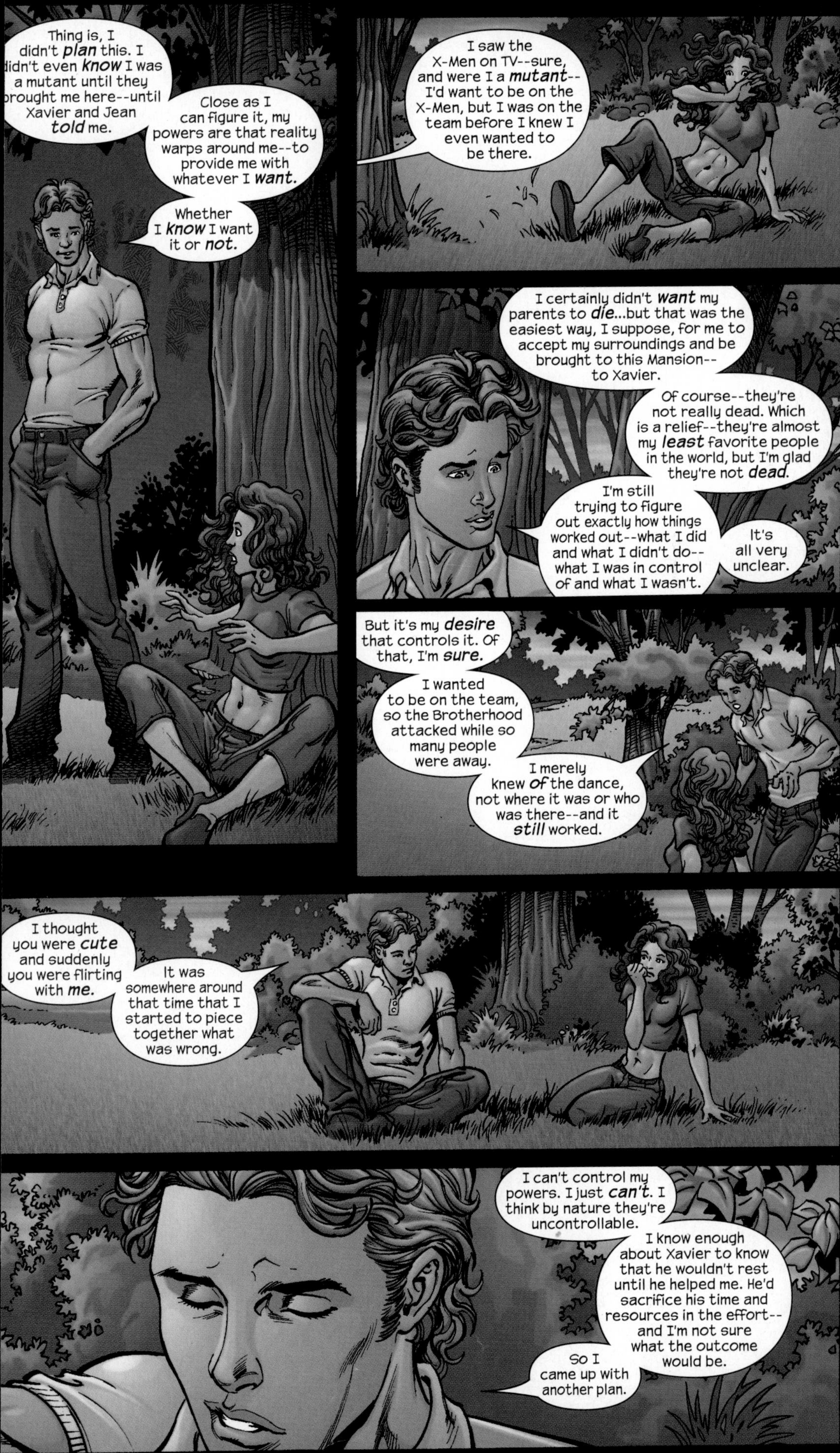

Thing is, I didn't plan this. I didn't even know I was a mutant until they brought me here--until Xavier and Jean told me.
Close as I can figure it, my powers are that reality warps around me--to provide me with whatever I want.
Whether I know I want it or not.
I saw the X-Men on TV--sure, and were I a mutant--I'd want to be on the X-Men, but I was on the team before I knew I even wanted to be there.
I certainly didn't want my parents to die...but that was the easiest way, I suppose, for me to accept my surroundings and be brought to this Mansion--to Xavier.
Of course--they're not really dead. Which is a relief--they're almost my least favorite people in the world, but I'm glad they're not dead.
I'm still trying to figure out exactly how things worked out--what I did and what I didn't do--what I was in control of and what I wasn't.
It's all very unclear.
But it's my desire that controls it. Of that, I'm sure.
I wanted to be on the team, so the Brotherhood attacked while so many people were away.
I merely knew of the dance, not where it was or who was there--and it still worked.
I thought you were cute and suddenly you were flirting with me.
It was somewhere around that time that I started to piece together what was wrong.
I can't control my powers. I just can't. I think by nature they're uncontrollable.
I know enough about Xavier to know that he wouldn't rest until he helped me. He'd sacrifice his time and resources in the effort--and I'm not sure what the outcome would be.
So I came up with another plan.

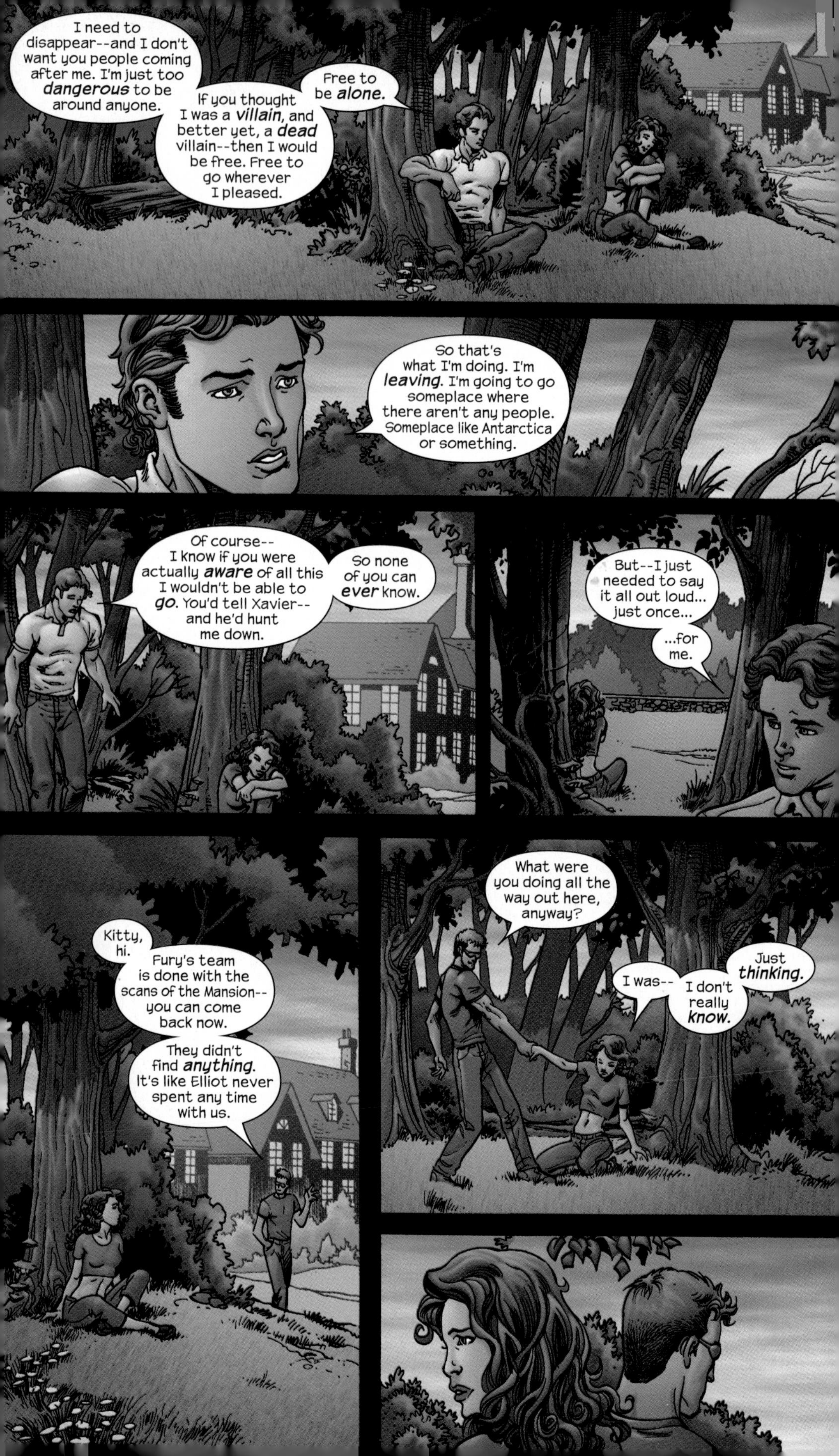
I need to disappear--and I don't want you people coming after me. I'm just too *dangerous* to be around anyone.
If you thought I was a *villain*, and better yet, a *dead* villain--then I would be free. Free to go wherever I pleased.
Free to be *alone.*
So that's what I'm doing. I'm *leaving*. I'm going to go someplace where there aren't any people. Someplace like Antarctica or something.
Of course-- I know if you were actually *aware* of all this I wouldn't be able to *go*. You'd tell Xavier-- and he'd hunt me down.
So none of you can *ever* know.
But--I just needed to say it all out loud... just once...
...for me.
Kitty, hi.
Fury's team is done with the scans of the Mansion-- you can come back now.
They didn't find *anything*. It's like Elliot never spent any time with us.
What were you doing all the way out here, anyway?
I was--
I don't really *know*.
Just *thinking*.

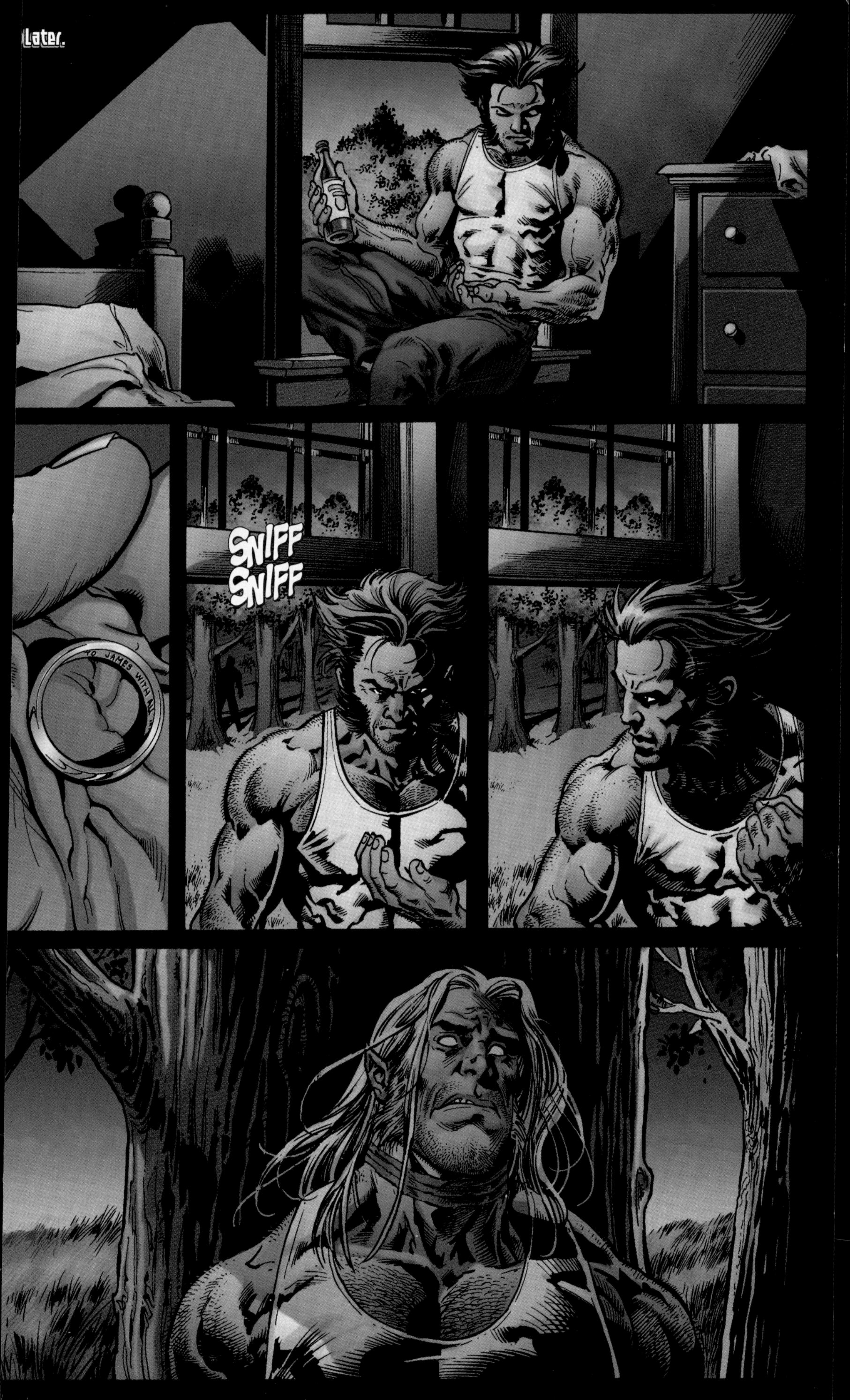
Later.
TO JAMES WITH ALL
SNIFF SNIFF

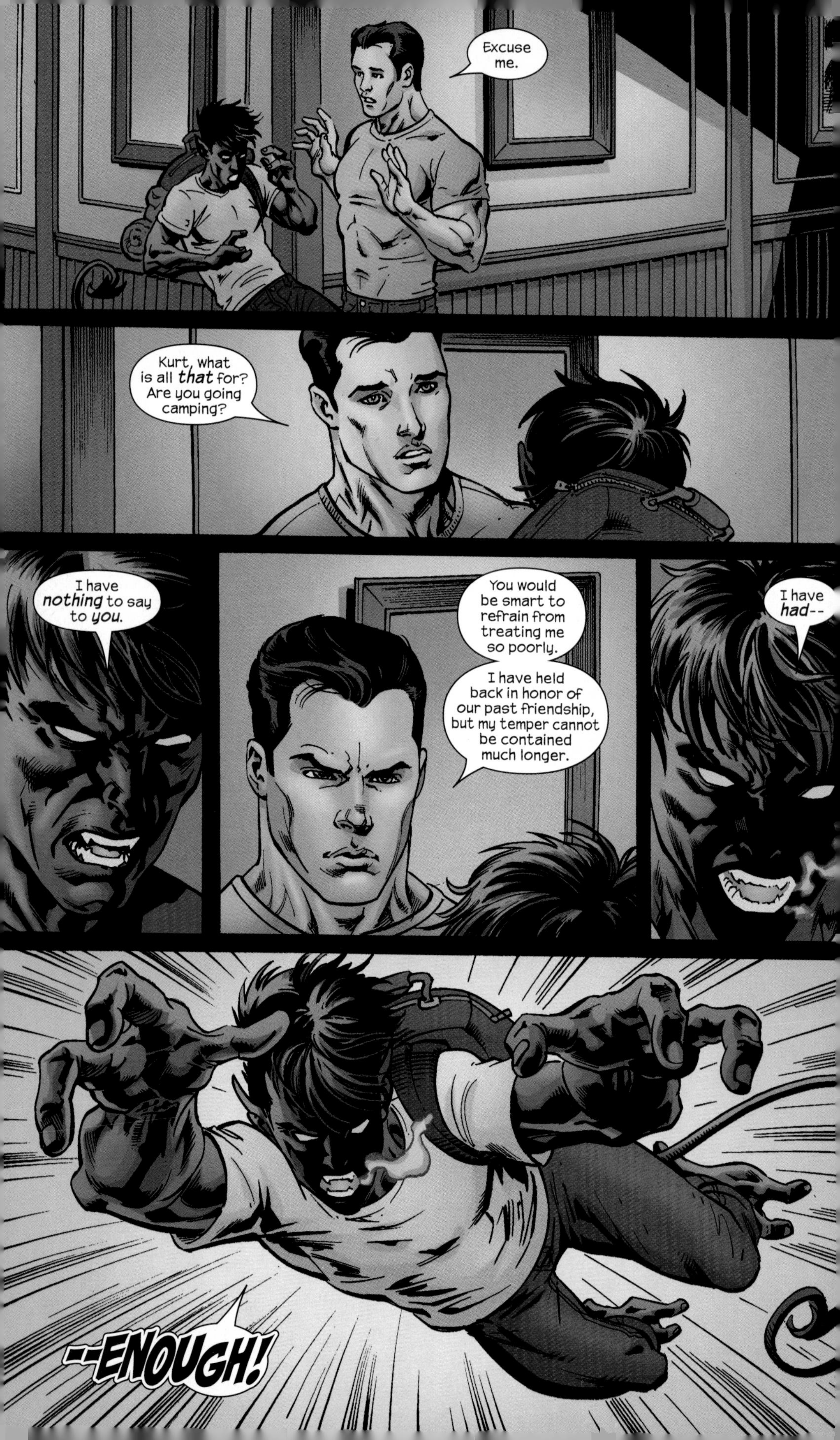
Excuse me.
Kurt, what is all *that* for? Are you going camping?
I have *nothing* to say to *you*.
You would be smart to refrain from treating me so poorly.
I have held back in honor of our past friendship, but my temper cannot be contained much longer.
I have *had*--
--ENOUGH!

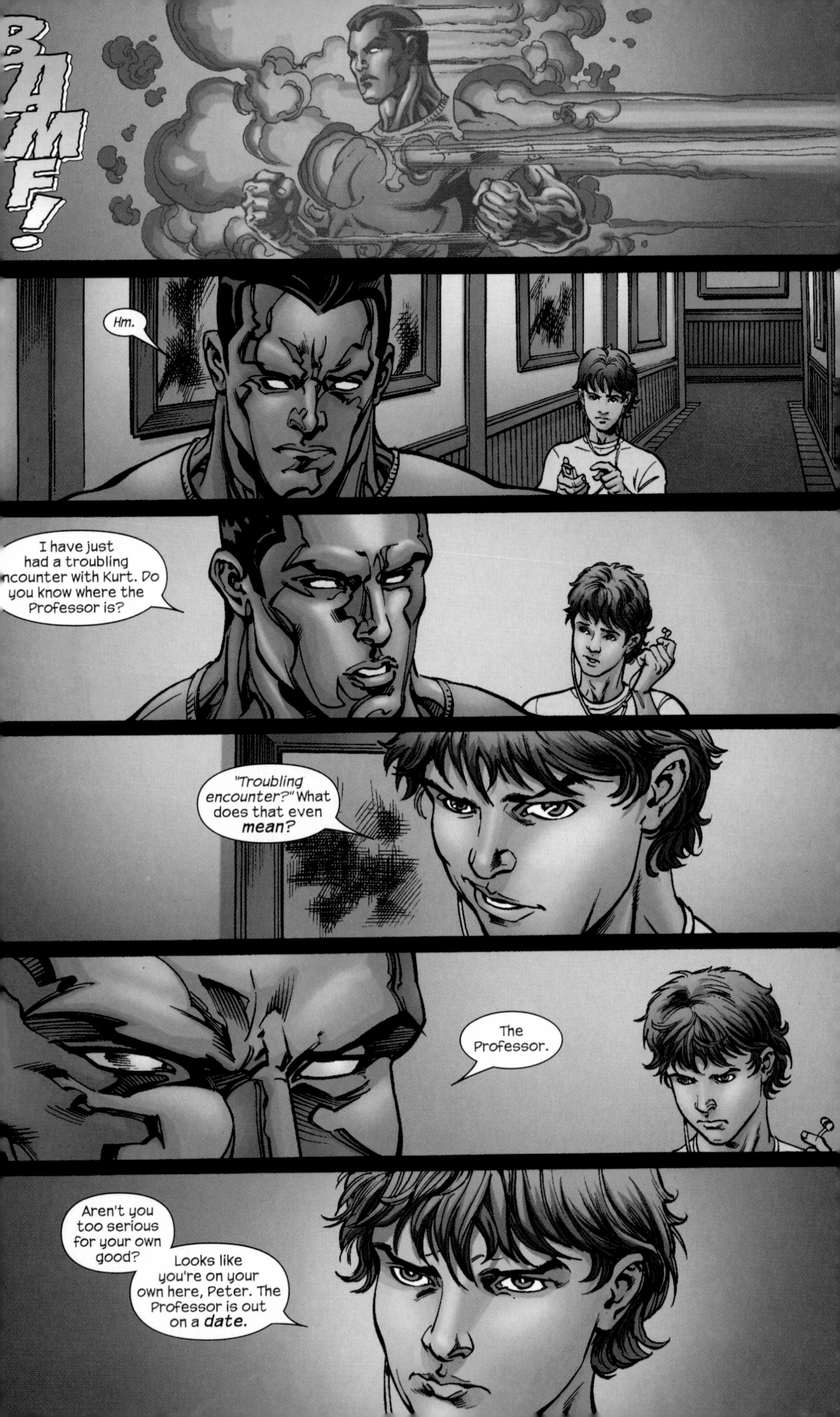
BAMF!
Hm.
I have just had a troubling encounter with Kurt. Do you know where the Professor is?
"Troubling encounter?" What does that even *mean?*
The Professor.
Aren't you too serious for your own good?
Looks like you're on your own here, Peter. The Professor is out on a *date.*

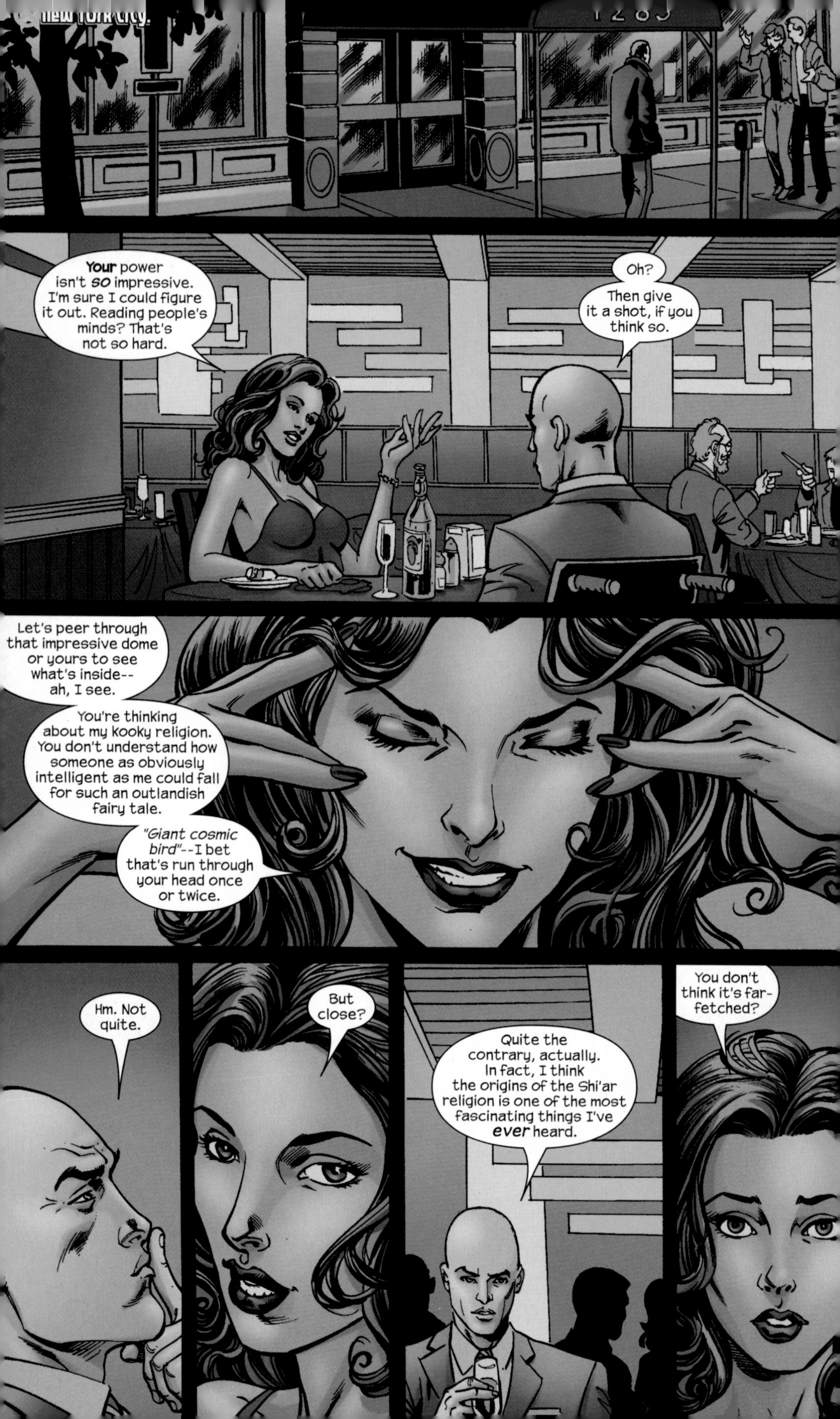
new york city.
Your power isn't SO impressive. I'm sure I could figure it out. Reading people's minds? That's not so hard.
Oh?
Then give it a shot, if you think so.
Let's peer through that impressive dome or yours to see what's inside--ah, I see.
You're thinking about my kooky religion. You don't understand how someone as obviously intelligent as me could fall for such an outlandish fairy tale.
"Giant cosmic bird"--I bet that's run through your head once or twice.
Hm. Not quite.
But close?
Quite the contrary, actually. In fact, I think the origins of the Shi'ar religion is one of the most fascinating things I've ever heard.
You don't think it's far-fetched?

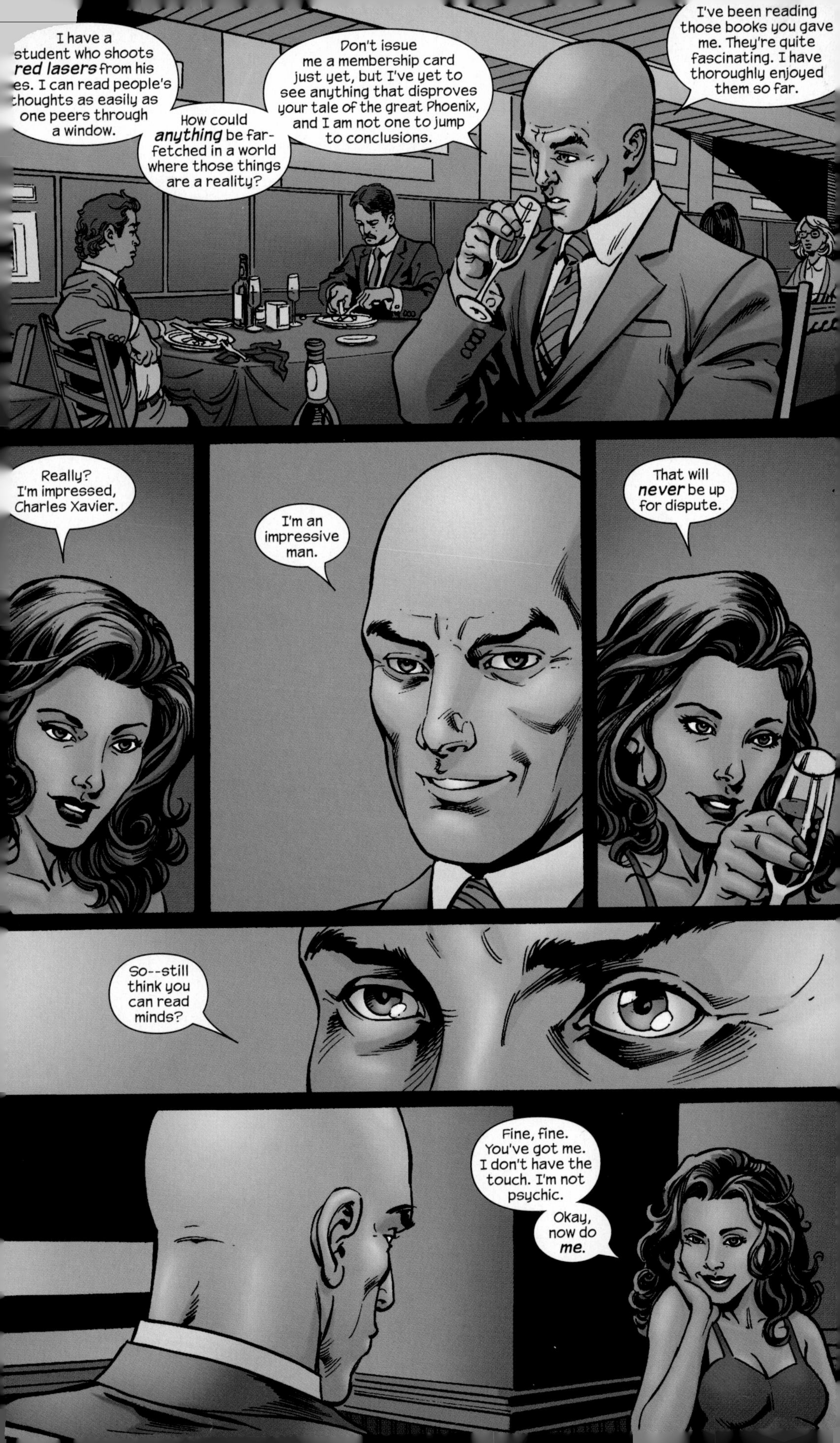
I have a student who shoots red lasers from his es. I can read people's thoughts as easily as one peers through a window.
How could anything be far-fetched in a world where those things are a reality?
Don't issue me a membership card just yet, but I've yet to see anything that disproves your tale of the great Phoenix, and I am not one to jump to conclusions.
I've been reading those books you gave me. They're quite fascinating. I have thoroughly enjoyed them so far.
Really? I'm impressed, Charles Xavier.
I'm an impressive man.
That will never be up for dispute.
So--still think you can read minds?
Fine, fine. You've got me. I don't have the touch. I'm not psychic.
Okay, now do me.

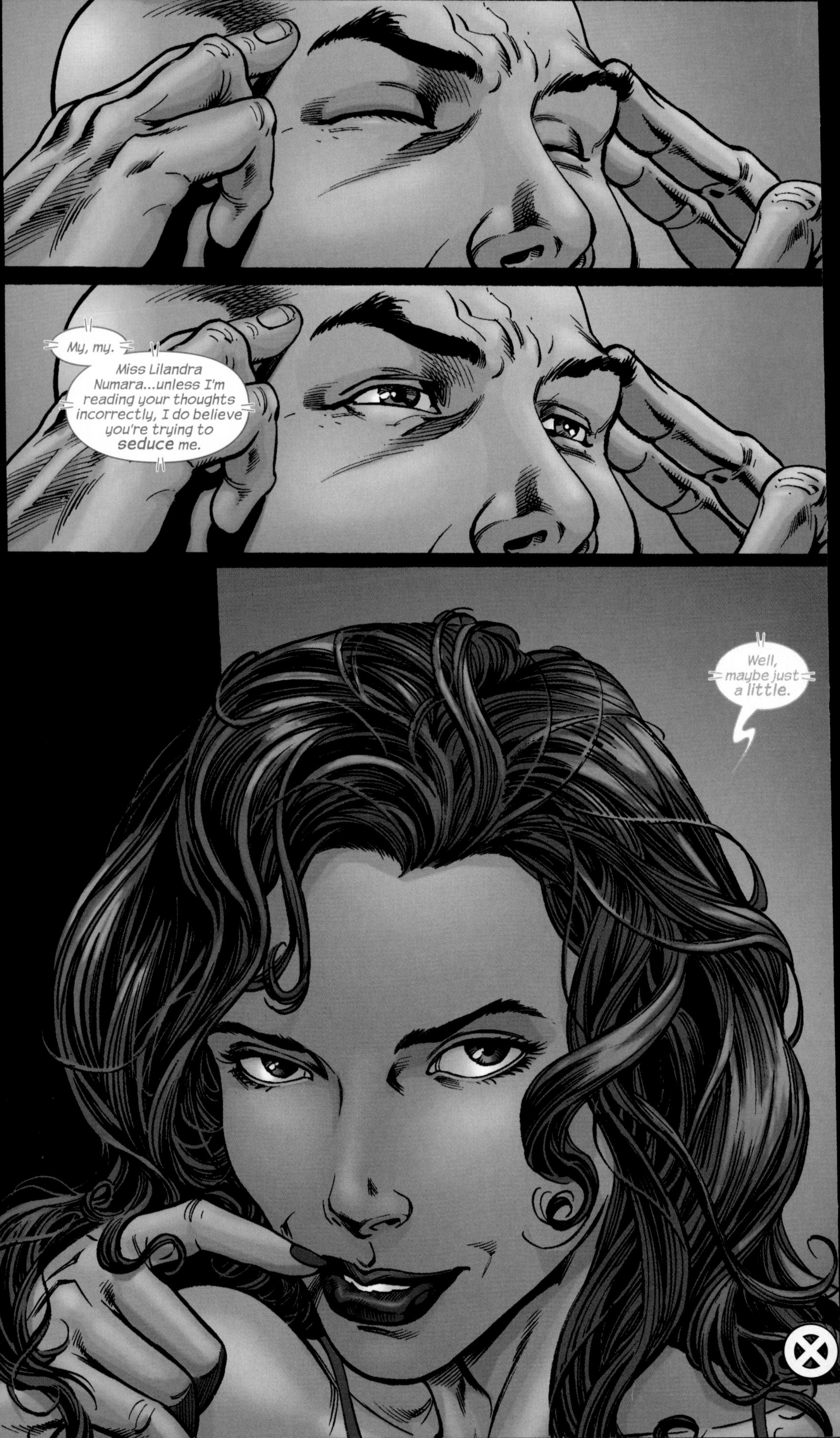
My, my.
Miss Lilandra Numara...unless I'm reading your thoughts incorrectly, I do believe you're trying to seduce me.
Well, maybe just a little.

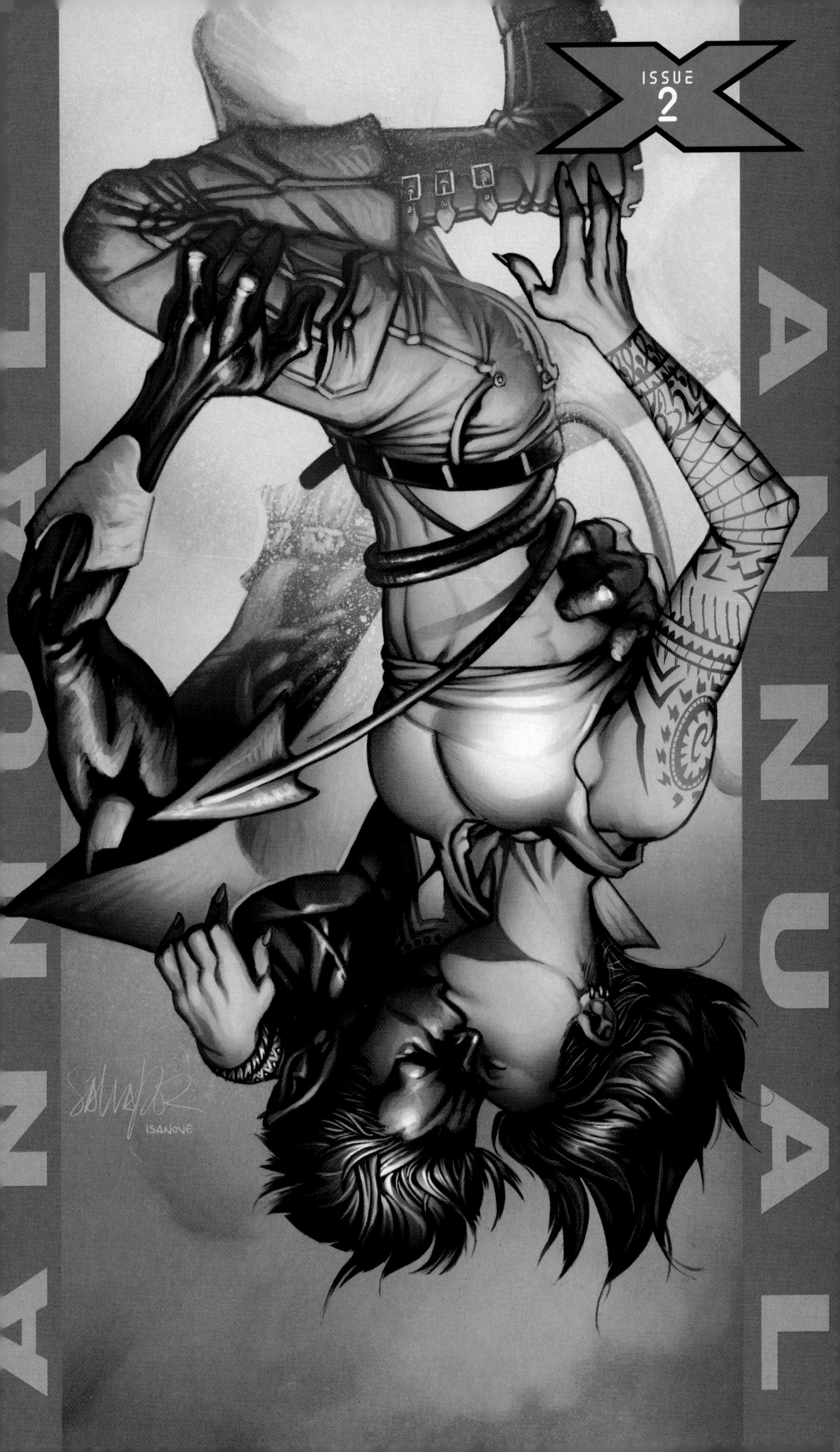
X
ISSUE
2
ANNUAL
ANNUAL

PREVIOUSLY IN ULTIMATE X-MEN

Born with strange and amazing abilities, the X-Men are young mutant heroes, sworn to protect a world that fears and hates them.

One member of the team—Alison Blaire, better known as the punk singer, Dazzler—has been in a coma for the past sever weeks, after she was injured in battle.

Her teammate, Nightcrawler, has been acting unusually since Dazzler's injury, frequently holding vigil in her hospital ro

Before joining the X-Men, Nightcrawler had been forced into working as an agent for the black-ops unit called Weapon which tortured mutants and turned them into killers...

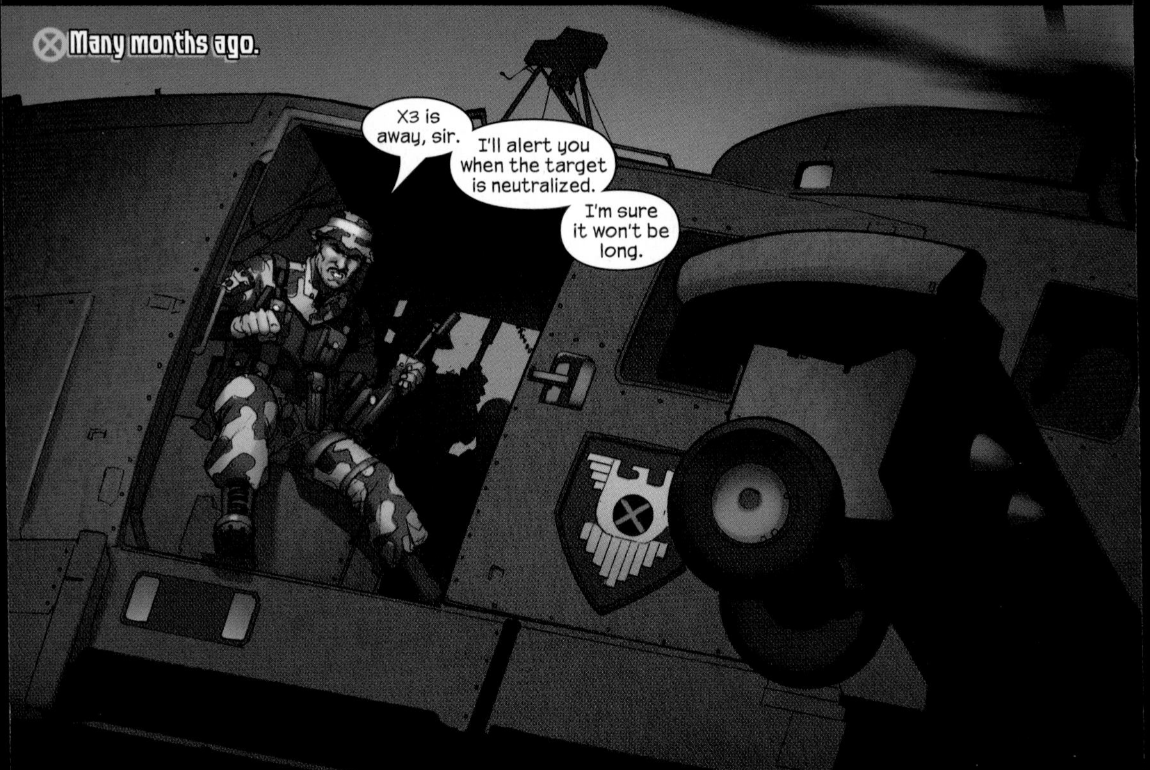
Many months ago.
X3 is away, sir.
I'll alert you when the target is neutralized.
I'm sure it won't be long.

BREAKING POINT

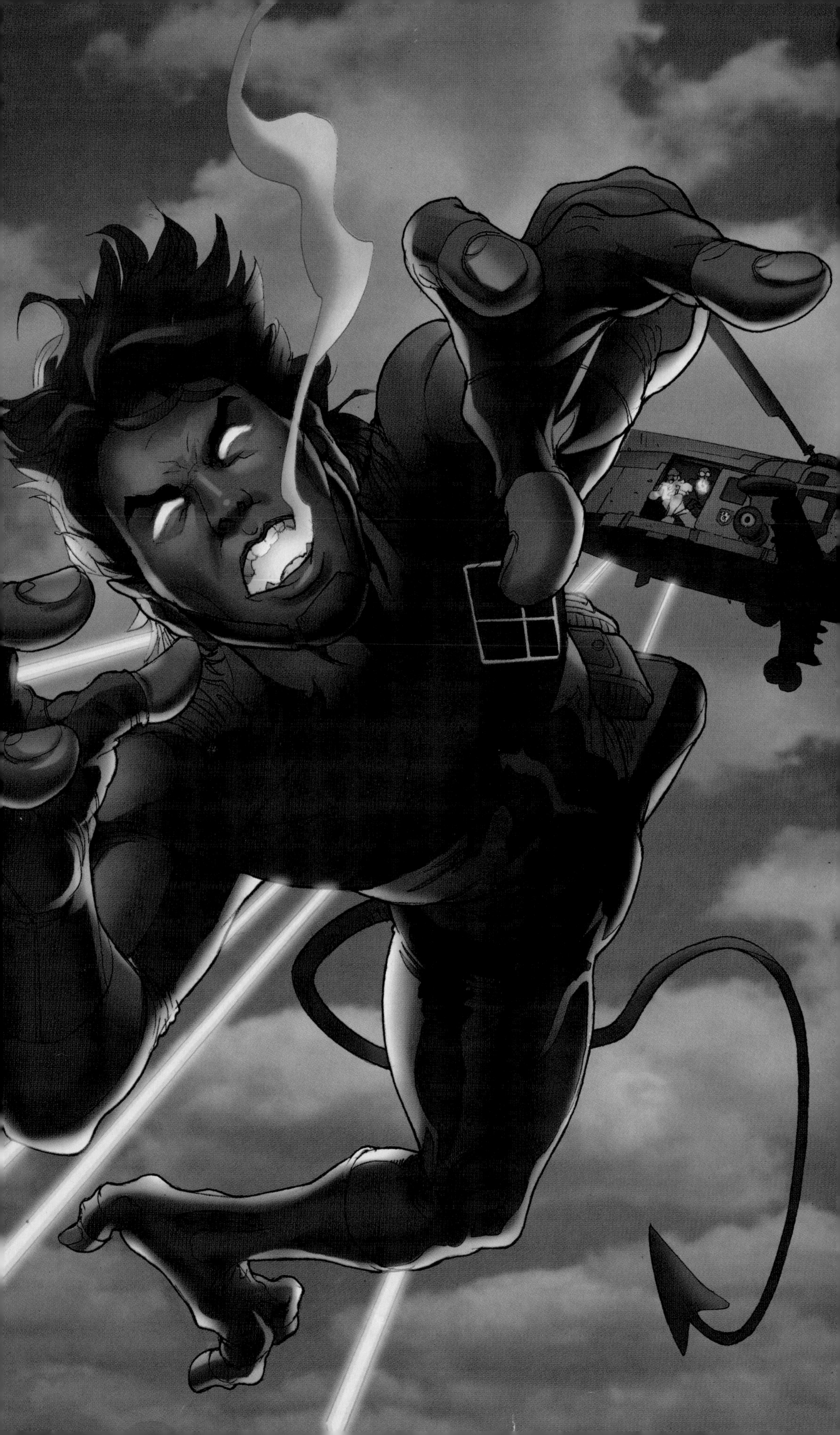

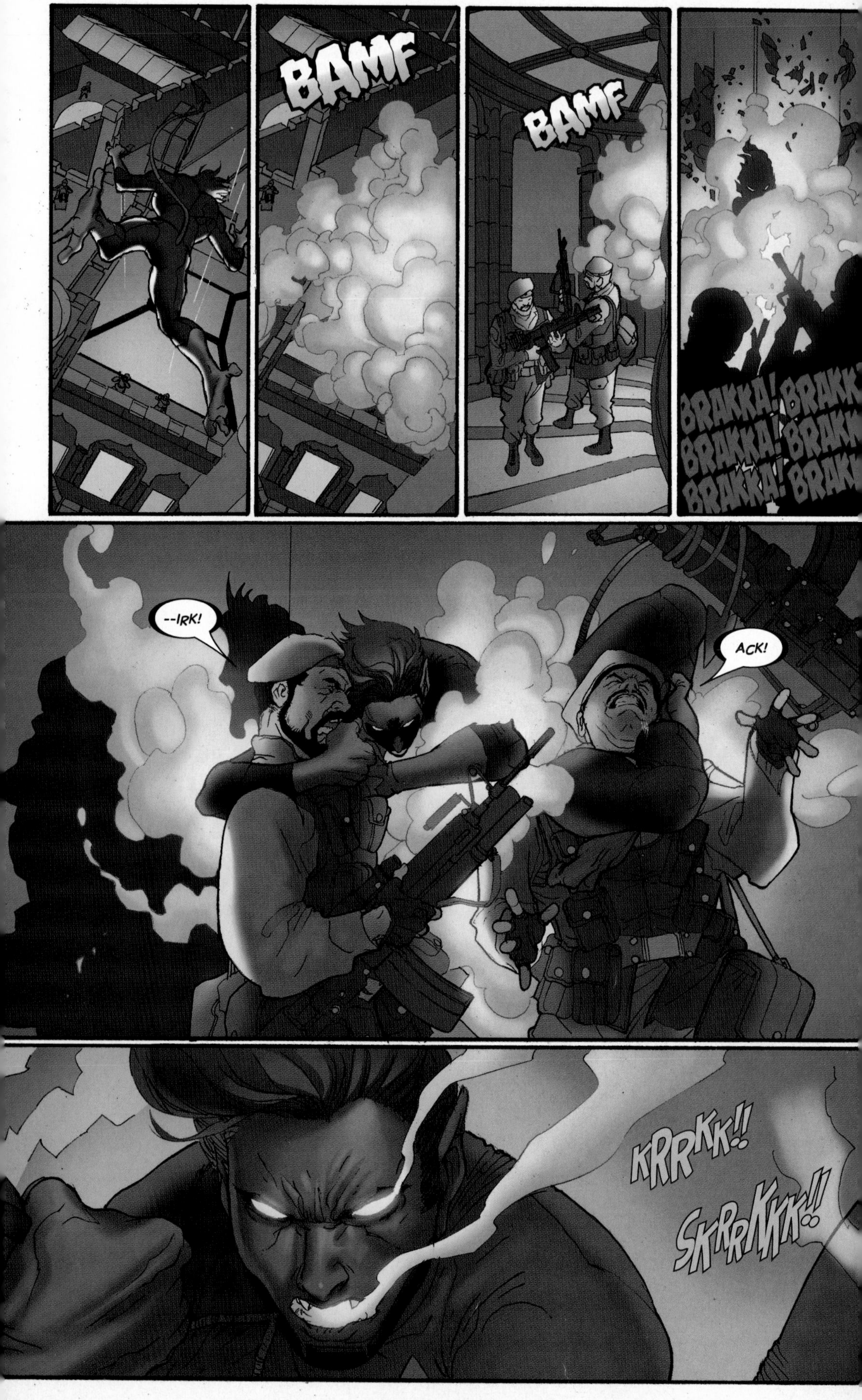
BAMF
BAMF
BRAKKA! BRAKKA! BRAKKA! BRAKKA! BRAKKA! BRAKKA!
--IRK!
ACK!
KRRKK!!
SKRRKKK!!

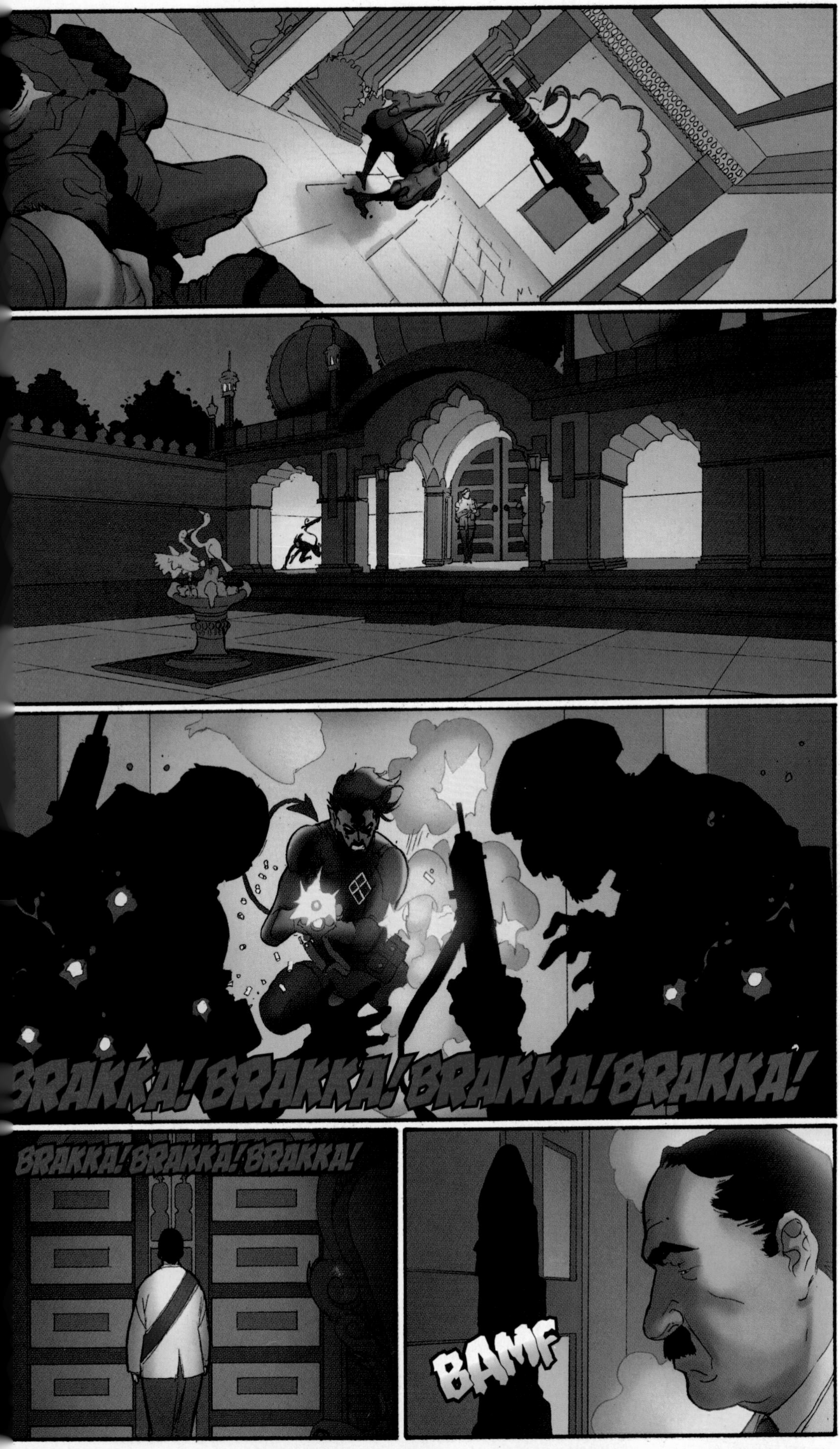

BRAKKA! BRAKKA! BRAKKA! BRAKKA!
BRAKKA! BRAKKA! BRAKKA!
BAMF

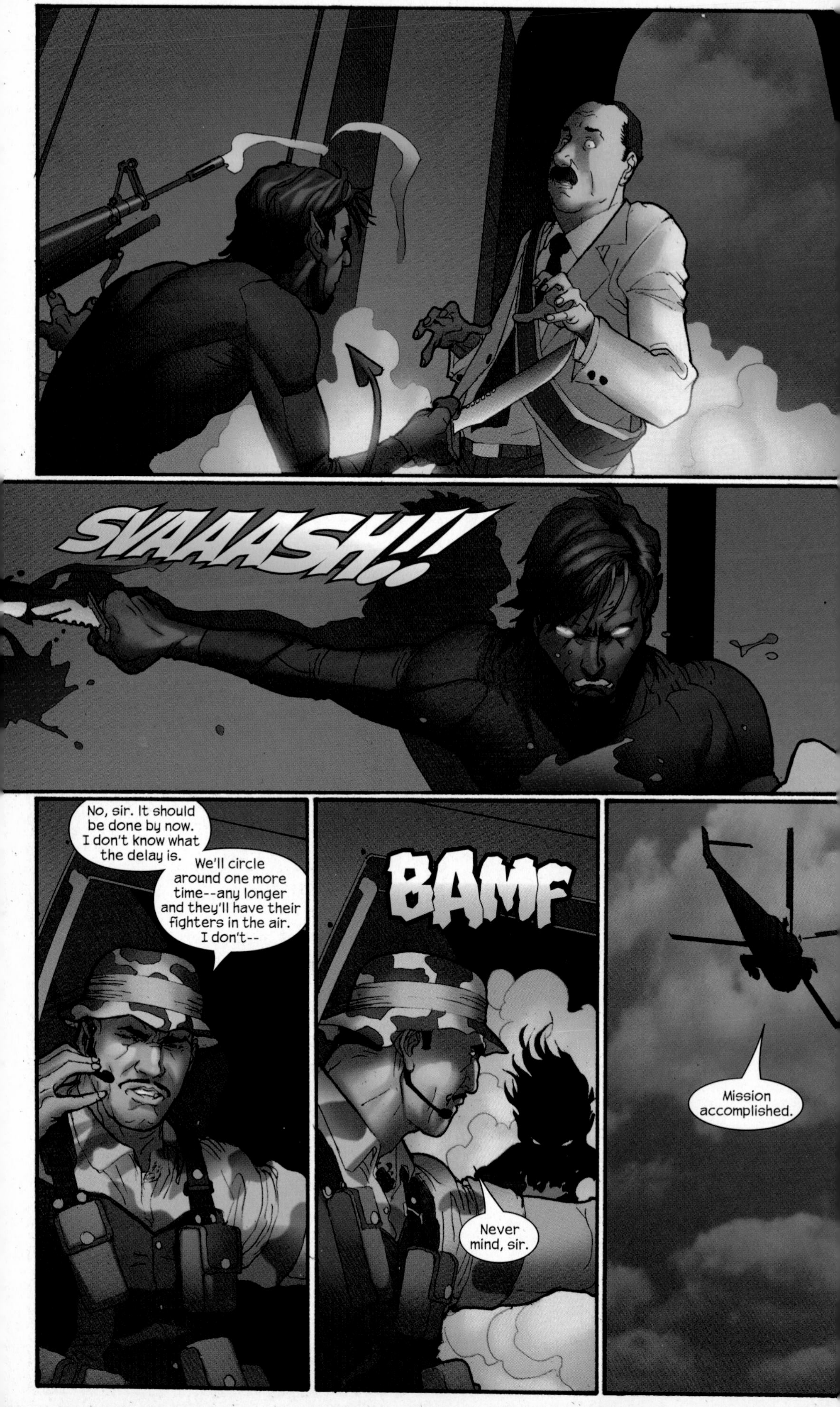
SVAAASH!!
No, sir. It should be done by now. I don't know what the delay is.
We'll circle around one more time--any longer and they'll have their fighters in the air. I don't--
BAMF
Never mind, sir.
Mission accomplished.

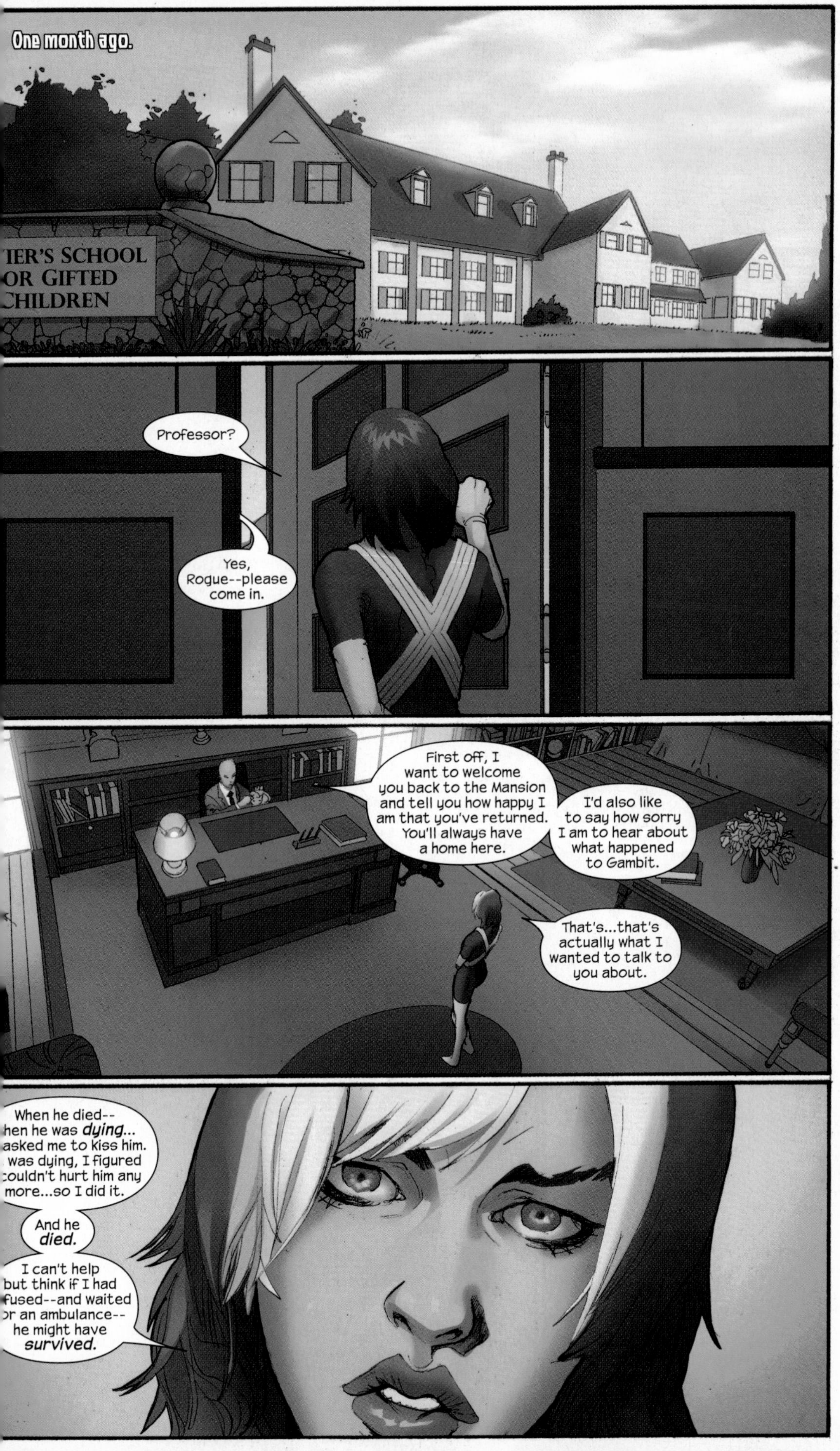

One month ago.
IER'S SCHOOL
OR GIFTED
CHILDREN
Professor?
Yes, Rogue--please come in.
First off, I want to welcome you back to the Mansion and tell you how happy I am that you've returned. You'll always have a home here.
I'd also like to say how sorry I am to hear about what happened to Gambit.
That's...that's actually what I wanted to talk to you about.
When he died-- hen he was *dying*... asked me to kiss him. was dying, I figured couldn't hurt him any more...so I did it.
And he *died.*
I can't help but think if I had fused--and waited or an ambulance-- he might have *survived.*

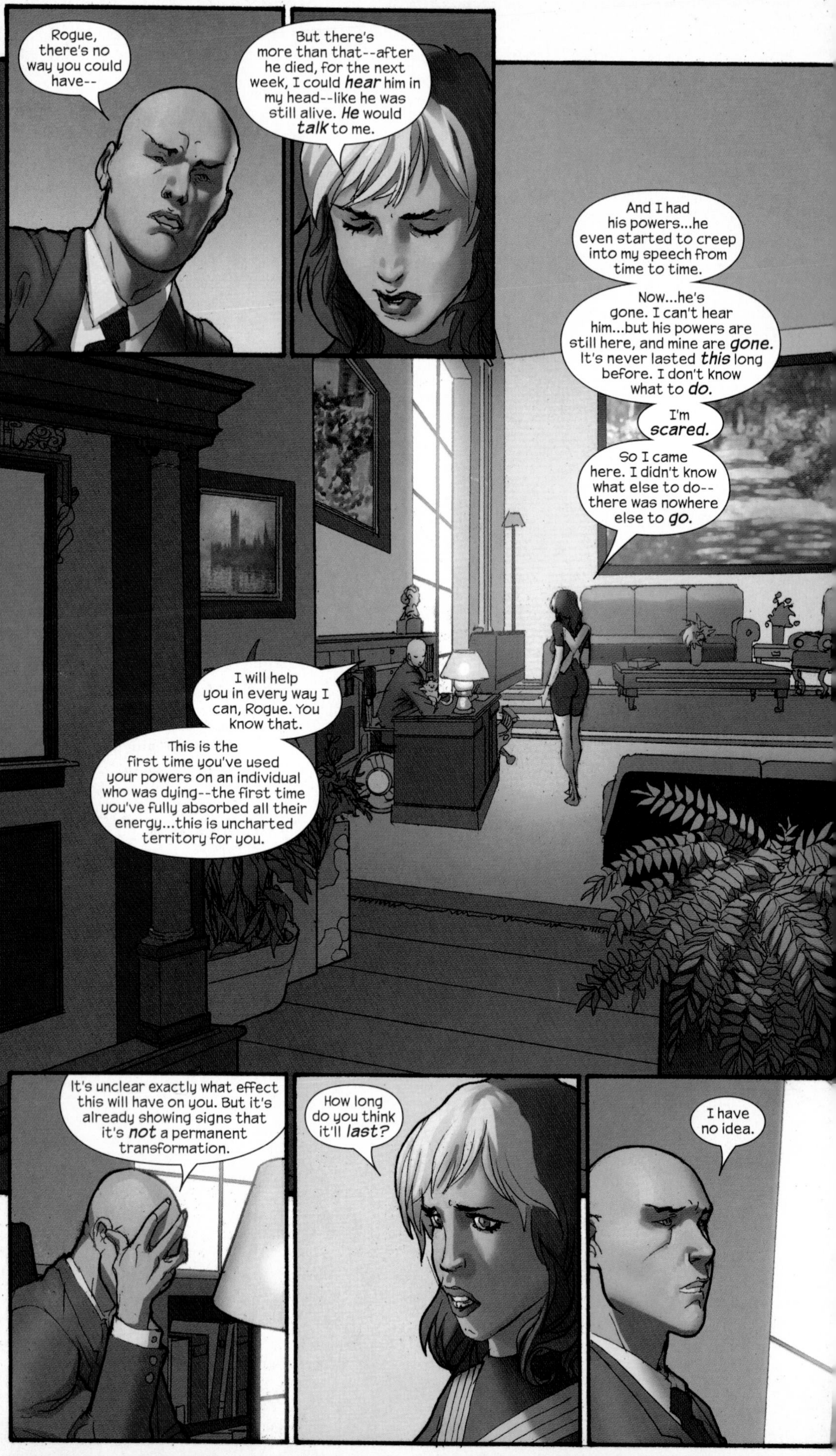
Rogue, there's no way you could have--
But there's more than that--after he died, for the next week, I could hear him in my head--like he was still alive. He would talk to me.
And I had his powers...he even started to creep into my speech from time to time.
Now...he's gone. I can't hear him...but his powers are still here, and mine are gone. It's never lasted this long before. I don't know what to do.
I'm scared.
So I came here. I didn't know what else to do--there was nowhere else to go.
I will help you in every way I can, Rogue. You know that.
This is the first time you've used your powers on an individual who was dying--the first time you've fully absorbed all their energy...this is uncharted territory for you.
It's unclear exactly what effect this will have on you. But it's already showing signs that it's not a permanent transformation.
How long do you think it'll last?
I have no idea.

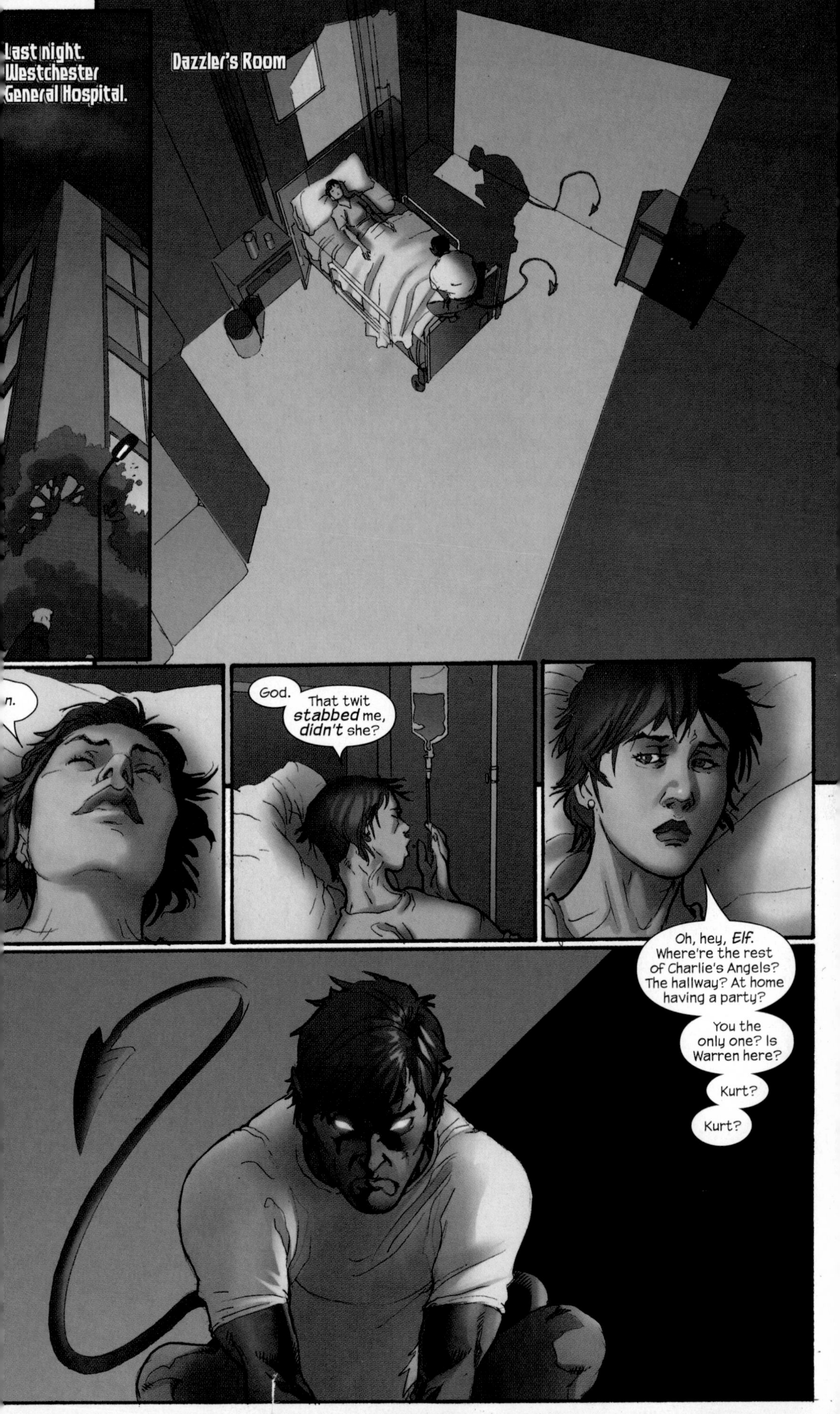

Last night. Westchester General Hospital.
Dazzler's Room
n.
God.
That twit *stabbed* me, *didn't* she?
Oh, hey, *Elf.* Where're the rest of Charlie's Angels? The hallway? At home having a party?
You the only one? Is Warren here?
Kurt?
Kurt?

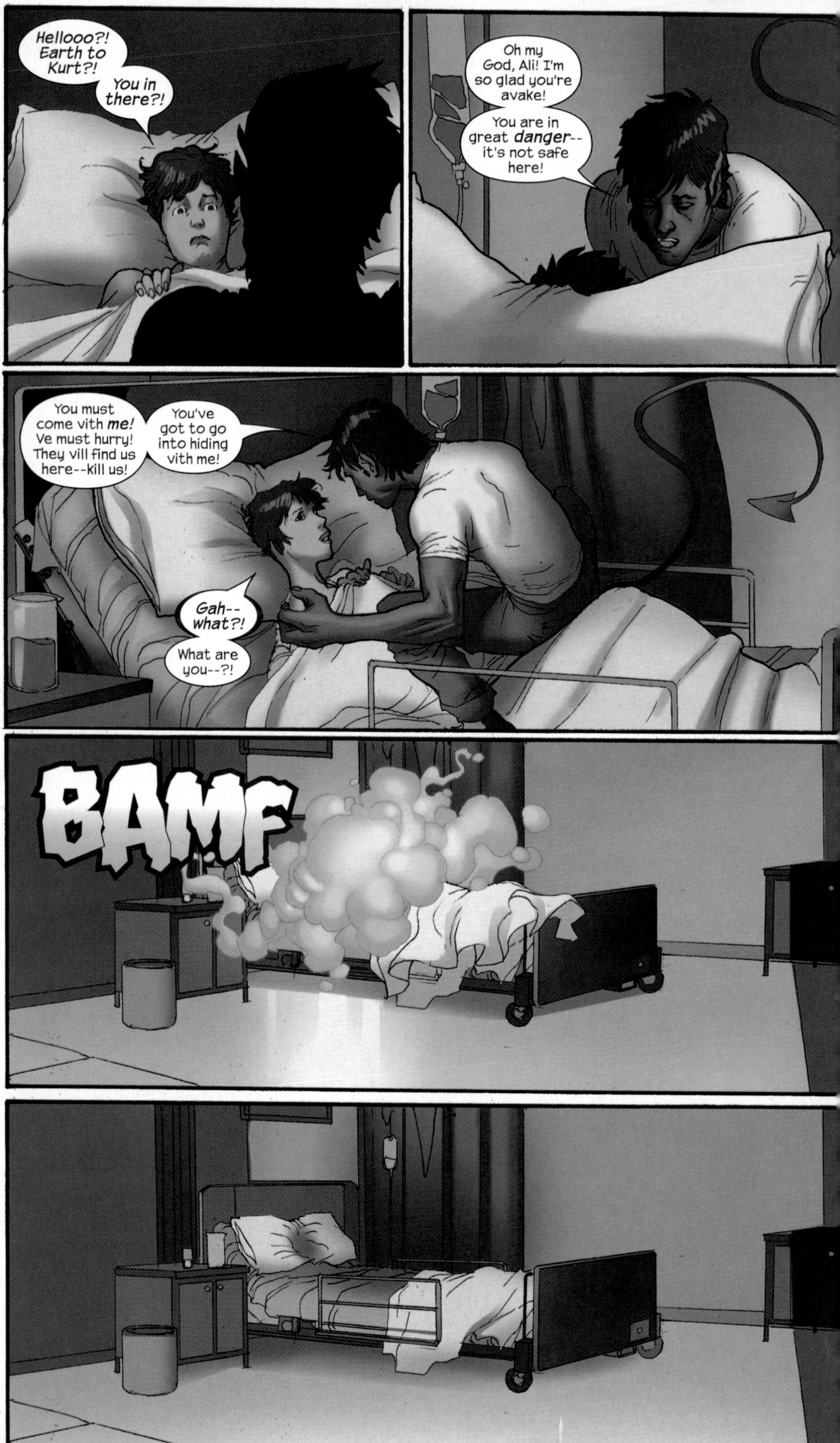
Hellooo?! Earth to Kurt?!
You in there?!
Oh my God, Ali! I'm so glad you're avake!
You are in great danger--it's not safe here!
You must come vith me! Ve must hurry! They vill find us here--kill us!
You've got to go into hiding vith me!
Gah--what?!
What are you--?!
BAMF

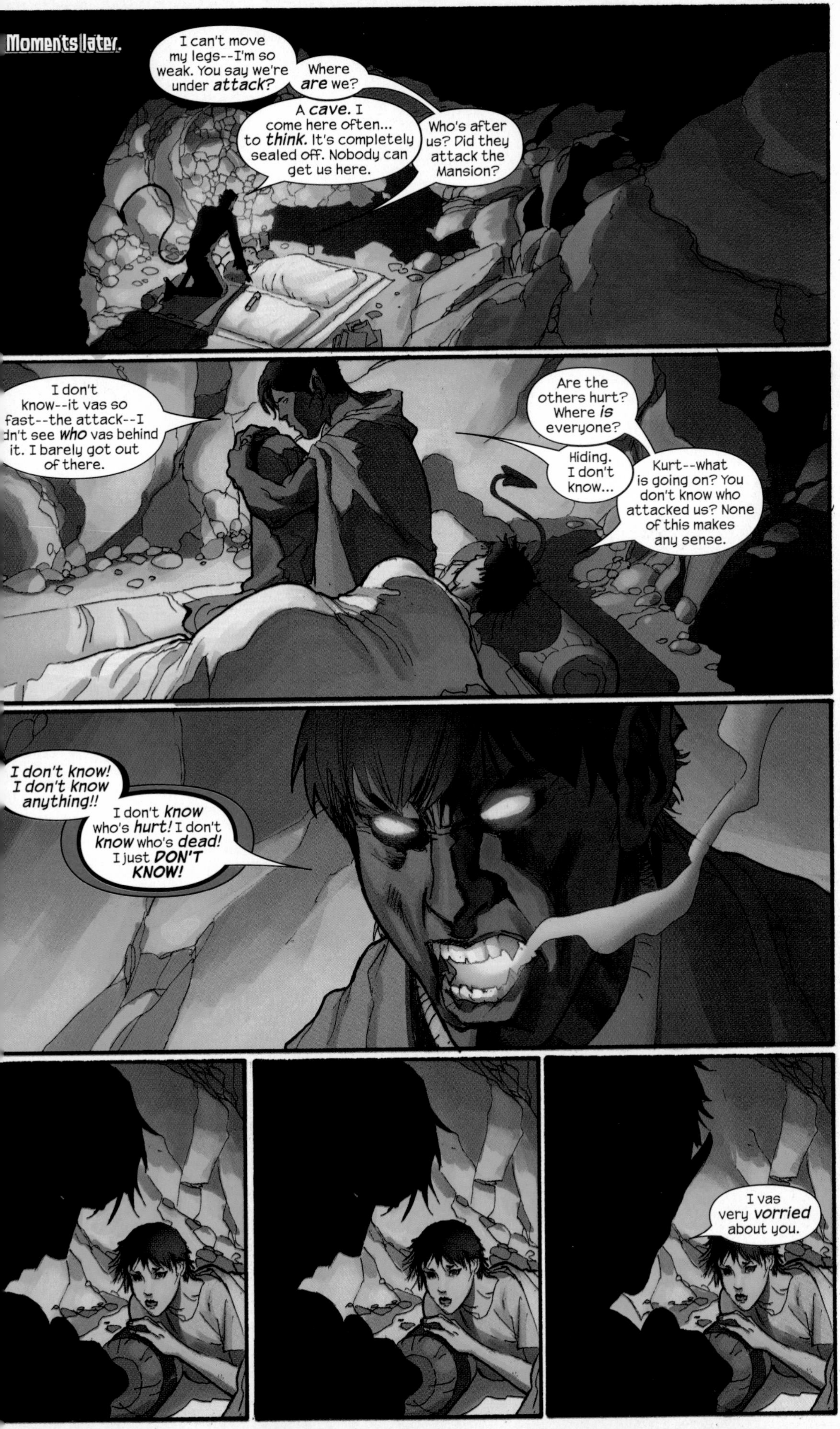

Moments later.
I can't move my legs--I'm so weak. You say we're under *attack*?
Where *are* we?
A *cave.* I come here often... to *think.* It's completely sealed off. Nobody can get us here.
Who's after us? Did they attack the Mansion?
I don't know--it vas so fast--the attack--I dn't see *who* vas behind it. I barely got out of there.
Are the others hurt? Where *is* everyone?
Hiding. I don't know...
Kurt--what is going on? You don't know who attacked us? None of this makes any sense.
I don't know! I don't know anything!!
I don't *know* who's *hurt!* I don't *know* who's *dead!* I just *DON'T KNOW!*
I vas very *vorried* about you.

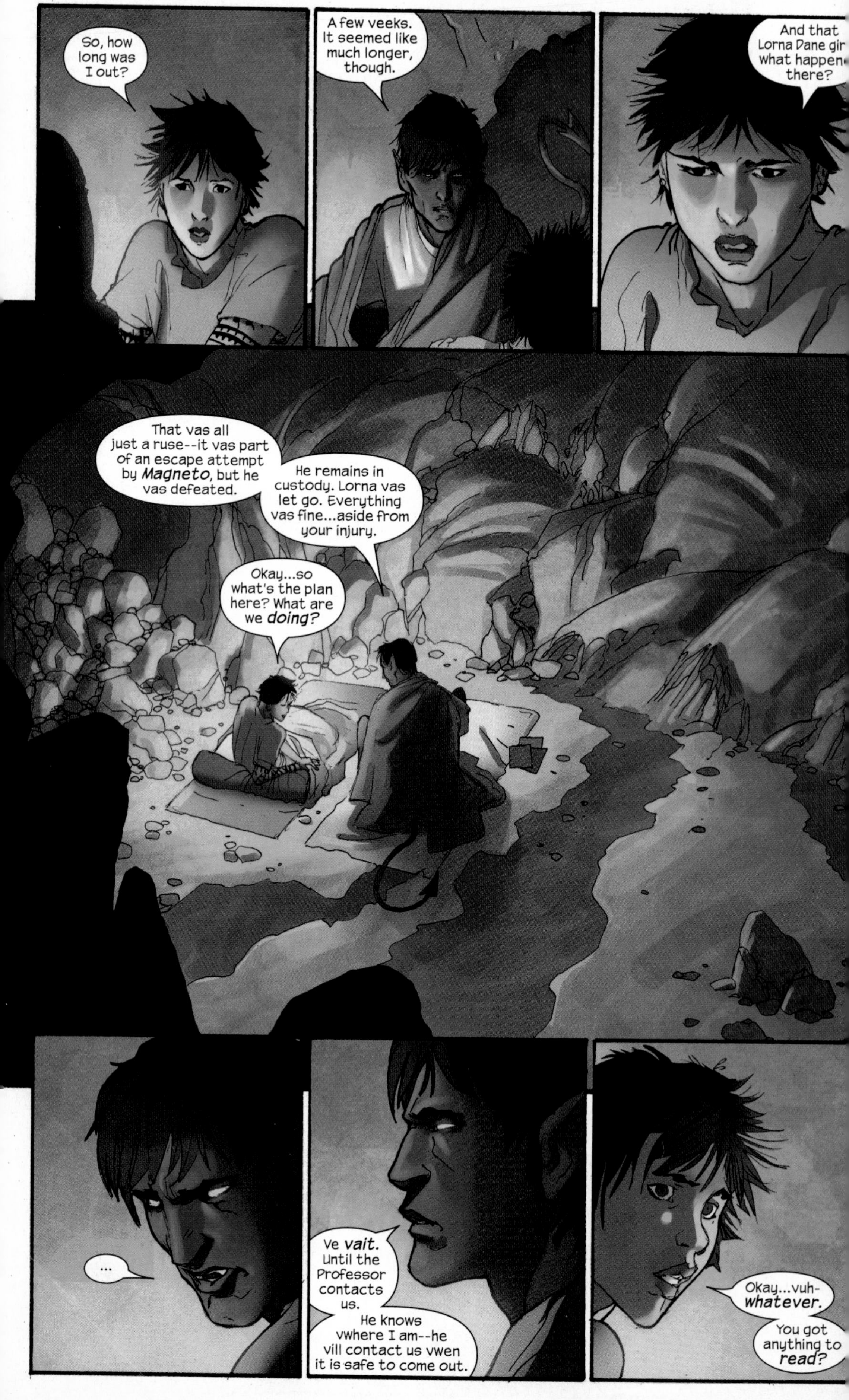
So, how long was I out?
A few veeks. It seemed like much longer, though.
And that Lorna Dane gir what happen there?
That vas all just a ruse--it vas part of an escape attempt by *Magneto*, but he vas defeated.
He remains in custody. Lorna vas let go. Everything vas fine...aside from your injury.
Okay...so what's the plan here? What are we *doing?*
...
Ve *vait.* Until the Professor contacts us.
He knows vwhere I am--he vill contact us vwen it is safe to come out.
Okay...vuh-*whatever.*
You got anything to *read?*

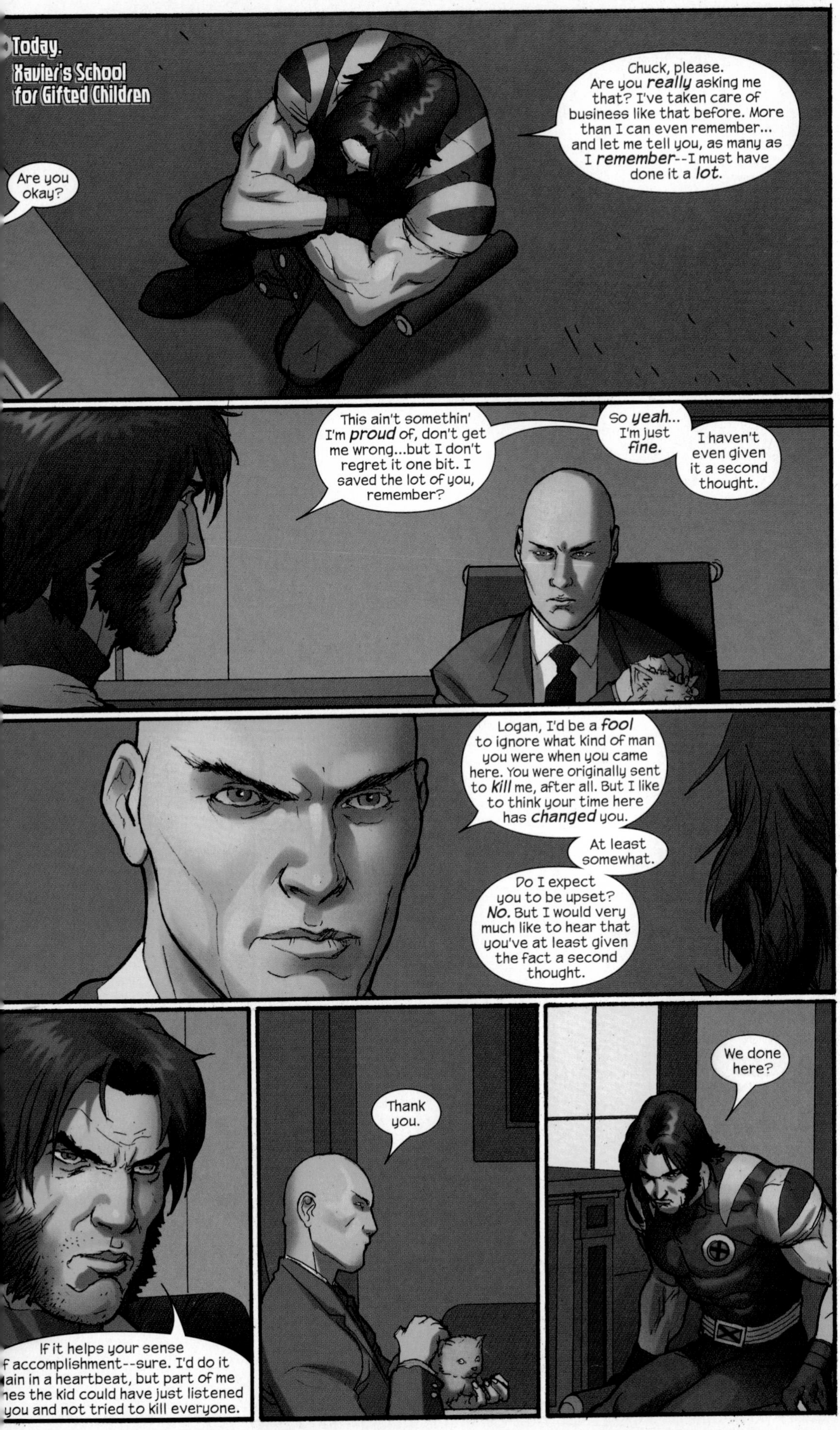
Today.
Xavier's School for Gifted Children
Are you okay?
Chuck, please. Are you really asking me that? I've taken care of business like that before. More than I can even remember... and let me tell you, as many as I remember--I must have done it a lot.
This ain't somethin' I'm proud of, don't get me wrong...but I don't regret it one bit. I saved the lot of you, remember?
So yeah... I'm just fine.
I haven't even given it a second thought.
Logan, I'd be a fool to ignore what kind of man you were when you came here. You were originally sent to kill me, after all. But I like to think your time here has changed you.
At least somewhat.
Do I expect you to be upset? No. But I would very much like to hear that you've at least given the fact a second thought.
If it helps your sense
f accomplishment--sure. I'd do it
ain in a heartbeat, but part of me
es the kid could have just listened
you and not tried to kill everyone.
Thank you.
We done here?

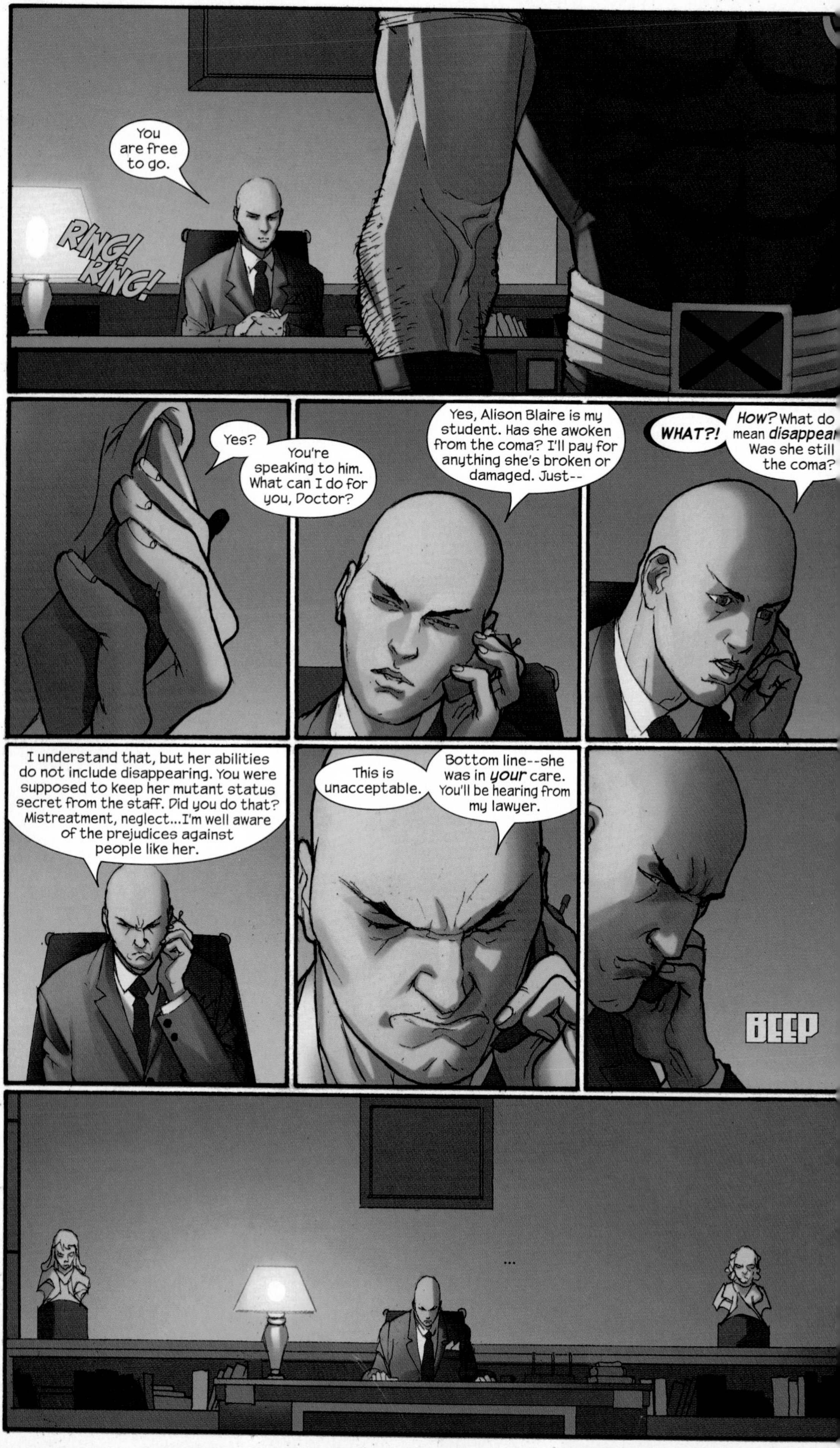
You are free to go.
RING! RING!
Yes?
You're speaking to him. What can I do for you, Doctor?
Yes, Alison Blaire is my student. Has she awoken from the coma? I'll pay for anything she's broken or damaged. Just--
WHAT?!
HOW? What do mean disappea Was she still the coma?
I understand that, but her abilities do not include disappearing. You were supposed to keep her mutant status secret from the staff. Did you do that? Mistreatment, neglect...I'm well aware of the prejudices against people like her.
This is unacceptable.
Bottom line--she was in your care. You'll be hearing from my lawyer.
BEEP
...

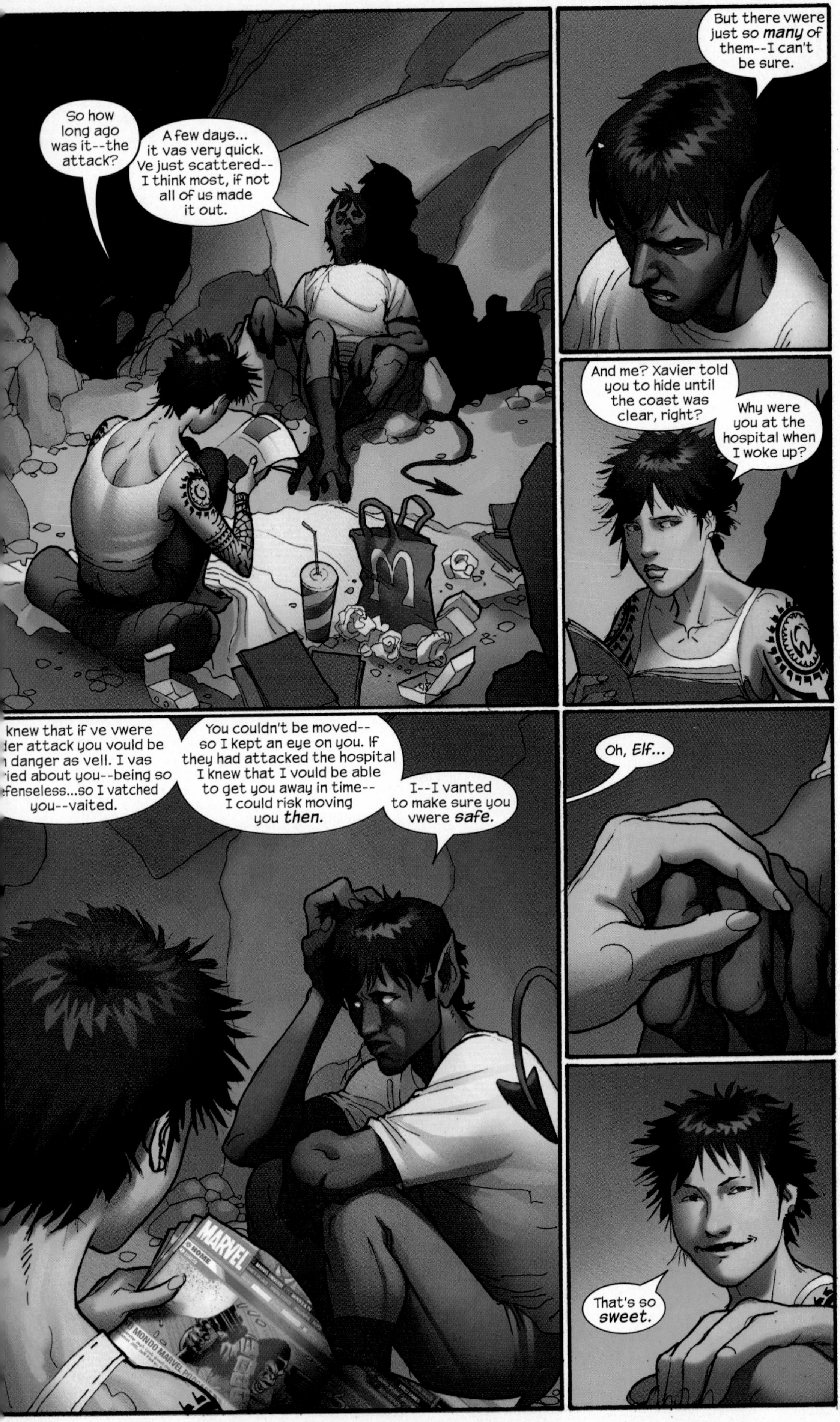
So how long ago was it--the attack?
A few days... it vas very quick. Ve just scattered-- I think most, if not all of us made it out.
But there vwere just so *many* of them--I can't be sure.
And me? Xavier told you to hide until the coast was clear, right?
Why were you at the hospital when I woke up?
knew that if ve vwere der attack you vould be danger as vell. I vas ied about you--being so efenseless...so I vatched you--vaited.
You couldn't be moved-- so I kept an eye on you. If they had attacked the hospital I knew that I vould be able to get you away in time-- I could risk moving you *then.*
I--I vanted to make sure you vwere *safe.*
Oh, *Elf*...
That's so *sweet.*
MARVEL

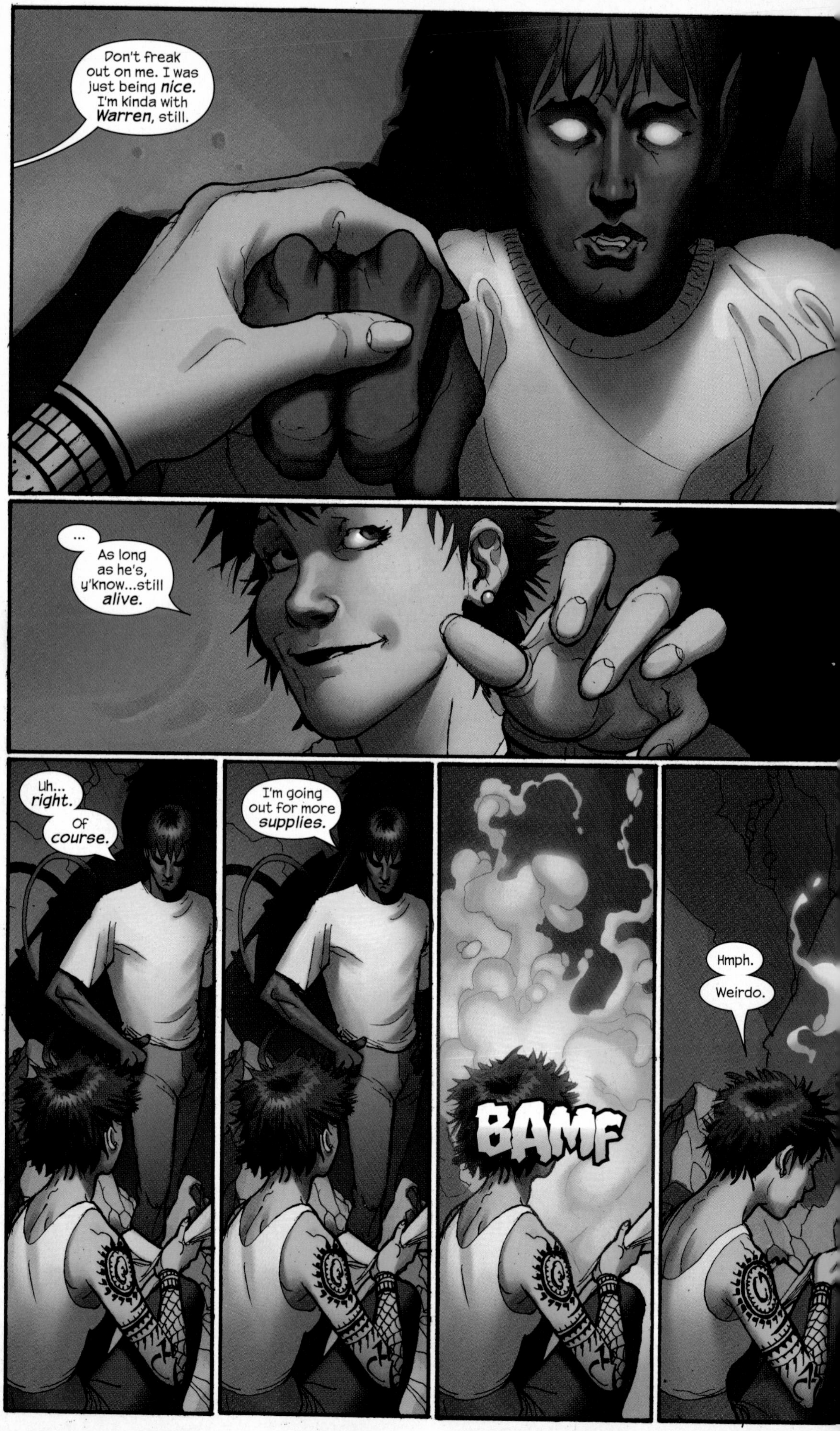
Don't freak out on me. I was just being *nice.* I'm kinda with *Warren*, still.
... As long as he's, y'know...still *alive.*
Uh... *right.*
Of *course.*
I'm going out for more *supplies.*
BAMF
Hmph.
Weirdo.

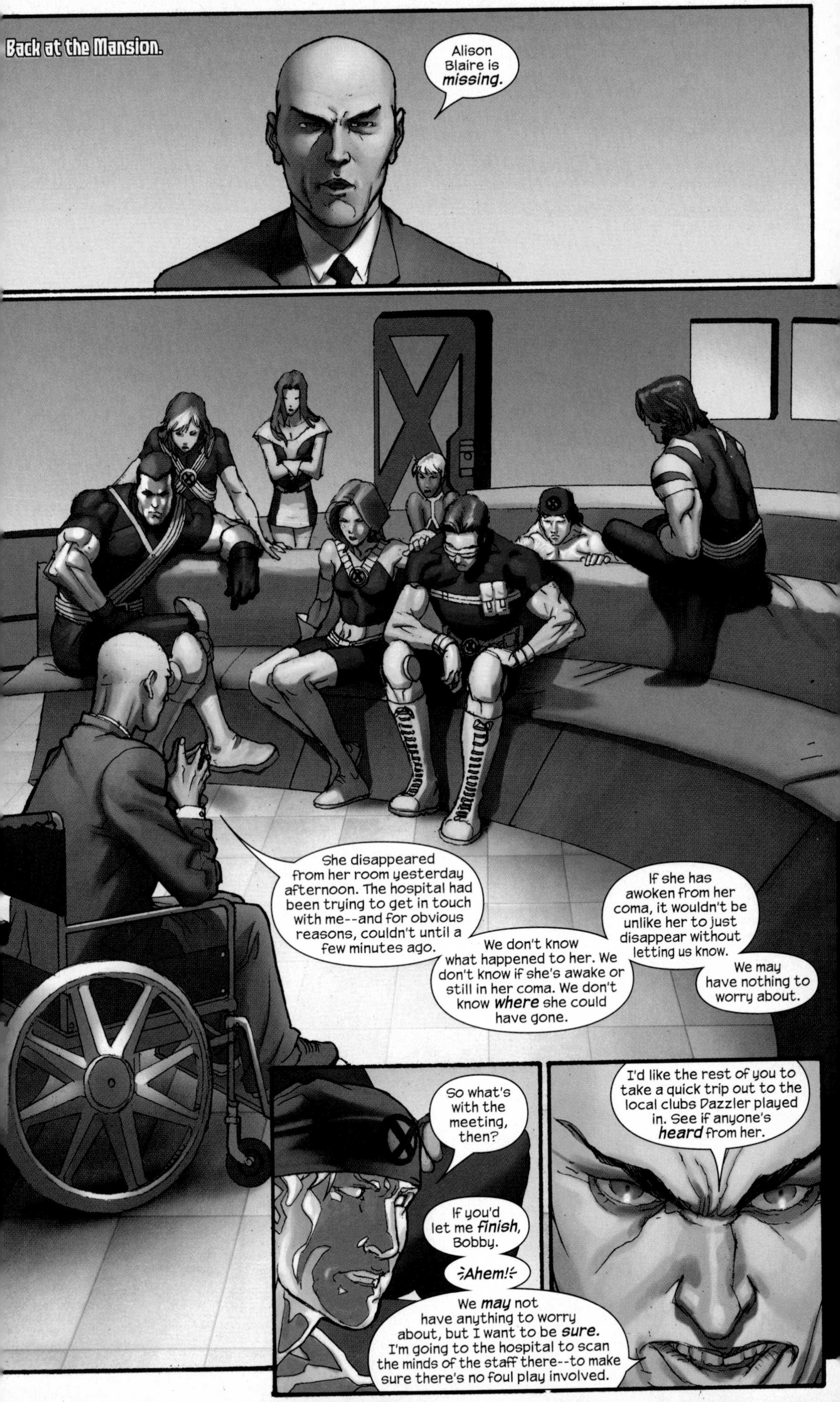

Back at the Mansion.
Alison Blaire is *missing.*
She disappeared from her room yesterday afternoon. The hospital had been trying to get in touch with me--and for obvious reasons, couldn't until a few minutes ago.
We don't know what happened to her. We don't know if she's awake or still in her coma. We don't know *where* she could have gone.
If she has awoken from her coma, it wouldn't be unlike her to just disappear without letting us know.
We may have nothing to worry about.
So what's with the meeting, then?
If you'd let me *finish*, Bobby.
Ahem!
We *may* not have anything to worry about, but I want to be *sure.* I'm going to the hospital to scan the minds of the staff there--to make sure there's no foul play involved.
I'd like the rest of you to take a quick trip out to the local clubs Dazzler played in. See if anyone's *heard* from her.

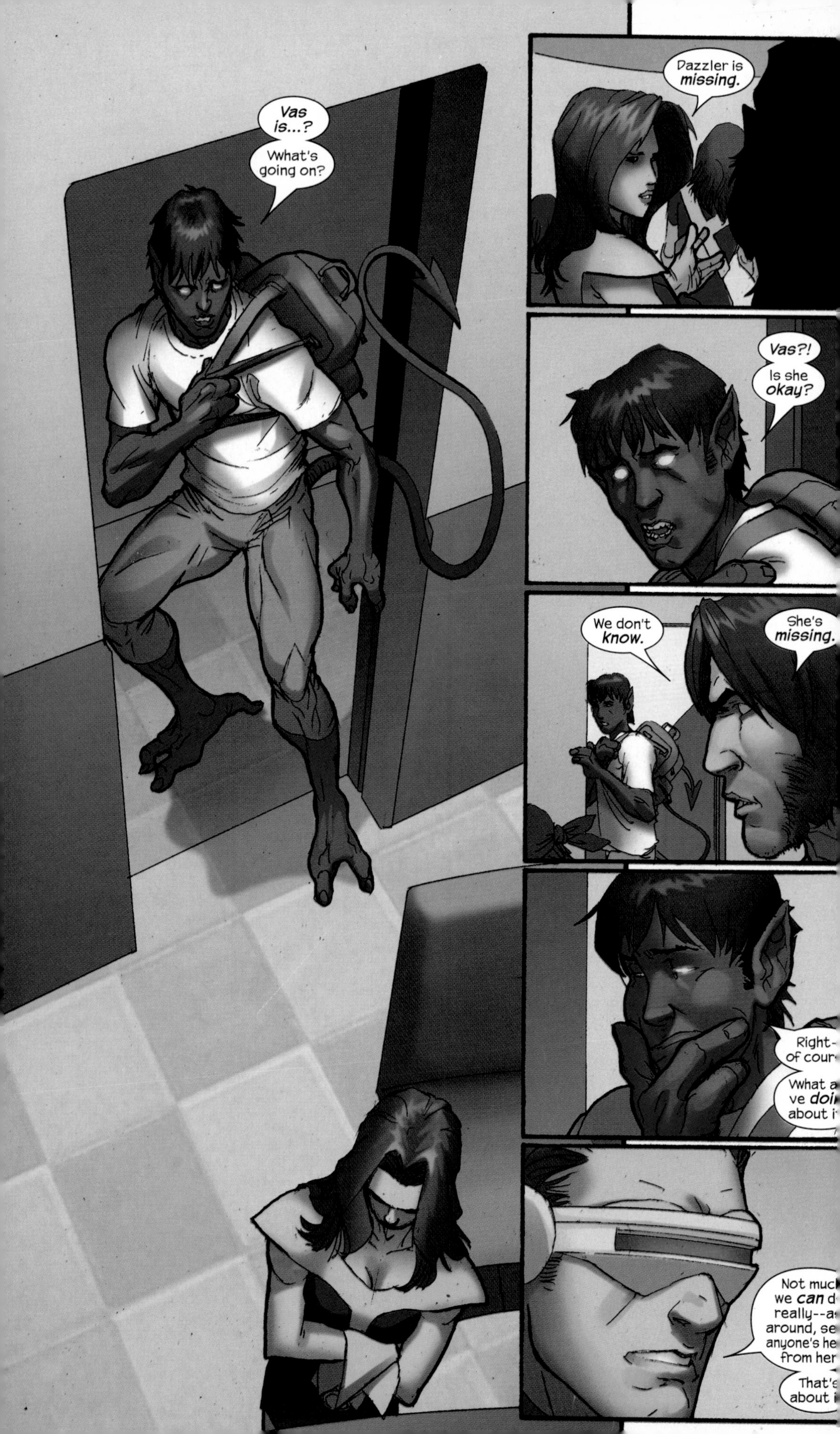

Vas is...?
What's going on?
Dazzler is missing.
Vas?!
Is she okay?
We don't know.
She's missing.
Right-
of cour
What a
ve doi
about i
Not muc
we can d
really--a
around, se
anyone's he
from her
That's
about i

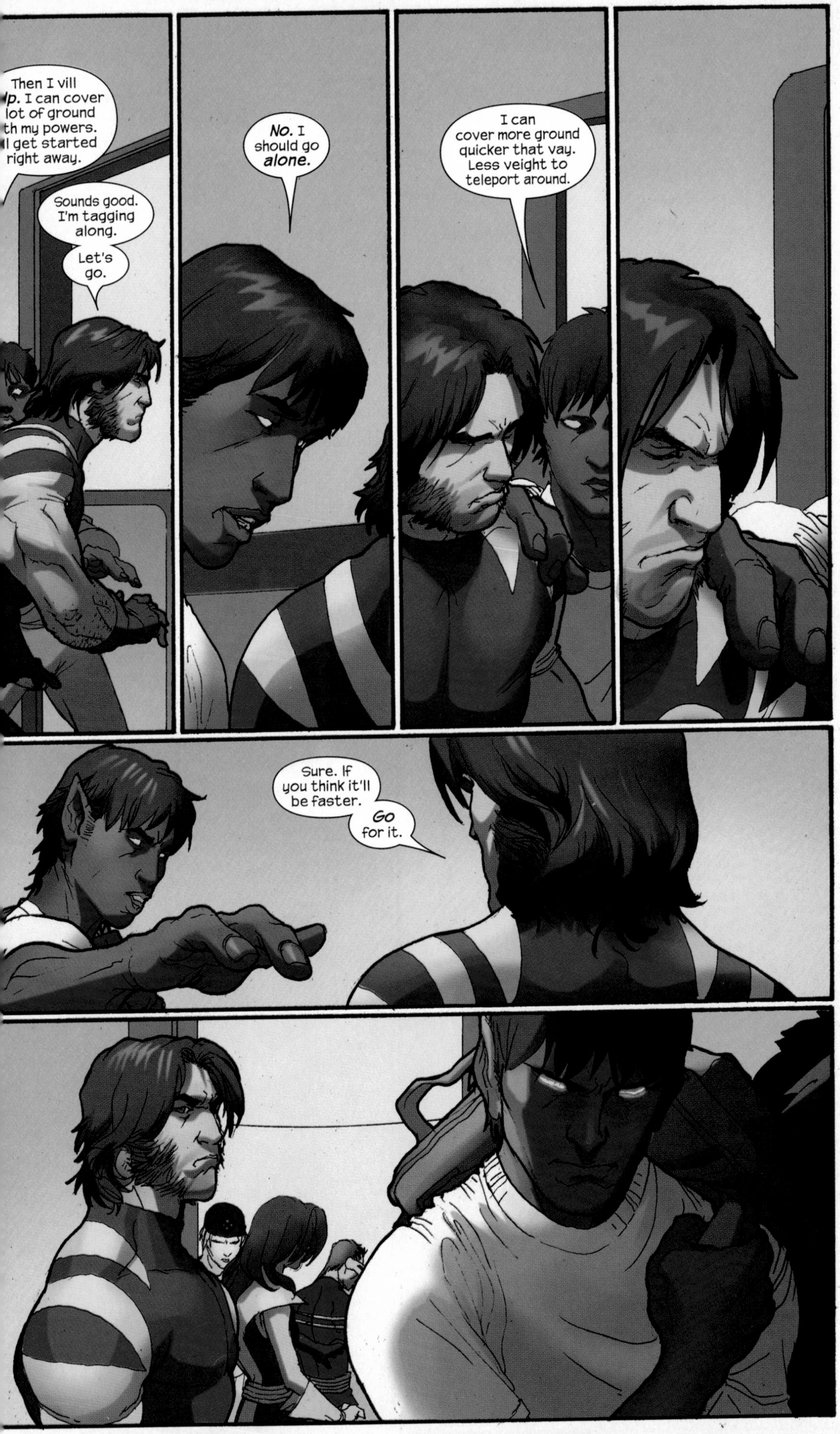

Then I vill ...p. I can cover ...lot of ground ...th my powers. ...l get started right away.
Sounds good. I'm tagging along.
Let's go.
No. I should go alone.
I can cover more ground quicker that vay. Less veight to teleport around.
Sure. If you think it'll be faster.
Go for it.

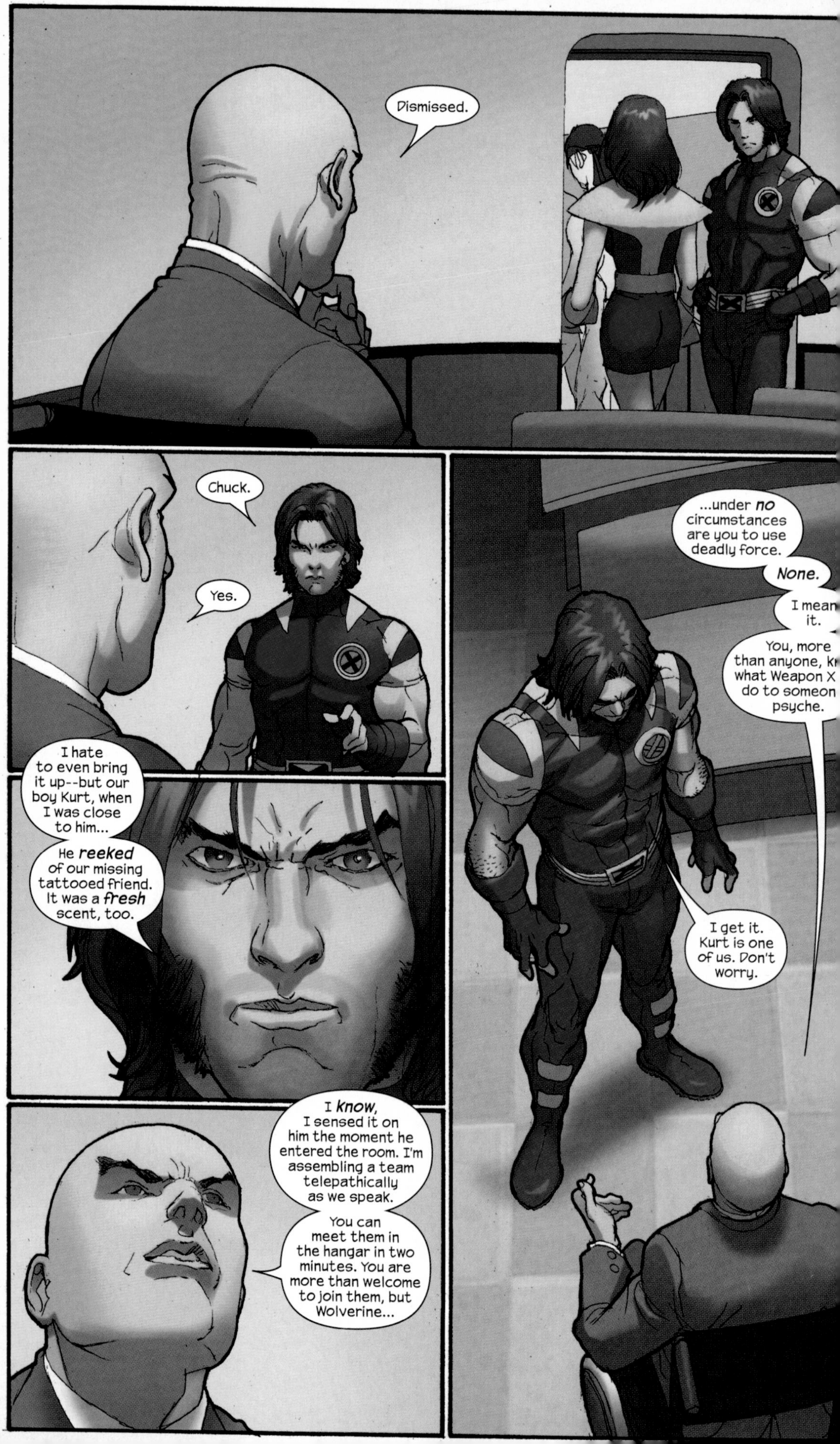
Dismissed.
Chuck.
Yes.
I hate to even bring it up--but our boy Kurt, when I was close to him...
He *reeked* of our missing tattooed friend. It was a *fresh* scent, too.
I *know*, I sensed it on him the moment he entered the room. I'm assembling a team telepathically as we speak.
You can meet them in the hangar in two minutes. You are more than welcome to join them, but Wolverine...
...under *no* circumstances are you to use deadly force.
None.
I mean it.
You, more than anyone, k
what Weapon X
do to someon
psyche.
I get it. Kurt is one of us. Don't worry.

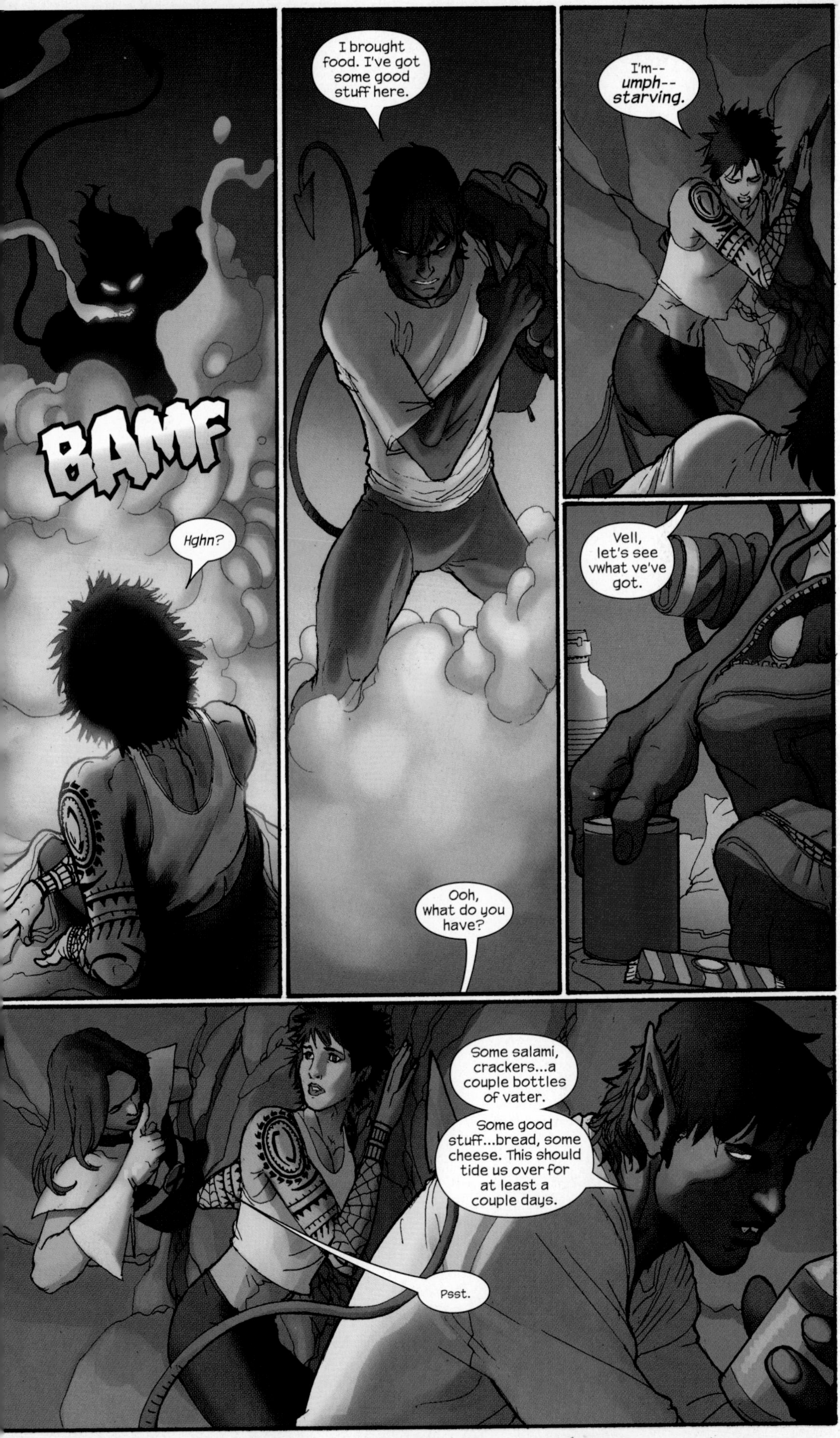
BAMF
Hghn?
I brought food. I've got some good stuff here.
Ooh, what do you have?
I'm-- *umph*-- *starving.*
Vell, let's see vwhat ve've got.
Some salami, crackers...a couple bottles of vater.
Some good stuff...bread, some cheese. This should tide us over for at least a couple days.
Psst.

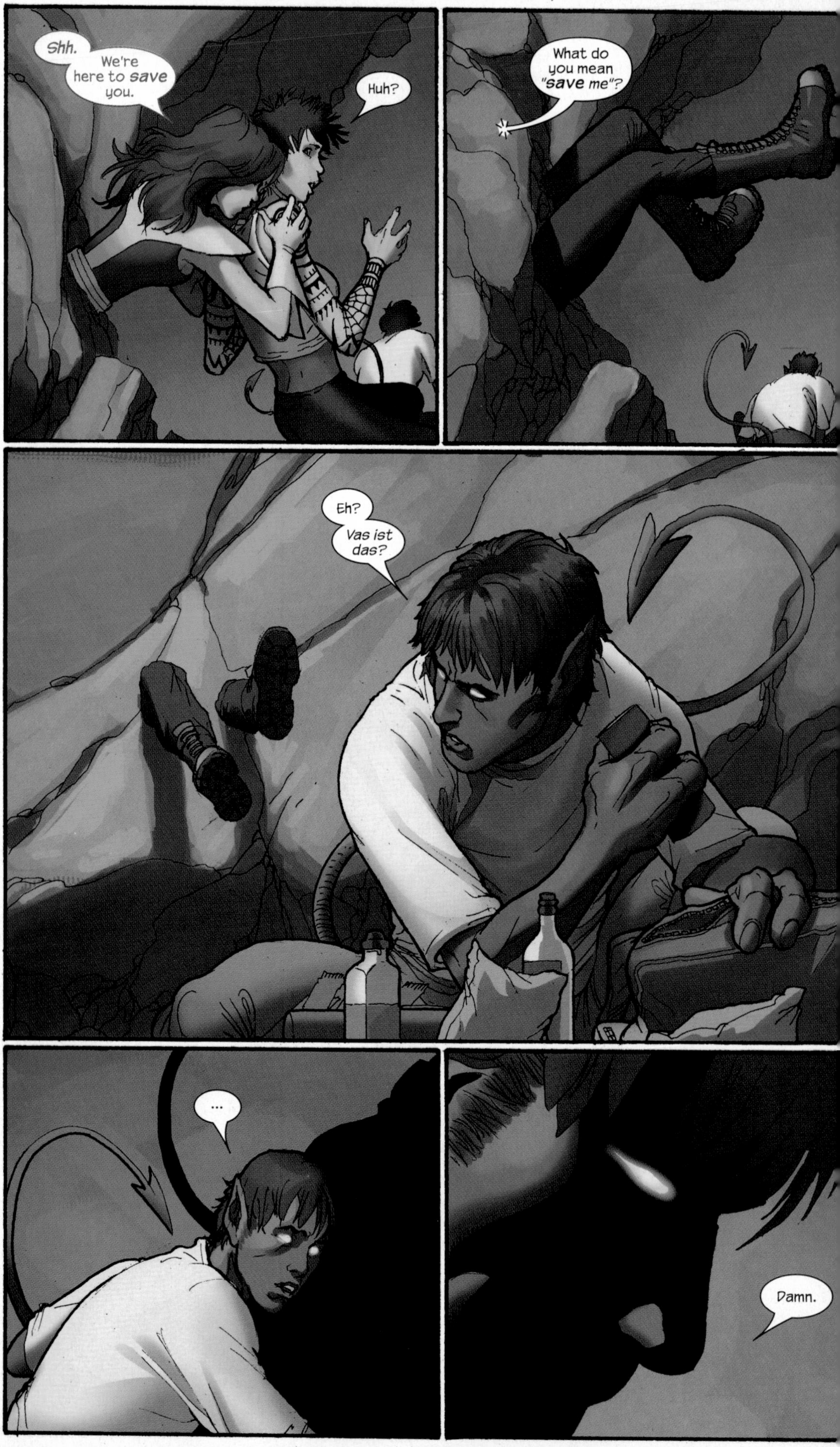

Shh.
We're here to *save* you.
Huh?
What do you mean "*save* me"?
Eh?
Vas ist das?
...
Damn.

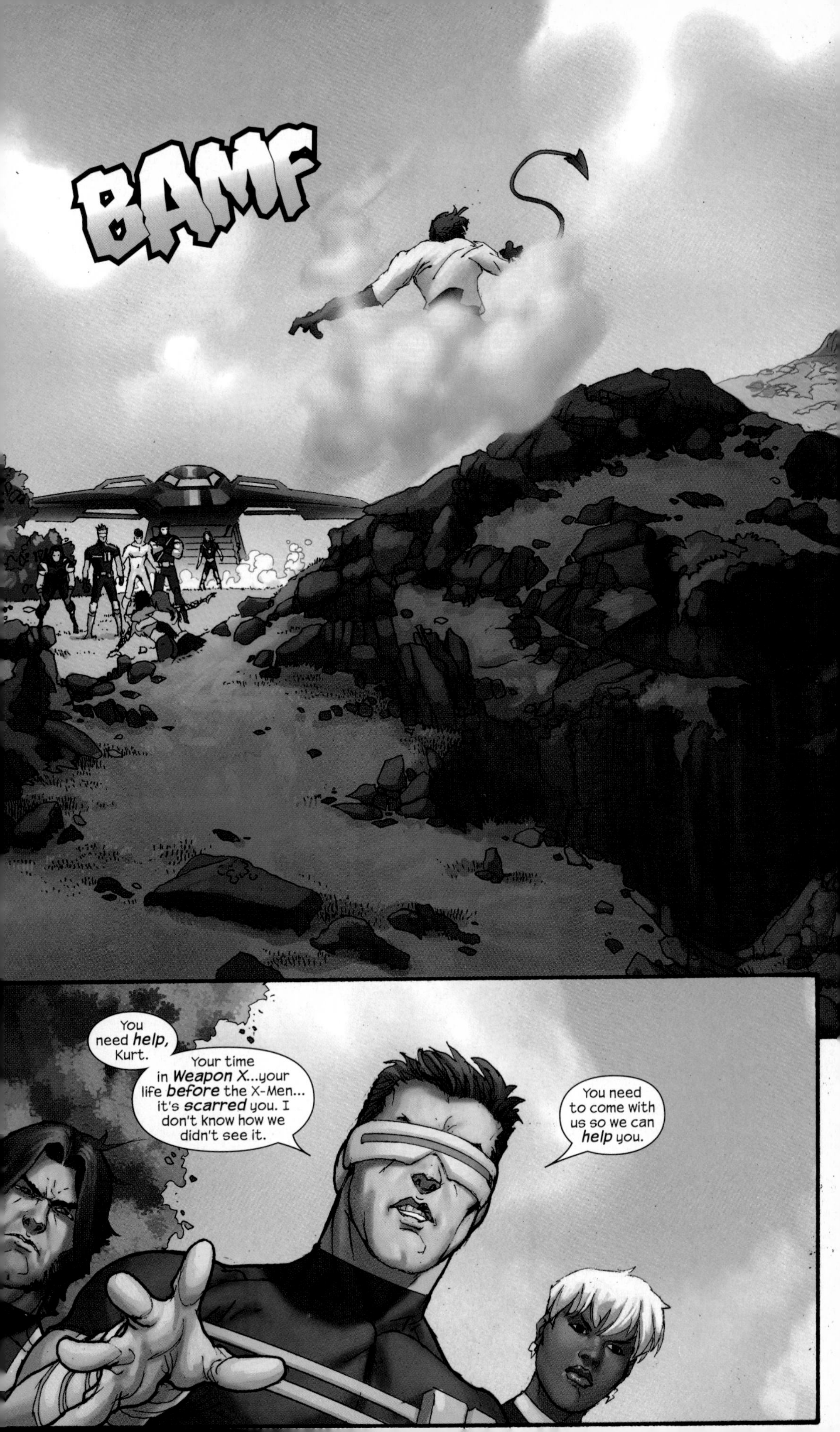
BAMF
You need *help,* Kurt.
Your time in *Weapon X*...your life *before* the X-Men... it's *scarred* you. I don't know how we didn't see it.
You need to come with us so we can *help* you.

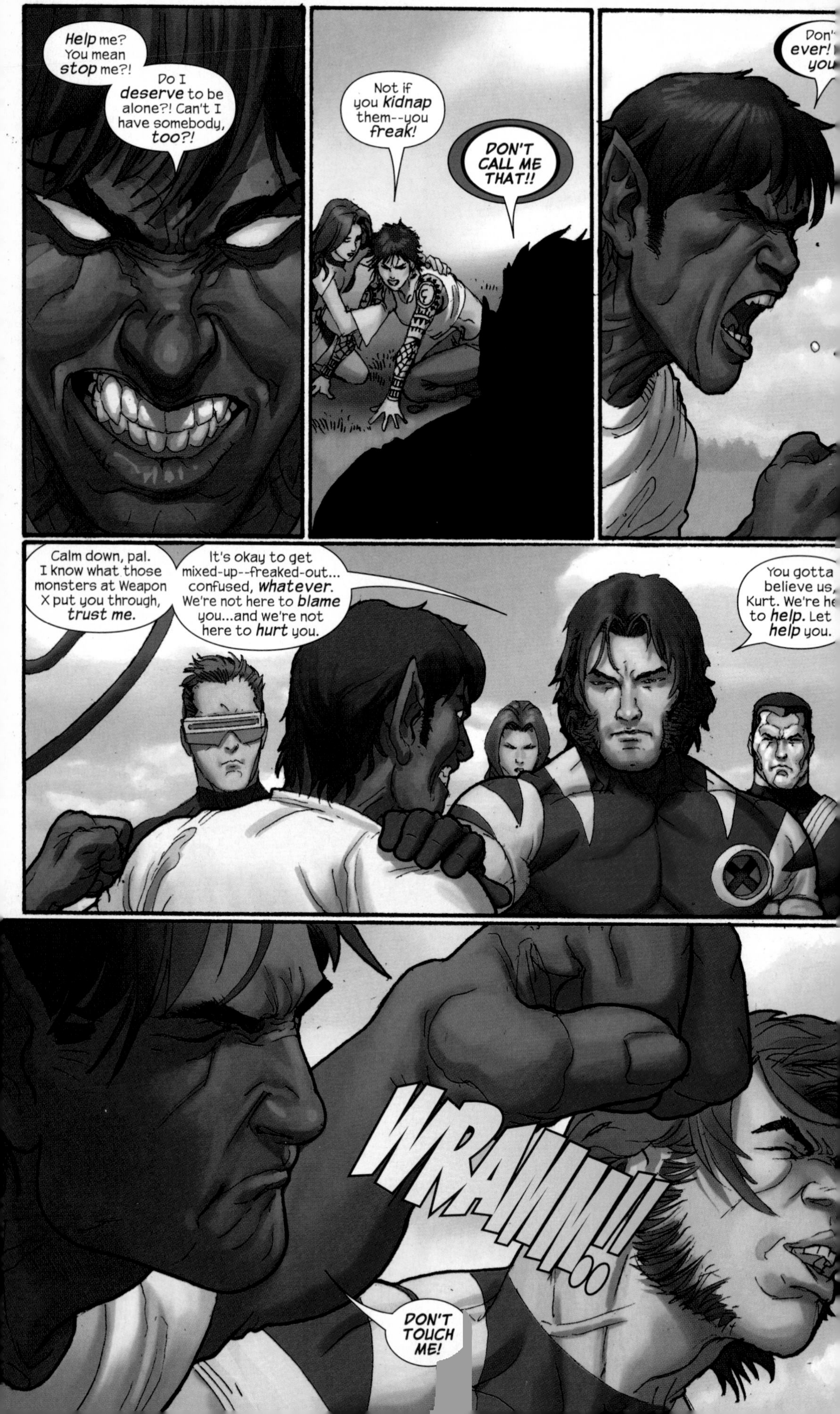
Help me? You mean stop me?!
Do I deserve to be alone?! Can't I have somebody, too?!
Not if you kidnap them--you freak!
DON'T CALL ME THAT!!
Don' ever! you
Calm down, pal. I know what those monsters at Weapon X put you through, trust me.
It's okay to get mixed-up--freaked-out... confused, whatever. We're not here to blame you...and we're not here to hurt you.
You gotta believe us, Kurt. We're he to help. Let help you.
WRAMM!!
DON'T TOUCH ME!

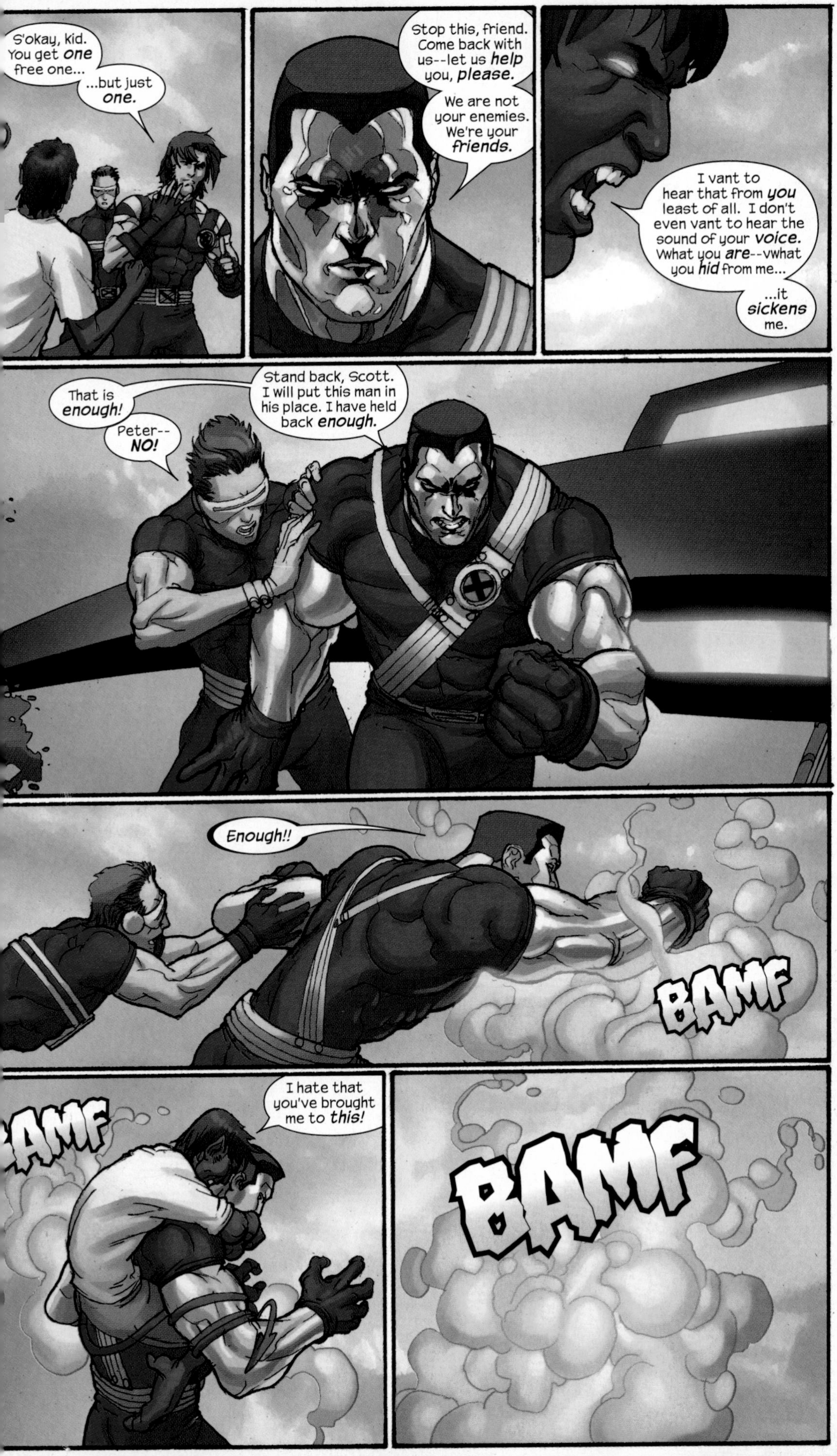
S'okay, kid. You get *one* free one...
...but just *one.*
Stop this, friend. Come back with us--let us *help* you, *please.*
We are not your enemies. We're your *friends.*
I vant to hear that from *you* least of all. I don't even vant to hear the sound of your *voice.* Vwhat you *are*--vwhat you *hid* from me...
...it *sickens* me.
That is *enough!*
Peter-- *NO!*
Stand back, Scott. I will put this man in his place. I have held back *enough.*
Enough!!
BAMF
AMF
I hate that you've brought me to *this!*
BAMF

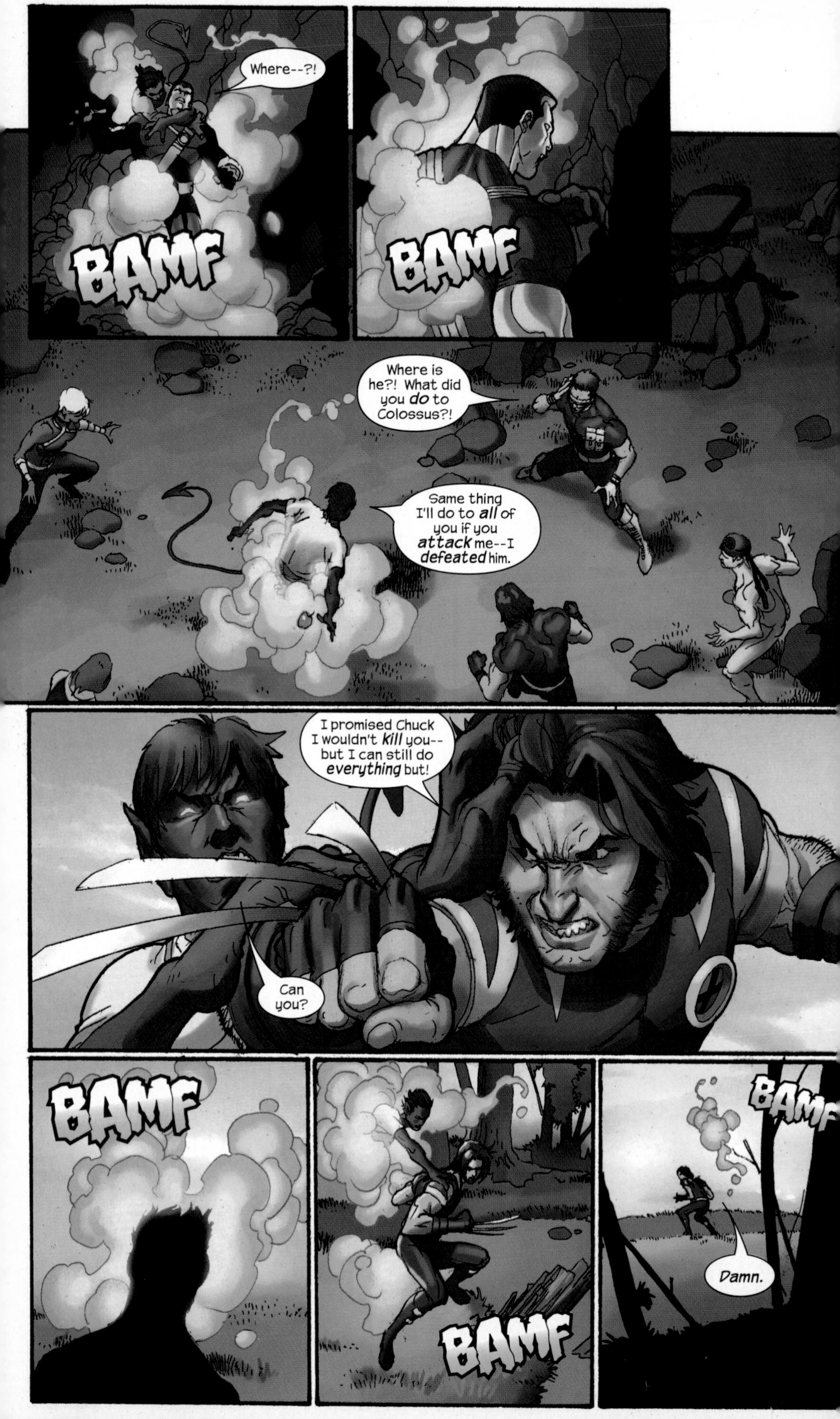
Where--?!
BAMF
BAMF
Where is he?! What did you do to Colossus?!
Same thing I'll do to all of you if you attack me--I defeated him.
I promised Chuck I wouldn't kill you--but I can still do everything but!
Can you?
BAMF
BAMF
BAMF
Damn.

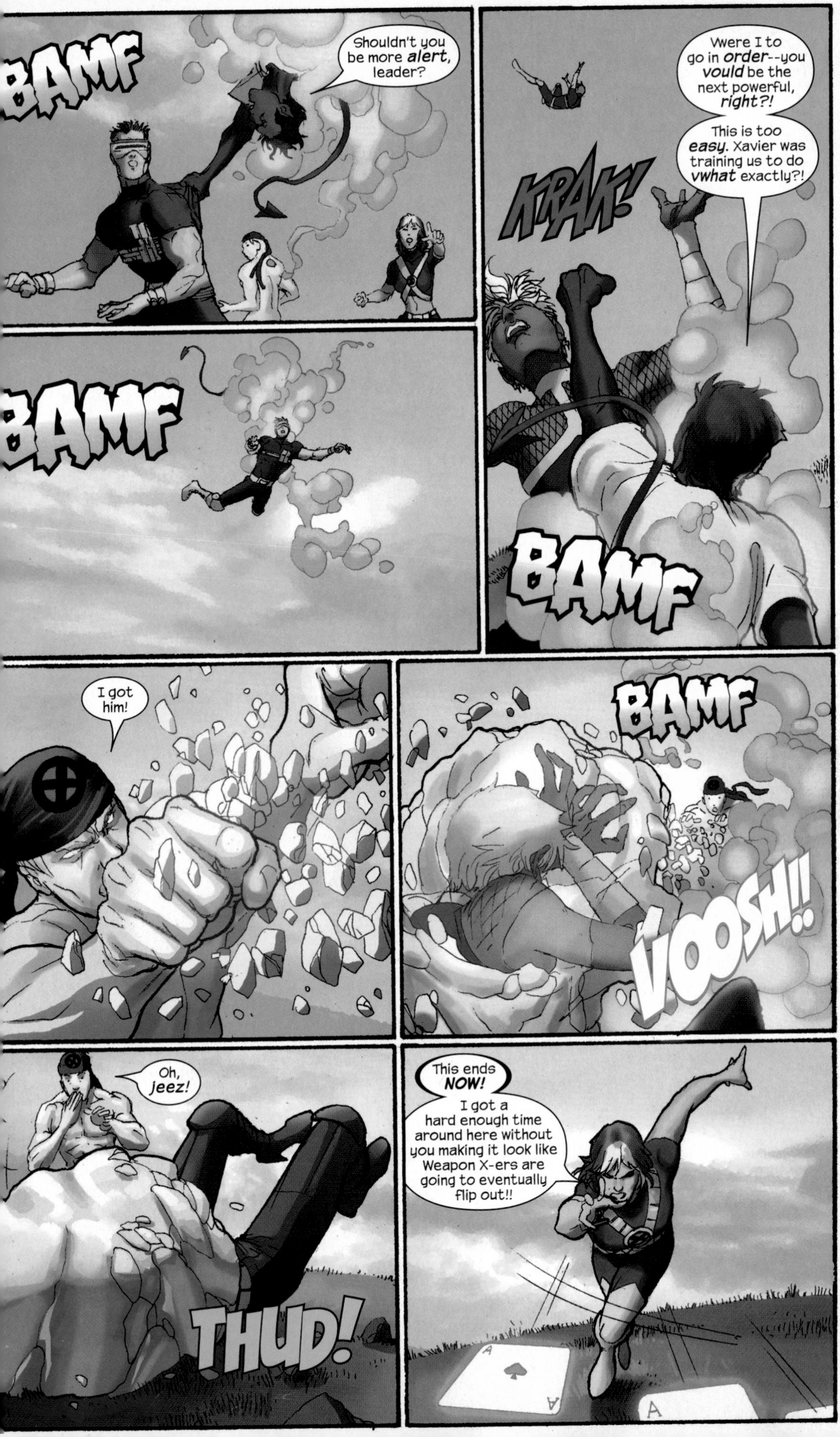
BAMF
Shouldn't you be more alert, leader?
BAMF
Vvere I to go in order--you vould be the next powerful, right?!
This is too easy. Xavier was training us to do vwhat exactly?!
KRAK!
BAMF
I got him!
BAMF
VOOSH!!
Oh, jeez!
THUD!
This ends NOW!
I got a hard enough time around here without you making it look like Weapon X-ers are going to eventually flip out!!

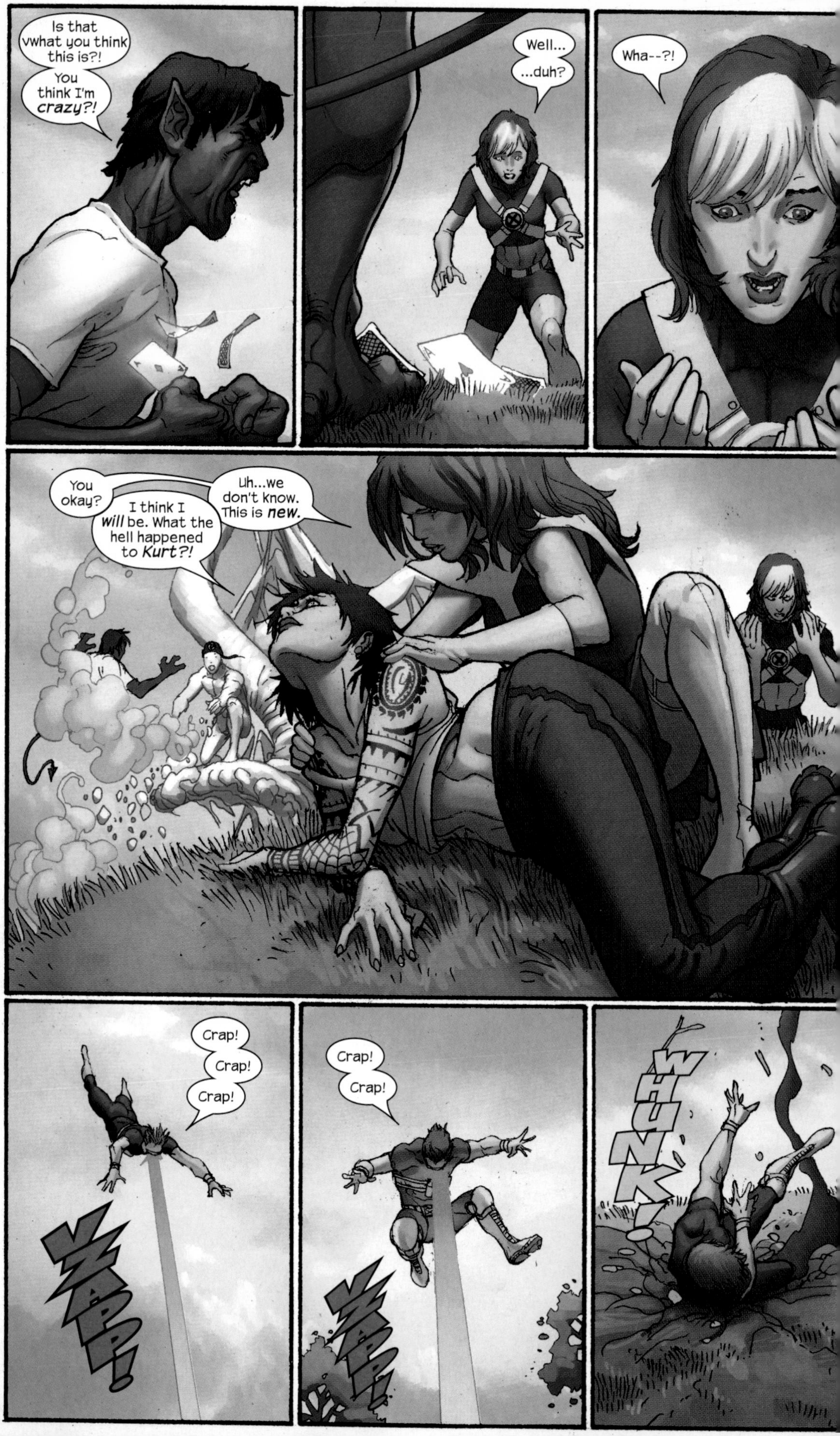
Is that vwhat you think this is?!
You think I'm *crazy?!*
Well...
...duh?
Wha--?!
You okay?
Uh...we don't know. This is *new.*
I think I *will* be. What the hell happened to *Kurt?!*
Crap!
Crap!
Crap!
VZAPP!
Crap!
Crap!
VZAPP!
WHUNK!

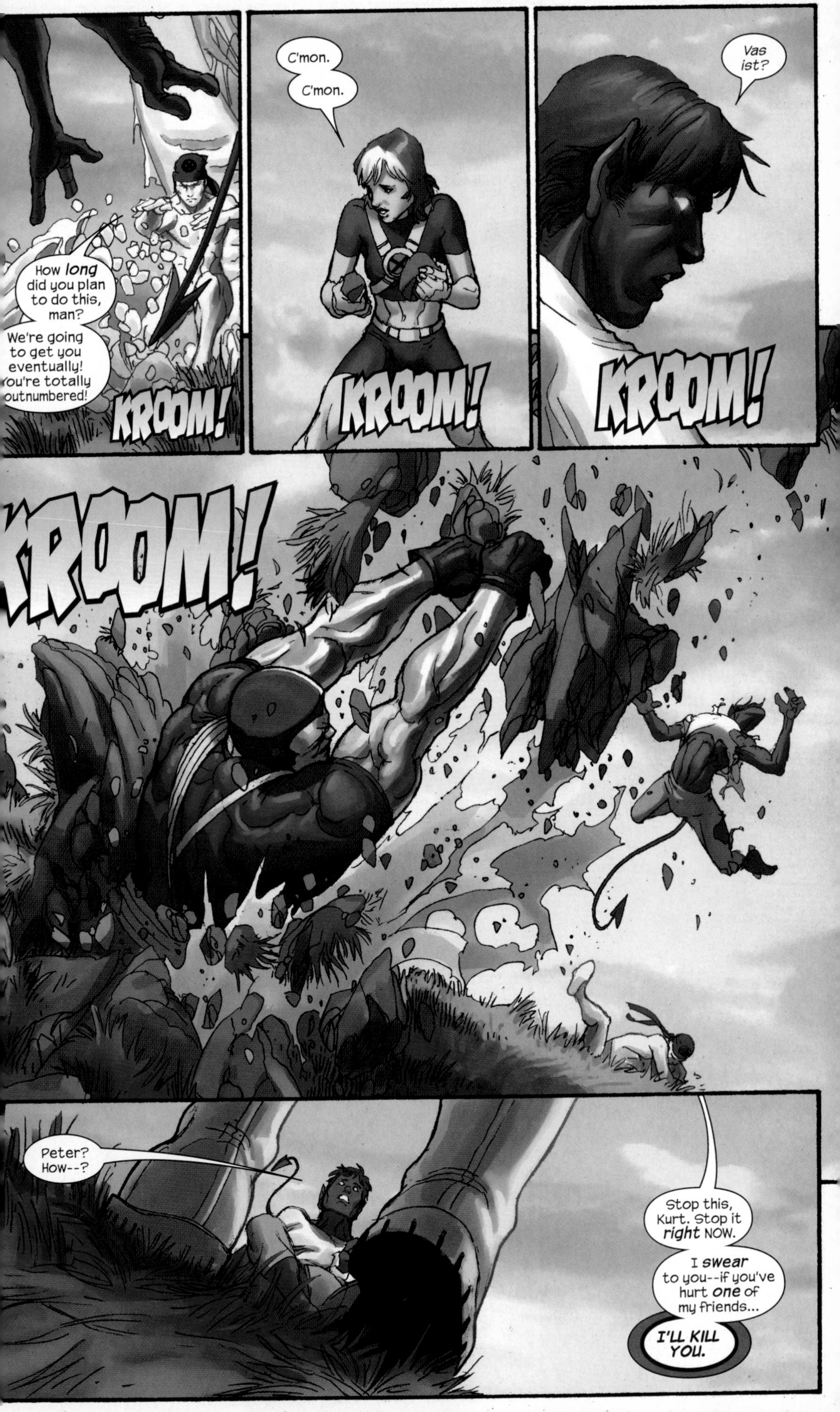
How long did you plan to do this, man?
We're going to get you eventually! You're totally outnumbered!
KROOM!
C'mon.
C'mon.
KROOM!
Vas ist?
KROOM!
KROOM!
Peter? How--?
Stop this, Kurt. Stop it right NOW.
I swear to you--if you've hurt one of my friends...
I'LL KILL YOU.

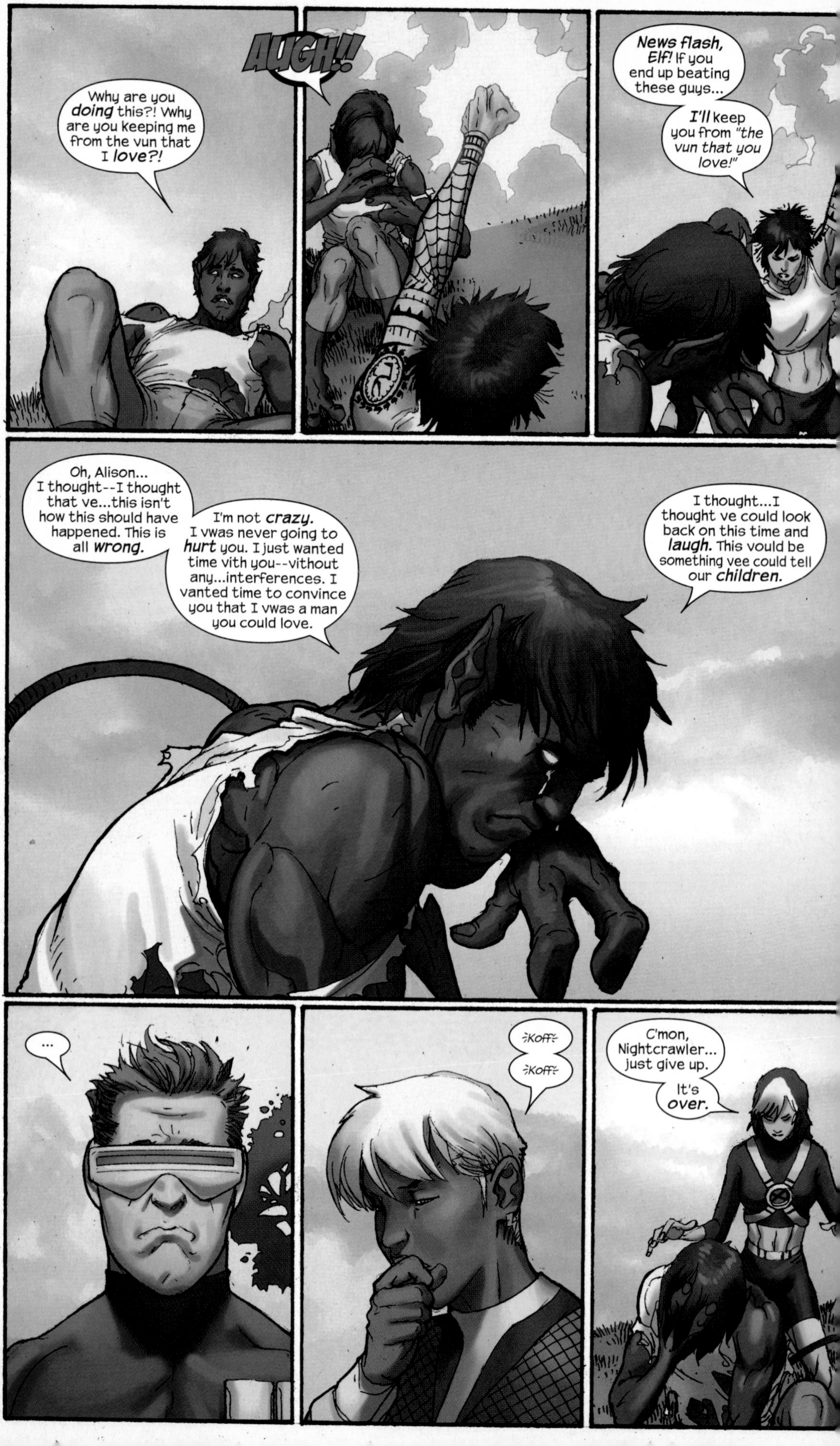

Vwhy are you doing this?! Vwhy are you keeping me from the vun that I love?!
AUGH!!
News flash, Elf! If you end up beating these guys...
I'll keep you from "the vun that you love!"
Oh, Alison... I thought--I thought that ve...this isn't how this should have happened. This is all wrong.
I'm not crazy. I vwas never going to hurt you. I just wanted time vith you--vithout any...interferences. I vanted time to convince you that I vwas a man you could love.
I thought...I thought ve could look back on this time and laugh. This vould be something vee could tell our children.
...
Koff
Koff
C'mon, Nightcrawler... just give up.
It's over.

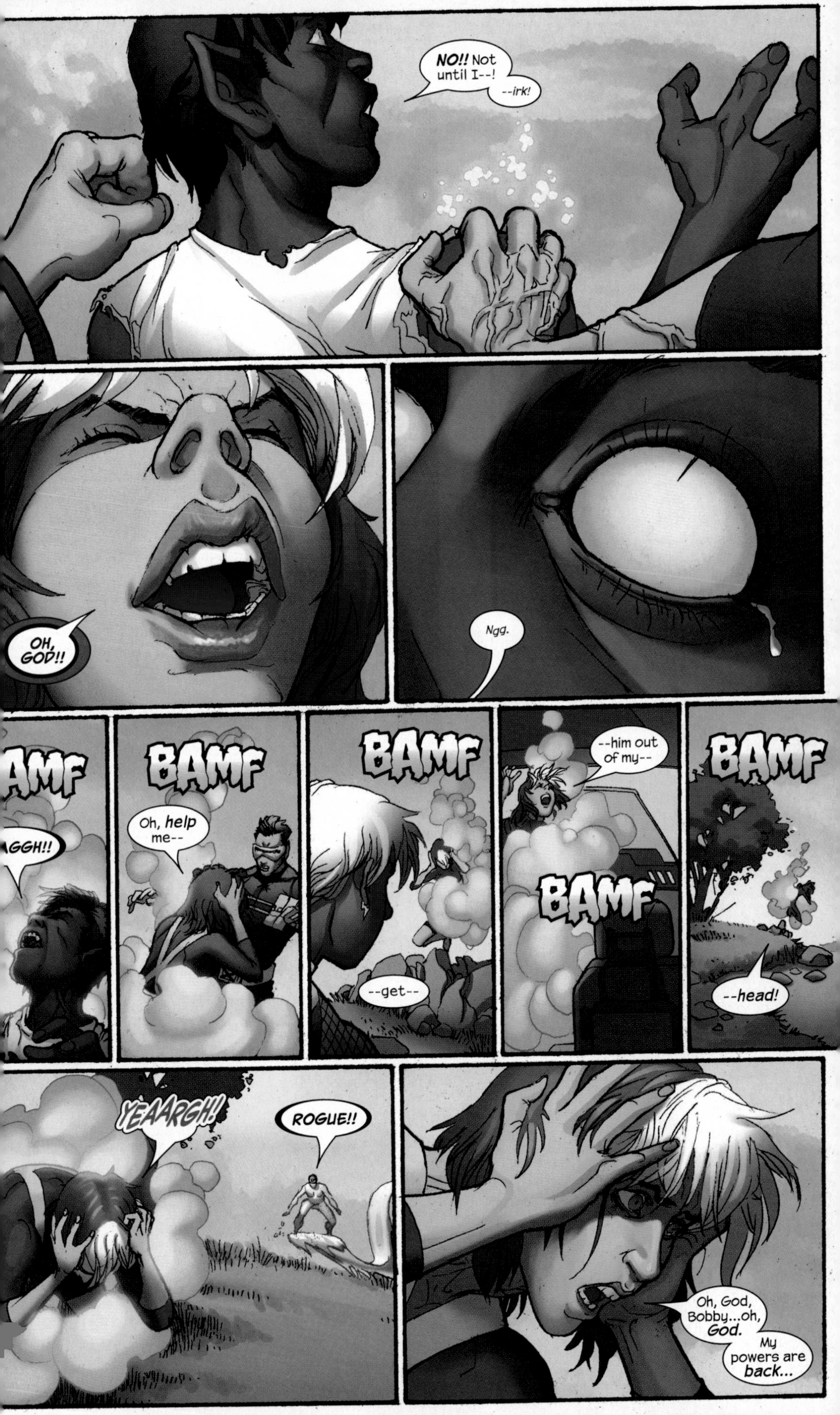
NO!! Not until I--!
--irk!
OH, GOD!!
Ngg.
AMF
AGGH!!
BAMF
Oh, help me--
BAMF
--get--
--him out of my--
BAMF
BAMF
--head!
YEAARGH!
ROGUE!!
Oh, God, Bobby...oh, God.
My powers are back...

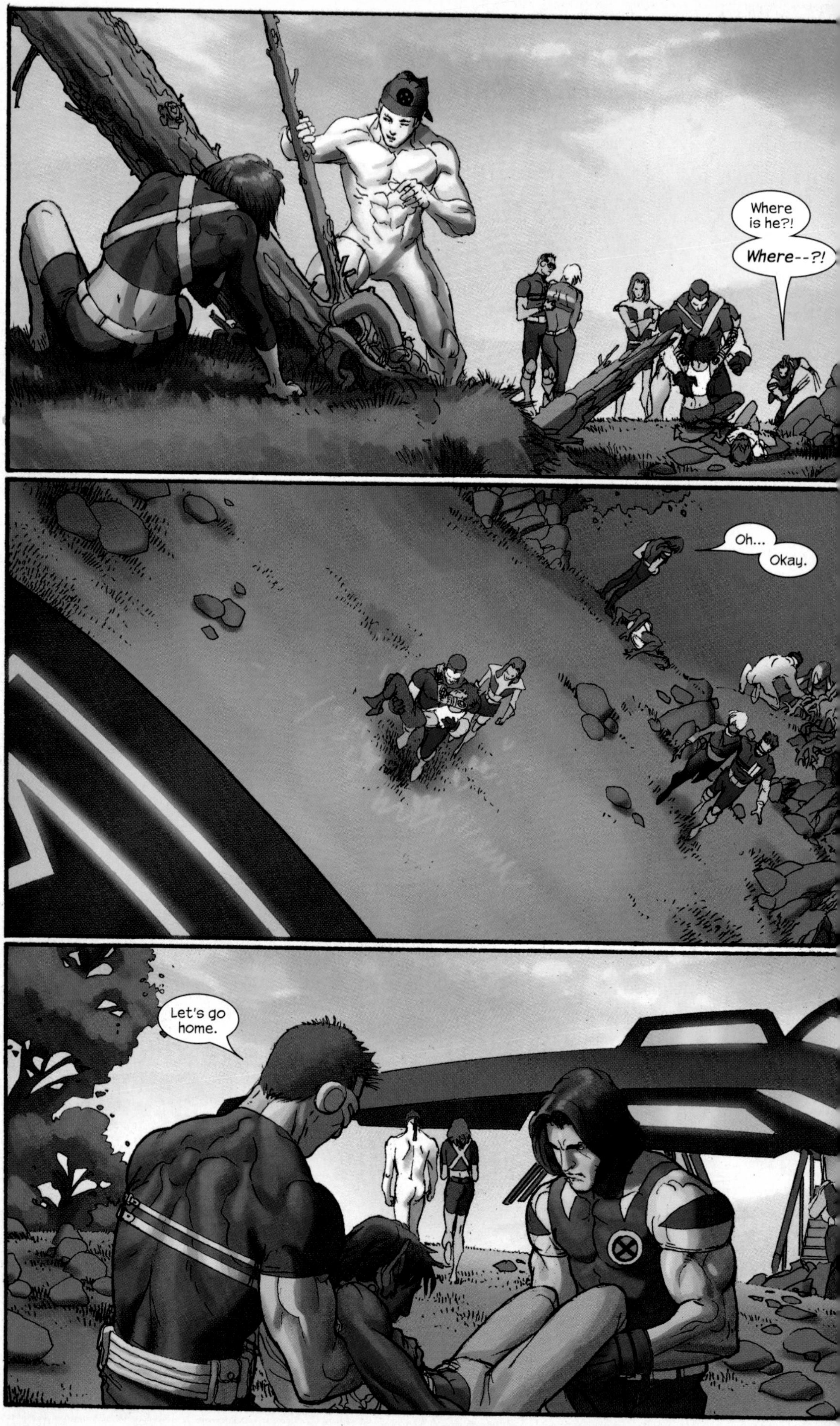
Where is he?!
Where--?!
Oh... Okay.
Let's go home.

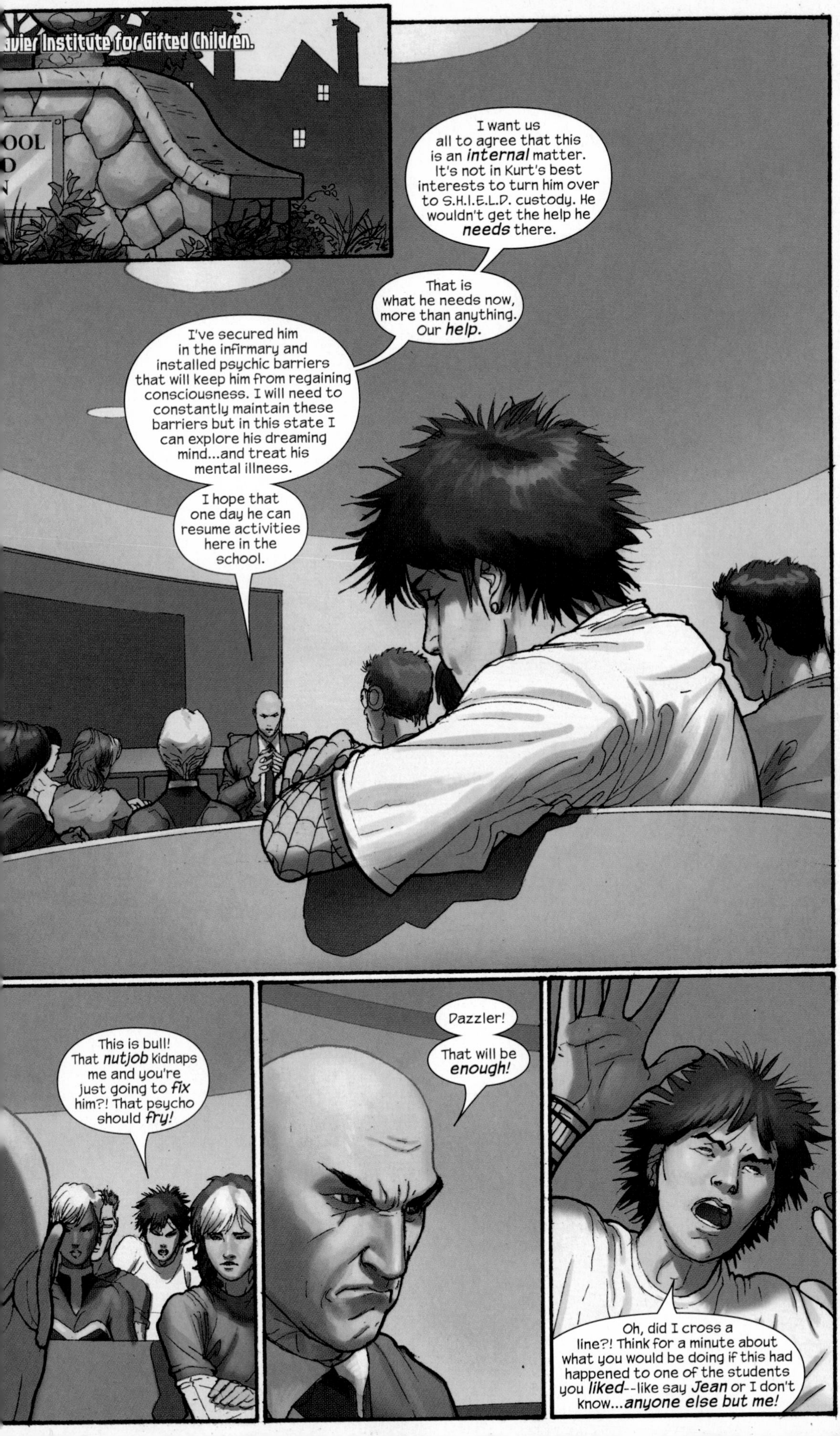
Xavier Institute for Gifted Children.
I want us all to agree that this is an *internal* matter. It's not in Kurt's best interests to turn him over to S.H.I.E.L.D. custody. He wouldn't get the help he *needs* there.
That is what he needs now, more than anything. Our *help.*
I've secured him in the infirmary and installed psychic barriers that will keep him from regaining consciousness. I will need to constantly maintain these barriers but in this state I can explore his dreaming mind...and treat his mental illness.
I hope that one day he can resume activities here in the school.
This is bull! That *nutjob* kidnaps me and you're just going to *fix* him?! That psycho should *fry!*
Dazzler!
That will be *enough!*
Oh, did I cross a line?! Think for a minute about what you would be doing if this had happened to one of the students you *liked*--like say *Jean* or I don't know...*anyone else but me!*

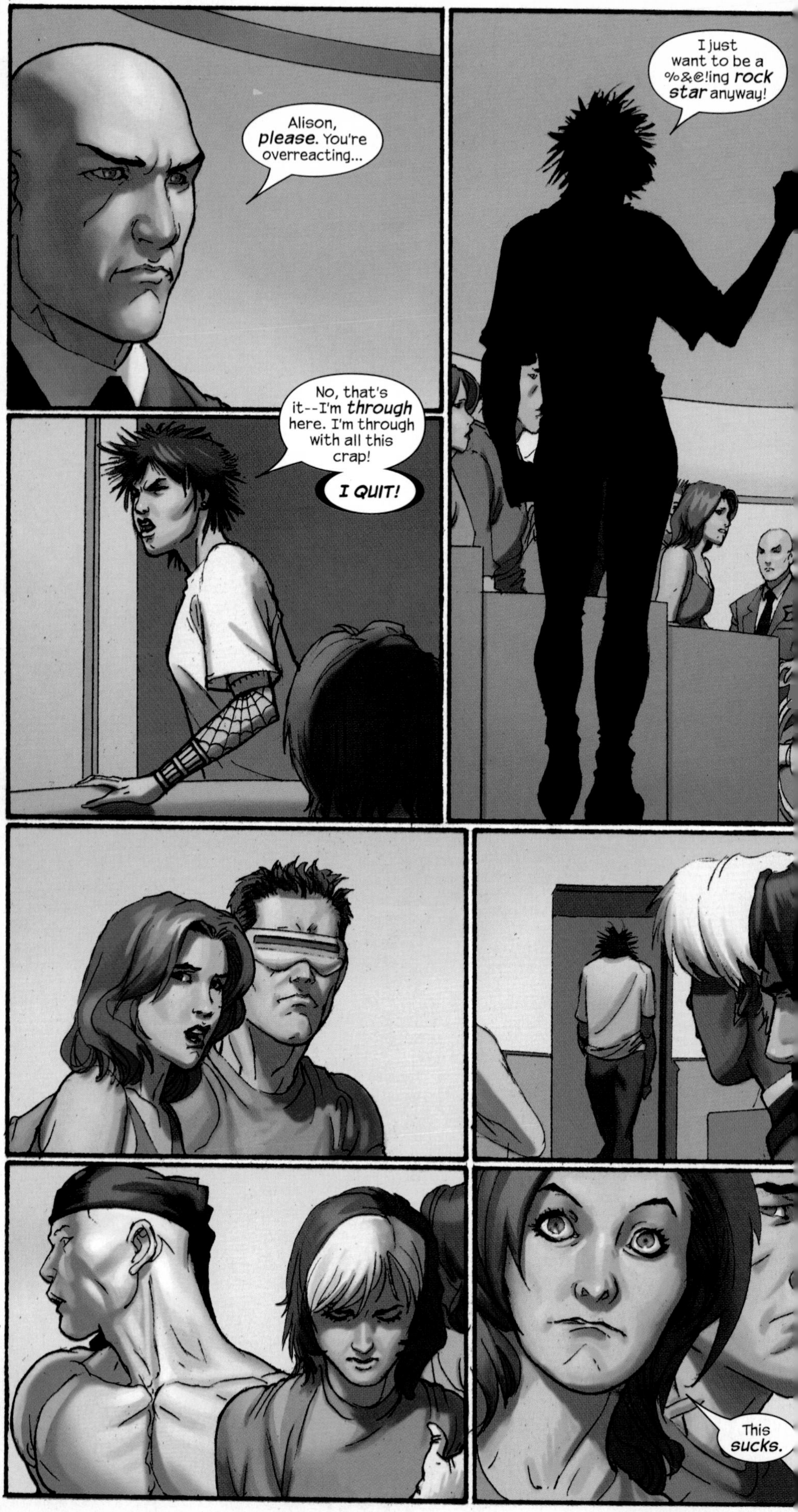
Alison, please. You're overreacting...
I just want to be a %&@!ing rock star anyway!
No, that's it--I'm through here. I'm through with all this crap!
I QUIT!
This sucks.

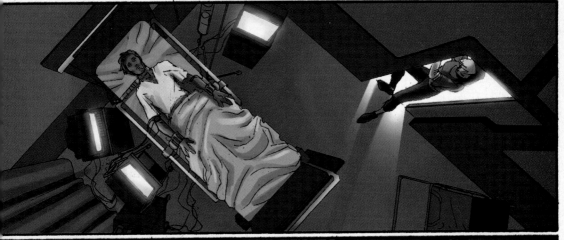

The Professor doesn't want us in here...and I don't even know if you can hear me anyway...so I'll make this *quick.*

I know what it's like to grow up being a mutant. To have people treat you a certain way just because you're different. I know about the ridicule, the isolation.

I know that it must be especially hard when you *look* different too. People who judged you just by the way you look...they probably thought you were a *monster.*

I just wanted to say that after being in your head...seeing what you *really* are...on the inside...

...I *know* you're a monster.

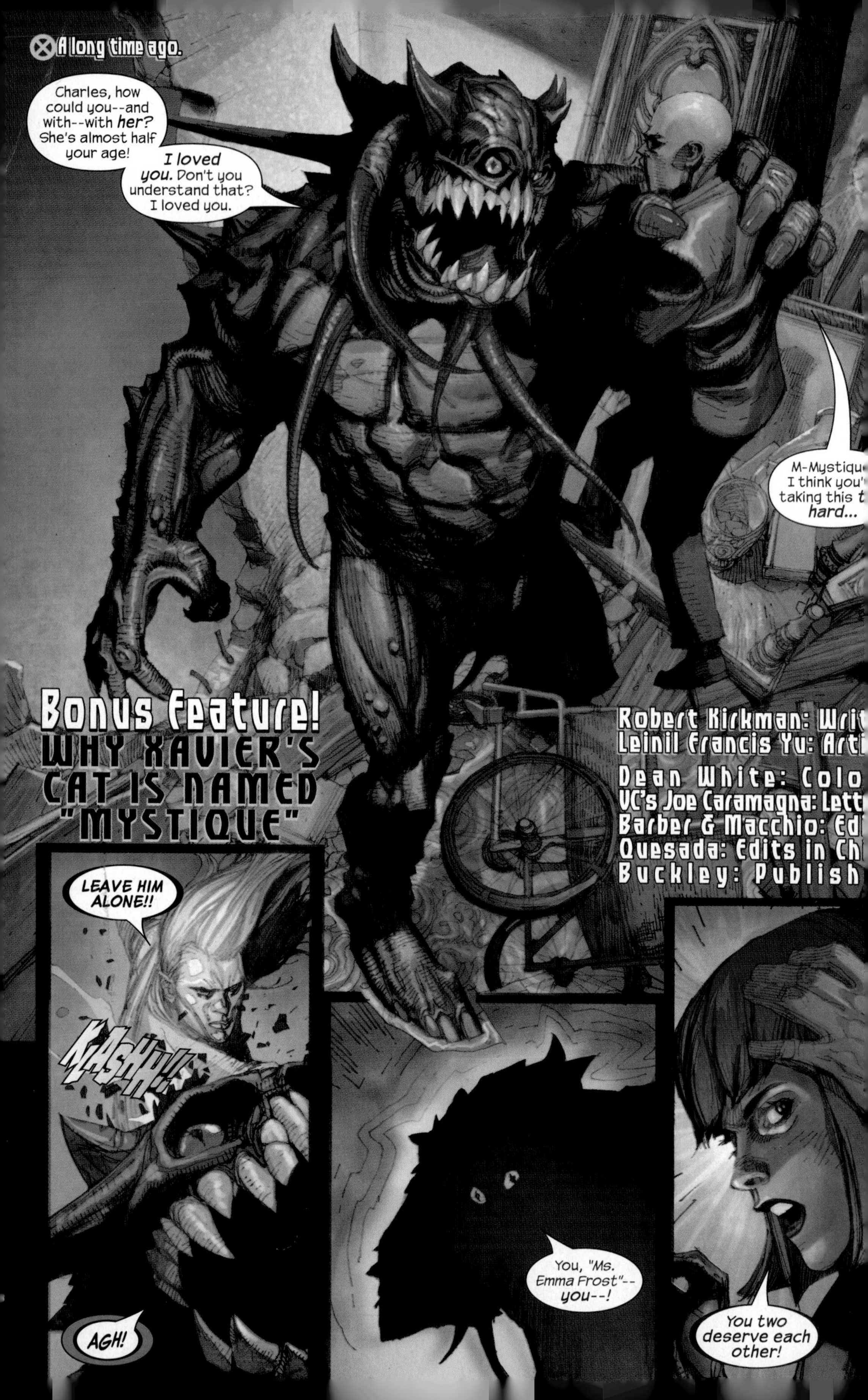
A long time ago.
Charles, how could you--and with--with *her*? She's almost half your age!
I loved you. Don't you understand that? I loved you.
M-Mystiqu I think you' taking this t *hard...*
Bonus Feature!
WHY XAVIER'S CAT IS NAMED "MYSTIQUE"
Robert Kirkman: Writ
Leinil Francis Yu: Arti
Dean White: Colo
VC's Joe Caramagna: Lett
Barber & Macchio: Edi
Quesada: Edits in Chi
Buckley: Publish
LEAVE HIM ALONE!!
KASHH!!
AGH!
You, "Ms. Emma Frost"-- *you*--!
You two deserve each other!

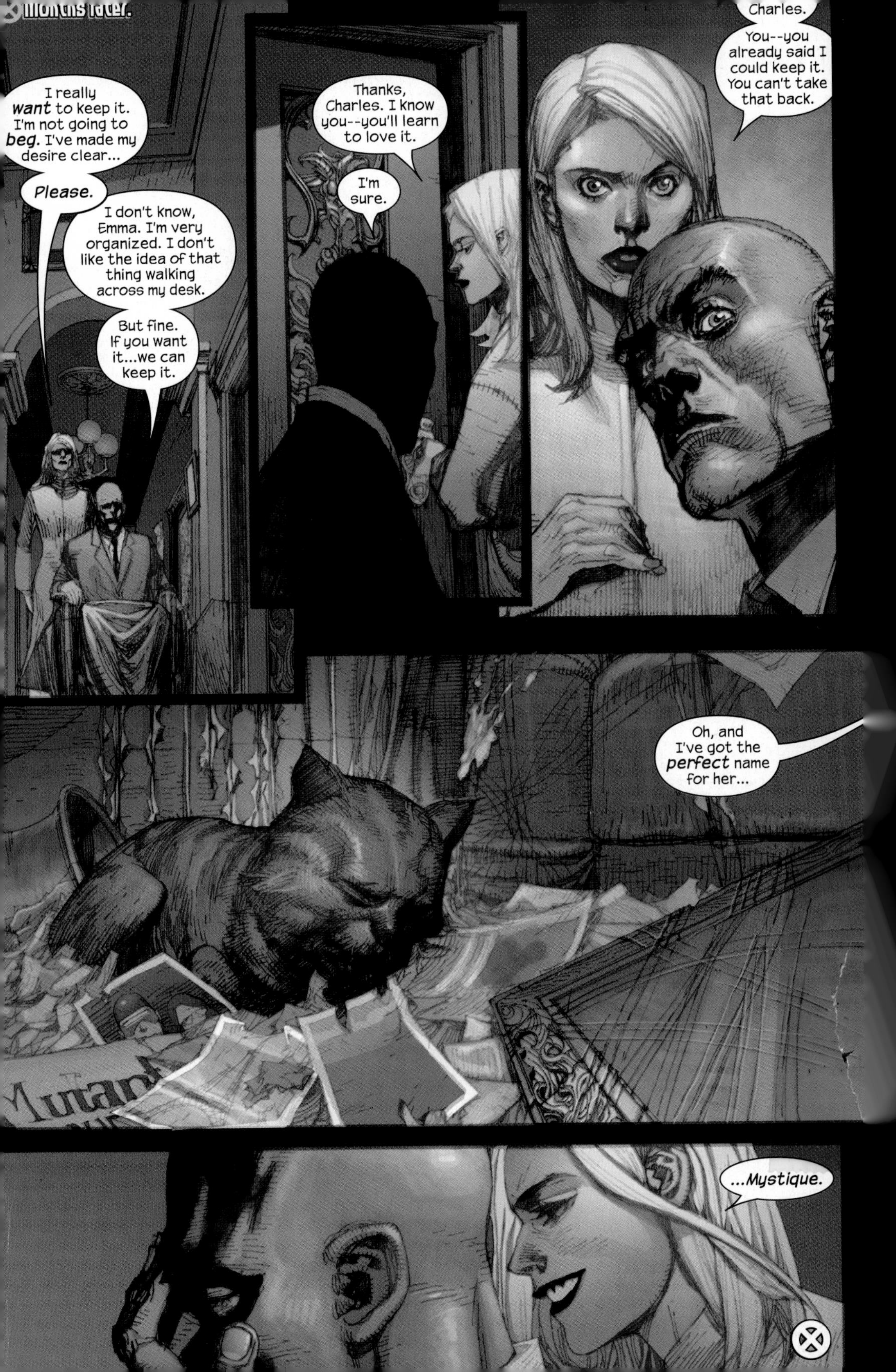
Months later.
I really want to keep it. I'm not going to beg. I've made my desire clear...
Please.
I don't know, Emma. I'm very organized. I don't like the idea of that thing walking across my desk.
But fine. If you want it...we can keep it.
Thanks, Charles. I know you--you'll learn to love it.
I'm sure.
Charles.
You--you already said I could keep it. You can't take that back.
Oh, and I've got the perfect name for her...
...Mystique.

by Tom Raney

A

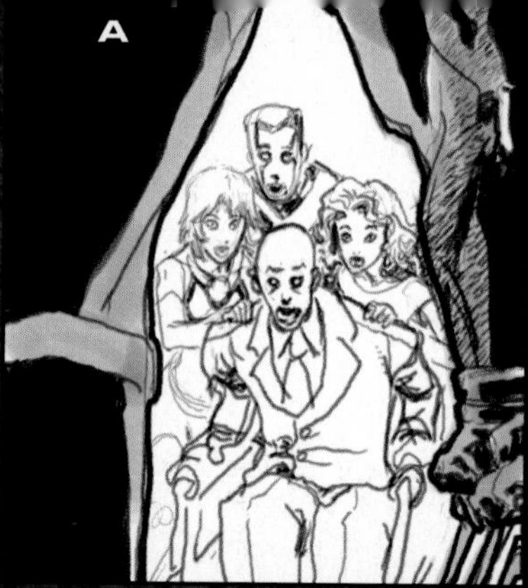

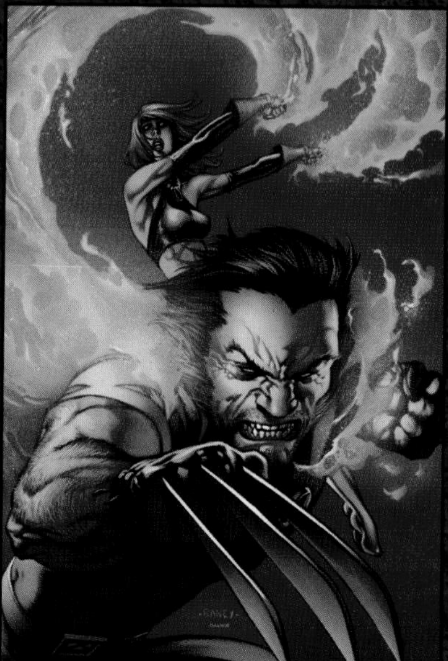

SKETCH
B

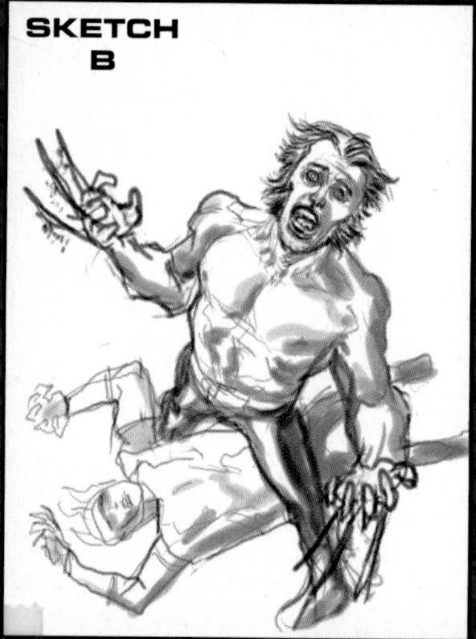

PENCILS

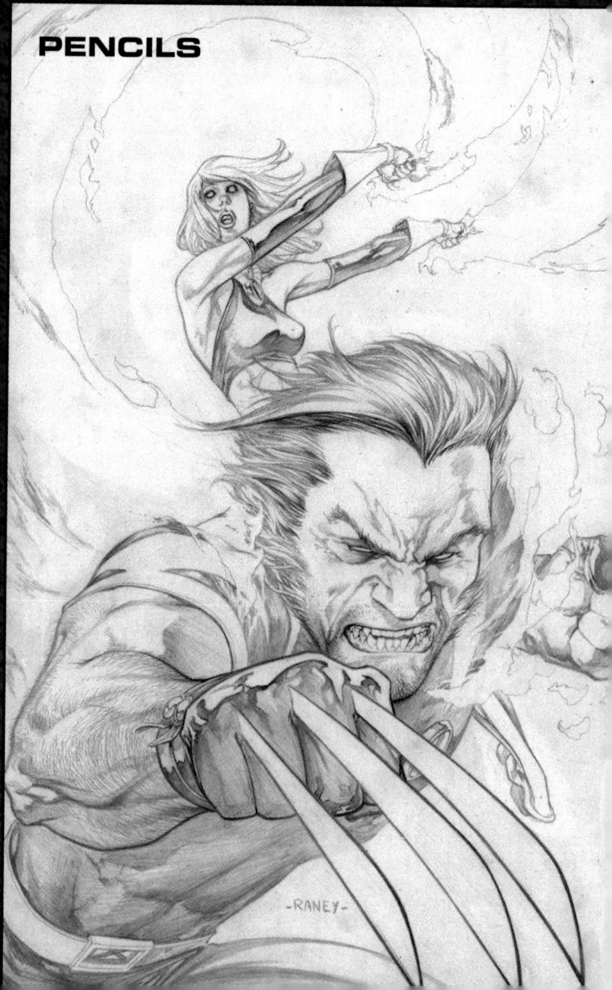
-RANEY-

SKETCH
C

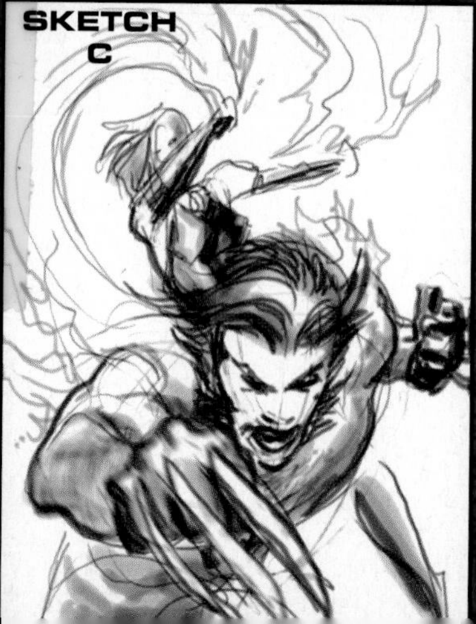